LAURIER AND A LIBERAL QUEBEC: A STUDY IN POLITICAL MANAGEMENT

LAURIER AND A LIBERAL QUEBEC: A STUDY IN POLITICAL MANAGEMENT

Edited and with an introduction by
Richard T. Clippingdale

H. BLAIR NEATBY

The Carleton Library No. 63
McClelland and Stewart Limited

The Carleton Library

A series of Canadian reprints and new
collections of source material relating to
Canada, issued under the editorial supervision
of the Institute of Canadian Studies of Carleton
University, Ottawa.

©McClelland and Stewart Limited, 1973

ALL RIGHTS RESERVED

0-7710-9763-8

The Canadian Publishers
McClelland and Stewart Limited
25 Hollinger Road, Toronto

Printed and Bound in Canada

CONTENTS

Introduction   ix

To John T. Saywell
who shared the pleasures of
archival research

Introduction

Sir Wilfrid Laurier's transformation of Quebec in the late nineteenth and early twentieth centuries from a Conservative into a
Liberal fortress, his struggle for political liberalism against ultramontane Catholicism, and his championing of a broad Canadian
"nationalism" as opposed to a narrow *nationaliste* or separatist
Quebec-oriented loyalty are the chief themes of this work. It was
prepared originally as a Ph.D. thesis under the supervision of the
late F. H. Underhill for the University of Toronto in 1956. Its
author, Dr. H. Blair Neatby, of the Department of History at
Carleton University, at first intended to follow it up with some
fuller treatment of Laurier, but an opportunity came along in 1958
to take up a portion of the Mackenzie King biography project.
William Lyon Mackenzie King, 1924-1932: The Lonely Heights[1]
was the first fruit of that labour; a second volume is in preparation.
Dr. Neatby now feels too far distanced in both time and interests to
return to the subject of his first serious professional research. Yet,
since *Laurier and a Liberal Quebec* was accepted by the University
of Toronto, it has won considerable respect among scholars of post-
Confederation politics as the most illuminating study available on
Laurier's relationship with his native province and on the origins of
that "solid Quebec" on which federal Liberalism has based its near-
monopoly of office since 1896. Microfilm and xerox copies have
been much in demand, and interlibrary loan services heavily em-
ployed – so that this unpublished study never has been allowed to
moulder in the archival obscurity to which so many "proofs" of
doctoral worthiness justly have been condemned. Recently, Dr.
Neatby yielded to the urgings of many friends and colleagues, and
agreed to its release in the Carleton Library Series.

From the original version a few things have been omitted, and
some alterations have been made. The author's original "Introduction," appendices concerning some Canadian constitutional documents, and his very thorough bibliography have been dropped,
principally to save space. However, I have drawn on these sources
for preparation of this introductory essay and for the brief "Note
on Sources and Suggestions for Further Reading" which is at the
end of the book. The text proper is almost exactly as first written,
with a few exceptions. Much of the quoted material in the thesis
was in French, and, not without regret, it was considered necessary

[1] (Toronto, 1963).

that it be translated so that the volume may have the widest possible circulation. For faults in the translation, I assume entire responsibility.

There is little other textual revision. No one but the author himself properly could have altered his original argument in any essential. I have merely tidied up a few of those typographical and stylistic slips which any unpublished thesis is bound to contain. In addition, where lines of a repetitive or peripheral nature could be cut without in any way altering the substance of the argument, this has been done. Very occasionally, some clarifying words or phrases have been added; and to a select number of footnotes references to material which has appeared since 1956 have been appended.

Sir Wilfrid Laurier's career, like Sir John A. Macdonald's, was lengthy, tinged with romance, full of drama and deeply tangled in the great issues of the day. Under his leadership the Liberals emerged from the shades of opposition, were released from the limitations of a basis in regional protests and attitudes of "voluble virtue[2]," and came to maturity as a pragmatic *national* party. He spent fifteen years, 1896-1911, as Prime Minister of Canada, the first French Canadian to hold the office. When he assumed the Liberal leadership in 1887 Canadians were by no means sure that their twenty-year old Confederation could survive the challenges which economic depression, provincialist particularism, American unfriendliness and English-French disharmony presented. Laurier was the man of "sunny ways" who healed some of the ethnic and sectarian wounds of the Manitoba Schools question and tried very hard to keep other such divisive issues from emerging. In addition, he presided over one of the greatest periods of economic development and population growth in Canadian history: Clifford Sifton's massive immigration successes and his own Grand Trunk Pacific Railway project were two major stages in the fleshing out of the skeleton of Macdonald's National Policy. He was Prime Minister at a time when the Great Britain of Joseph Chamberlain[3] and the Canada of the Anglo-Saxon imperialists pined for closer connection and a fuller Canadian participation in the responsibilities and burdens of Empire. "Fifteen years of saying no"[4] to those ideas under

[2] The phrase is J. S. Willison's, quoted, F. H. Underhill, "Edward Blake and Canadian Liberal Nationalism," in R. Flenley, ed., *Essays in Canadian History* (Toronto, 1939), 135.
[3] Chamberlain was the British Colonial Secretary from 1895 to 1903.
[4] The phrase is J. W. Dafoe's in his *Laurier: A Study in Canadian Politics* (Toronto, 1922). In the 1963 Carleton Library edition, p. 50.

Laurier, a number of his biographers have argued, were the essential prelude to World War One and Versailles nationhood under Sir Robert Borden and to the "autonomy" status arranged by Mackenzie King.

Laurier was a gifted leader of men and a keen philosopher of politics who knew how to take advantage of his opportunities and give a touch of nobility to his causes. His support of Reciprocity with the United States in 1911 and his opposition to conscription in 1917 brought his two great electoral defeats, but while he lived he remained what Governor-General Lord Minto had called him in 1898 – " . . . far the biggest man in Canada. . . . "[5] And his party, though shaken in his last years, endured as *the* federal governing instrument.

Virtually none of Laurier's accomplishments – indeed, little of his career itself – would have been possible if he had not established mastery of his own province. Blair Neatby lists Laurier's success in this regard as ranking in importance in the history of Canadian political parties with the coming together of English Canadians and French Canadians in the Macdonald-Cartier Liberal-Conservative party in the 1850's and 1860's and with Mackenzie King's incorporation of dissident western radicals into the Liberal party in the 1920's. "Of these three," he judges, "the emergence of a Liberal Quebec was possibly the most startling."[6] He considers it nothing less than "a political revolution,"[7] in which Laurier was the central figure. In explaining how and why the transformation occurred he has drawn a fascinating portrait of Quebec politics from Confederation to the years of the First World War and of that other Laurier, not the "national" figure but the manager of his province.

Quebec, it is claimed, is "not a province like the others." Neatby displays for us the distinctiveness of Quebec politics in the immediate post-Confederation years. Features included a complicated and uneasy Church-State relationship, schismatic warfare within both the Church and the parties, incredibly bitter personal vendettas, and a fondness for classic orations, dramatic legal suits, exciting *assemblées contradictoires*, stirring manifestos and insulting pamphlets. It was not a place for what J. W. Dafoe has termed the "Sir Galahad" side of Laurier, although this was sometimes displayed; rather it was an environment for the exercise of his Machiavellian talents.[8] As we can see in this book, it was no mean tactician and strategist who faced successfully the clerical storm, subverted the

[5] Cited, J. Buchan, *Lord Minto: A Memoir* (London, 1924), p. 159.
[6] "Introduction" to the unpublished thesis, i.
[7] *Ibid.*, ii.
[8] Dafoe (1963 edition), p. 24.

Quebec Conservative party and stood firm against the *nationaliste* challenge.

As early as 1903, the first of Laurier's English-Canadian biographers, J. S. Willison, saw his career as "remarkable for consistent and unchanging devotion to three great objects: the assertion and maintenance of the principles of federalism, ardent and unflinching championship of civil and religious freedom, patient and courageous resistance to the denationalizing tendencies of racialism, sectarianism and provincialism."[9] Dr. Neatby, with his focus on Quebec, devotes less attention to "the principles of federalism" than do the general biographers, but his treatment of all three themes is quite in keeping with the Willison guidelines.

He begins by looking at Quebec politics in the 1860's and 1870's, when the province was being shaken by the aggressive ultramontane[10] clericalism which had been imported from the counter-revolutionary Catholic Europe of Pope Pius IX, to be merged with certain elements of the French-Canadian nationalist tradition. The Liberal Party in which Laurier was beginning to climb in the 1870's was tainted in the eyes of ultramontane clergymen and lay leaders by its origins in the radical republicanism and anti-clericalism of Louis-Joseph Papineau's *Rouge* group in the 1840's and 1850's. Laurier himself was involved with the *Rouges* during their anti-Confederation phase in the mid-1860's – he even served briefly as editor of one of the party's newspapers, *Le Défricheur*. It is not entirely clear in this book, or in any other account for that matter, just how much anti-clericalism and what might be termed "radical liberalism" of the continental European variety Laurier had to disavow in his celebrated speech on Political Liberalism in 1877. It was in his interests, of course, not to admit to having been a very serious *Rouge* in directions like these. Indeed, in that address, to which Dr. Neatby quite properly devotes considerable attention, Laurier strove to identify his party with the political principles of moderate British Liberalism rather than the Papally-condemned ones of the continental European brand, in order to turn aside the Church's

---

[9] J. S. Willison, *Sir Wilfrid Laurier and the Liberal Party* (Toronto, 1903), II, 355.

[10] See below, Chapter One for a discussion of the European and French-Canadian meanings of the term "ultramontane." Simply stated, it was a reverence for Papal authoritarianism within the Church and a belief in the Church's right and duty to exercise primacy over secular government wherever and whenever it believed the interests of faith and morals required. In practice, this could mean a thorough supervision by prelates and priests over politics generally.

wrath, especially as expressed so potently during elections.[11] He may have been partially successful in this, although other factors – such as the lessening hold of ultramontanism on the Church both in Quebec and at the Vatican – had an important effect.

One of the most interesting points of view in this study concerns the internecine warfare within Quebec Conservatism in the 1880's and 1890's over the degree of clerical influence or even dictation to which the party's politicians should be subject. The bitter conflict was between the doctrinaire ultramontane *Castor* wing and J.-A. Chapleau's more moderate, more materialistic "school of Cartier." "It was this dissension . . . ," Neatby contends, "rather than national issues, which was to make possible the emergence of a 'solid Liberal Quebec'."[12] In the mid-1890's, Chapleau led many of his followers into Laurier's camp, leaving the *Castor* Conservatives politically isolated. The theme was not entirely new with this study when it was completed in 1956: in particular, some of the outlines were present in Robert Rumilly's *Histoire de la province de Québec*.[13] But Neatby's development of it in this work and in his important article with J. T. Saywell, "Chapleau and the Conservative Party in Quebec,"[14] represented a significant new emphasis in the interpretation of French-Canadian politics in the 1880-1896 period. The province's Conservative to Liberal shift could be explained no longer as wholly, or even primarily, a consequence of the execution of Louis Riel and the *parti national* furor which sprang from it. Neatby demonstrates how Laurier's "quiet diplomacy" over Manitoba Schools came to seem to Chapleau and his friends preferable to the procrastination and bad faith of the federal Conservatives. In 1896 Laurier won Quebec with their support and took office in Ottawa. He and the provincial Liberals, who assumed power in 1897, soon cemented the alliance by patronage means and through a co-operative attitude towards the Church. In addition, by 1902 Laurier's unwillingness to be stampeded by Imperialism was evident to most French Canadians. Neatby concludes:

After 1902, Laurier's control of the province was never challenged by the national Conservative party. The only political party which could weaken Laurier in Quebec would have to be a third party – a provincial party with a French-Canadian nationaliste platform so extreme that Laurier would appear almost English in comparison.[15]

[11] A full text of the speech, in French, is appended to Vol. II of Willison's *Laurier* (1903).
[12] See below, p. 12.
[13] Especially in Vol. VIII.
[14] *Canadian Historical Review*, XXXVII (March, 1956), 1-22.
[15] See below, pp. 148-149.

Laurier's contest with just such a group, the *nationalistes* led by Henri Bourassa, is the focus of most of the rest of this study. For Neatby, the *nationalistes'* dogmatic assertions of rigid, strictly French-Canadian positions on Canada's Imperial relationship, concerning minority school and language rights outside Quebec, and in response to what they saw as external threats to the French and Catholic character of their own province were "not only futile but dangerous to political unity."[16] They certainly were dangerous to Laurier's hold on office, since their undermining in 1911 of his Quebec power base helped to hand power to the federal Conservatives. Neatby calls attention to the *nationalistes'* failures as defenders of the French-Canadian people because they were unable to force the new regime to take the sensibilities and interests of that population properly into account during the terribly divisive wartime period after 1914.[17] He notes Laurier's view in 1916 that the *nationalistes* had made important contributions to these divisions.[18]

Given that interpretation and the fact that in 1956, when this work was completed, Canada was basking in the warmth of the national unity optimism of consensus Liberalism, with a French-Canadian Prime Minister once more, and with all – or almost all – quiet on the French-English front, Neatby's final general conclusion is not especially surprising:

. . . . events subsequent to Laurier's death suggest that the compromises accepted during his lifetime have so firmly established Confederation that it can never again be seriously challenged.[19]

Today that judgement can hardly stand unchallenged – at the very least it requires substantial modification. The "Not-so-Quiet Revolution" in Quebec, the debates over bilingualism and biculturalism and the challenges to federalism or even the continuance of Canada which have been features of the 1960's and early 1970's have tended to throw doubt on the adequacy of a number of the past "compromises" of Confederation, including some in which Laurier was involved.

Of course, there have always been doubters. *Nationalistes*, separatists and near-separatists in Quebec in Laurier's time and since have tended to regard his career, in the words of Armand Lavergne, one of Bourassa's lieutenants, as "a great illusion," rather than a work of French-English reconciliation and the protection of the

[16] *Ibid.*, pp. 165-166.
[17] *Ibid.*, p. 204.
[18] Cited, below, pp. 215-216.
[19] See below, p. 231.

French-Canadian minority in Canada.[20] The historian Michel Brunet has catalogued some of the reasons for that point of view:

The unsatisfactory compromise Laurier was compelled to accept on the Manitoba school problem; Canada's intervention in the South African War, which fostered and gave vent to the pan-British nationalism of the English-speaking Canadians; Laurier's retreat on the school rights of the Catholic minority when the provinces of Saskatchewan and Alberta were created; the slow progress of bilingualism outside of Quebec; the imperialistic propaganda and the frequent violent outbursts of francophobia and anti-Catholicism of the Anglo-Canadians – reminded the French Canadians that the country in which they lived could not yet be considered as their fatherland.[21]

Admittedly, the movement against meaningful linguistic dualism outside Quebec – which began before Laurier was Prime Minister but which in office he did little to counter – has helped make an emotional loyalty to Canada as a whole increasingly difficult for a good many French Canadians in later generations. Still, Laurier was hardly a prime "culprit" in this regard: his "sins" were more of omission than of commission, and English-speaking Canada in his day was too Anglo-Saxonist, too North American, too multicultural through immigration from continental Europe, and too Protestant for there to be much of an opening for a pragmatic French-Canadian Roman Catholic politician to dare to champion even a very mild bilingualism and biculturalism very forcefully. And while on issues associated with Imperialism and war in Europe he ultimately failed personally to bridge the English-French gulf which developed, it was not for lack of trying. What is more, it is hard to discern that any other Canadian of the time did better.

Yet that is not all: there is a vitally significant socio-economic side of the rise of Laurier Liberalism to dominance in Quebec which scarcely rates mention in Neatby's account but which relates to what we now can see has been one of the most divisive "compromises" of Confederation – the continuing social and economic domination of Quebec life by English Canadians and the eventual resentment thus bred among French-speaking Quebecers. It was one of the key elements in the Confederation scheme of things in the 1860's that there had to be a pan-Canadian united economy. Cartier's *Bleus* represented, among other things, an alliance of the French-Canadian political elite, mostly of the liberal professions,

---

[20] A. Lavergne, *Trente ans de vie nationale* (Montréal, 1934), p. 70 (translation).

[21] M. Brunet, "The French Canadians' Search for a Fatherland," in P. Russell, ed., *Nationalism in Canada* (Toronto, 1966), pp. 53-54.

with entrepreneurs and financiers, mainly English-speaking.[22] Cartier's involvement with the Grand Trunk Railway symbolized this, and the attacks of the *Castors* on Chapleau in the 1880's were based in part on their horror of such connections. When the "school of Cartier" came Laurier's way in the mid-1890's it brought along its friendship towards business and its support for tariff protection. And Laurier as he came nearer power at this time and jettisoned Unrestricted Reciprocity was the perfect pragmatist in reassuring businessmen that tariff protection would be safe with him.[23]

As the years passed, the alliance solidified. The protectionist Fielding Budget which the Laurier government brought down in 1897 helped.[24] The former *Bleu*, Israel Tarte, told Laurier the same year that the Liberals could best assure their survival in office by linking themselves to "the power of capital."[25] That did not make it so, of course, but when Tarte was pushed out of the ministry in 1902 over calling for higher protectionism he was succeeded as representative for Montreal by Raymond Préfontaine whom Neatby terms an "avowed protectionist."[26] Then, too, at the provincial level in Quebec the Liberal governments after 1897 co-existed very comfortably indeed with the resource and manufacturing concerns which were proliferating very rapidly. It was *nationalistes* like Henri Bourassa and Olivar Asselin who worried about the social implications of an economic development pursued in many cases through enterprises in which French Canadians were rarely involved above the lowest levels.[27] But of course, the politicians themselves were no mere hewers of wood or drawers of water: when two years after Laurier's death Mackenzie King formed a Liberal administration at Ottawa, it was the leaders of the Quebec contingent with their

[22] Jean Hamelin and Yves Roby, "L'évolution économique et sociale du Québec, 1851-1896," *Recherches sociographiques*, x, 2-3 (mai-décembre 1969), p. 167, term the "professionals" as "socio-political agents between the people and power", both clerical and business.

[23] R. C. Brown, *Canada's National Policy, 1883-1900: A Study in Canadian-American Relations* (Princeton, 1964), pp. 262-268. In R. Rumilly, *Histoire de la province de Québec*, VIII, p. 58 there is special reference to the very considerable Liberal effort in this regard in Quebec.

[24] See below, p. 136.

[25] Cited, below, p. 132.

[26] See below, p. 140.

[27] Among the many accounts of Bourassa and the *nationalistes* J. Levitt's *Henri Bourassa and the Golden Calf: The Social Program of the Nationalists of Quebec, 1900-1914* (Ottawa, 1969), deals in most detail with this.

rigid protectionism and their many directorships in finance and industry who constituted the greatest single bar to his hopes of accommodation with the anti-protectionist Progressives of the West.[28] It was not merely "political liberalism" which the Laurier Liberal party came to represent; the party was also generally favourable to business, despite the pro-Reciprocity strategy in 1911. Governing parties in Quebec – and federally as well as provincially they have been mostly Liberal since 1896 – traditionally have been aligned with the business and financial power in the province, chiefly English-speaking. The political "power of capital" in Quebec was as significant as elsewhere in North America, and there was little in the way of a "progressive tradition" to counter it very much.

The Liberals' possession of political mastery did not bring, until recently at least, an energetic effort to encourage or to educate French-speaking Quebecers to run their own economy. The *nationalistes* of Bourassa's time were all too easily diverted from socioeconomic issues to the more traditional ones concerning Imperialism, school rights and the like.[29] But separatism today, especially of the more radical leftist variety, among other things feeds on the yearning of the young to possess control of their own economic life and thus, as they see it, not only to look after their individual futures but also to provide security for the collective French fact. In this sense then, Laurier Liberalism, along with the parties associated with leaders such as Cartier, Chapleau, Taschereau and Duplessis, held and exercised power politically for French-speaking Quebec without daring, or even dreaming, of coming to grips with the challenges to the province's French-Canadian distinctiveness inherent in the increasing domination of its economy, and hence in some ways its culture, by *les Anglais*. Laurier, the man more than any other who brought political hegemony in Quebec to the Liberal party, played a not insignificant role in the process whereby some of the economic developments under Confederation have led to very serious problems for the national unity to which clearly he was so devoted. But it has not generally been the habit of our historians of politics – especially Liberal politics – to mess with these sorts of things. They have been much more at home with personalities and

[28] R. M. Dawson, *William Lyon Mackenzie King: A Political Biography, 1874-1923* (Toronto, 1959), pp. 260-261; F. W. Gibson, "The Cabinet of 1921," in the volume he edited on *Cabinet Formation and Bicultural Relations: Seven Case Studies* (Ottawa, 1970), pp. 67-69, 73-104.

[29] R. Cook, *Canada and the French-Canadian Question* (Toronto, 1966), p. 95, calls nationalism, because it encouraged such diversions, "the Achilles heel" of social reform-oriented organizations like the *Ligue nationaliste*.

their principles and with heroic struggles in defence of national unity or some other such laudable end. This has been a rather limited view of history.

To be sure, it seems that Quebec politicians generally in Laurier's day did debate politics publicly mainly along such lines. Laurier understood well the game as it was then played, and he played it to win, although usually with a commendable commitment to ideals and principles. Even fifty-two years after his death he is virtually impossible to dislike. He was more than just a gifted political manager, although surely somewhat less than the saint he is sometimes depicted as having been. He *was*, however, a very impressive human being, and this had not a little to do with the establishment of his incredible hold on the political loyalty of his province. Blair Neatby's book may lack something of the social analysis the historians of the 1970's – including, one suspects, he himself – would be drawn to attempt. Yet it is, for the most part, a clear window on one of the great "political revolutions" of Canadian history, the building of a Liberal Quebec.

RICHARD T. CLIPPINGDALE
Carleton University,
Ottawa

November, 1971.

LAURIER AND A
LIBERAL QUEBEC:
A STUDY IN POLITICAL
MANAGEMENT

1.
Catholic-Liberalism

In the early 1880's, the Liberals in the province of Quebec were reconciled to the fact that Quebec was a Conservative province, and likely to remain so. L. O. David, a prominent Liberal, frankly admitted this after the provincial elections of 1881.

The elections which have just taken place have proven once again that the province of Quebec is Conservative, and wants to be governed by Conservatives. The Liberals will come to power only thanks to special circumstances, to transitory causes. The people may be disoriented for a time, but they will revert to their first loyalties.[1]

Laurier himself, at this time, considered "twenty-two counties as the fair average strength of the party."[2] The Liberals, however, should not have been despondent about this situation. In 1881 the Liberal party was still in existence, after a struggle with the Roman Catholic Church which had threatened to destroy the party completely.

In the 1850's, the *Rouge* party in Quebec had been openly anti-clerical. The leaders of the party – the Dorions, Laflamme and Doutre – were able men who had been influenced by contemporary European liberal movements. In *L'Avenir*, Eric Dorion, *l'Enfant Terrible*, advocated a political platform which was the Canadian version of the Declaration of the Rights of Man. It was unequivocally egalitarian, demanding "equal rights, equal justice for all citizens," "electoral reform based on universal suffrage," and "education as widely available as possible." The separating of church and state was to be achieved by the "abolition of the system of tithes, the ending of the Protestant Clergy Reserves," and also by transforming parishes into municipalities.[3]

In the province of Quebec, the *Rouge* party could never be successful. The separation of politics and religion was itself anathe-

---

[1] Montreal *Tribune*, n.d., cited, R. Rumilly, *Histoire de la province de Quebec*, III, 120. This multi-volume study, published in Montreal, began appearing in 1940.

[2] Ontario Archives, Blake Papers, Laurier (hereinafter W. L.) to Blake, 7 Dec., 1881.

[3] The platform is printed in *L'Avenir*, 7 May, 1851.

ma to the Roman Catholic Church. Even more serious was the suspicion that the *Rouges* were more radical than their platform suggested, and there was evidence to support the suspicion. The *Rouges* had formed a political alliance in the 1850's with George Brown, who was not noted for his tolerance of the church. They also advocated annexation to the United States, where secularization was far advanced. Even more dangerous was the interest taken by the *Rouges* in education. Their educational policy was made explicit by a motion in the legislature in 1855:

to establish throughout the province a general and uniform system of free elementary education, maintained wholly at the cost of the State..., all schools thus established should be open without discrimination, without exposing any (children)... to having their religious beliefs injured in any manner.[4]

Clericals believed the Church could not give up control over education without lessening its influence over the shaping of society along properly Catholic lines.

Thus it is not surprising that the breach between the *Rouge* party and the Roman Catholic Church occurred over a question of education. The *Institut Canadien* was not originally a *Rouge* society, although many prominent *Rouges* were members. According to Article Two of the Montreal *Institut* charter, "the object of l'Institut *Canadien* is to extend and develop a taste for science, art and literature."[5] The *Institut* included in its membership both English- and French-Canadians, Protestants and Roman Catholics. To the ultramontane Bishop Bourget of Montreal this meant that the *Institut* was tainted with heresy.[6] More serious in his view, was the use of the large library of the *Institut*, which included some books on the Index. In a Pastoral Letter of 1858, he explained that the *Institut* had rejected his suggestion that the undesirable books should be withdrawn from circulation.

The cardinal error [of the Institut] *is manifest in the following, to wit: That the Institut has always been, and is alone competent to judge the morality of its library... and that the Committee of*

[4] O. D. Skelton, *The Life and Letters of Sir Wilfrid Laurier* (Toronto, 1921), I, 94. An excellent short treatment of the *Rouges'* policies is in J. Monet, "French-Canadian Nationalism and the Challenge of Ultramontanism," Canadian Historical Association, *Report*, 1966, pp. 41-55.

[5] J. Dougall, "History of the Guibord Case" (Montreal, 1875), p. 5.

[6] "Ultramontane" is to be understood in the sense of extreme doctrinaire.

Administration is sufficient for the management of the affairs of the Institut, and to see to the administration of the library.[7]

To this, Bourget could make only one reply.

And, in effect, it would follow that no Catholic can any longer belong to this Institut. . . . These unfortunate results will be the unavoidable consequence of the anti-Catholic attitude which the Institut has taken, while persisting in its revolt against the Church.[8]

To many of the Roman Catholic members of the *Institut*, this ultimatum was decisive. Many withdrew to form the *Institut Canadien Française.*[9] The Roman Catholics who remained, less tractable men, believed that they could be members of both the *Institut* and the church. It was natural that men of such temperament should also believe that they could separate their politics from their religion. So it was that many of those who remained loyal to the *Institut* were *Rouges*. The ultramontane suspicion of the *Rouges* was confirmed.

In 1865, some members of the *Institut* appealed to Rome against Bishop Bourget's denial to them of the sacraments. Bourget, in a Circular from Rome a few years later, explained that Rome had decided against the *Institut*.

Thus, so long as the Institut Canadien is not reformed in such a way as to provide the necessary guarantees, Catholics ought to be removed from it; and if they decline to obey, they must be treated as rebels against the Church in a grave matter.[10]

Some *Rouges*, such as L. A. Dessaulles and Joseph Doutre,[11] continued to resist Bourget. This led to the *cause célèbre*, the Guibord case, in which the right of the church to refuse burial in consecrated ground was challenged by the *Institut* before the Privy Council. Few Roman Catholics were willing to go to this extreme, and the

---

[7] *Mandements, lettres pastorales, circulaires et autres documents publiés dans le diocèse de Montréal*, VI (Montréal, 1887), 25, Pastoral Letter, 30 April, 1858.

[8] *Ibid.*, 37.

[9] "History of the Guibord Case," 7.

[10] *Mandements*, VI, 43, 16 July 1869.

[11] Dessaulles (1819-1895) was a member of the Legislative Council of Canada, 1856-1863, and was president of the *Institut*. Doutre (1825-1886), a leading *Rouge*, was one of the founders of the *Institut*.

Institut membership declined rapidly after 1869. Among the resignations were those of A. A. Dorion and F. Geoffrion.[12]

Thus, by 1870, the *Rouges* had become identified with the *Institut* and with anti-clericalism. In politics, however, the opposition party had adopted the name of Liberal. This party included many Roman Catholics whose devotion was unquestioned, some having joined the party because of their opposition to Confederation.[13] But the Liberal party also included the *Rouges*. To the ultramontanes, Liberals who associated with former *Rouges* were equivalent to the "fellow-travellers" of our own day. And even the name "Liberal" was identified with French radicalism and the revolutions of 1848. For the Liberal party, the decade of the 1870's was a long struggle to avoid the fate of the *Institut*.

One abortive attempt was made by the Liberals in the 1870's to secure the neutrality of the clergy by founding the *Parti National*. As Honoré Mercier wrote in 1872:

Our clergy is national by its glorious traditions and equally by its patriotic aspirations; the day it realizes that we are working sincerely for the prosperity of the country, and that our cause is that of religion and of the nation, it will give us its friendship and will support with its immense strength the great causes that we seek to further.[14]

It was no secret that the new party was composed of Liberals. One of its pamphlets describes it as the party "which has been labelled, in order to ostracize it, under the names *rouges, communists* and *socialists*, but which finally took its proper designation as *parti national*."[15] A provincial party such as this could not hope to challenge the government at Ottawa. In Quebec it failed to gain the confidence of the clergy, and there was no reason to maintain the subterfuge. The *Parti National* disappeared after the election of 1872.

[12] "History of the Guibord Case," 10. Dorion (1818-1891), the leading *Rouge* politician, was a minister in a number of pre-Confederation Canadian administrations and served as federal minister of justice, 1873-1874. He was Chief Justice of the Queen's Bench in Quebec, 1874-1891. Geoffrion (1832-1894) was a member of both the pre-Confederation and post-Confederation Canadian parliaments and was a minister in the federal Liberal government in the 1870's.

[13] Included among these new recruits were Honoré Mercier (1840-1894), later provincial Liberal leader and premier, and L. O. David (1840-1926), provincial legislator and then a Senator, who was a close personal friend of Laurier.

[14] C. Langelier, *Souvenirs politiques*, I (Quebec, 1909), 17.

[15] C. J. Lafrance, "Nos divisions politiques," (Quebec, 1873).

It was in vain for the Liberals to plead that they were devout Roman Catholics. Liberals were denounced for being guilty of the sin of Catholic-liberalism. Catholic-liberalism had been condemned in the Syllabus of Errors of 1864, as the mistaken belief "that the Roman Pontiff can and ought to reconcile himself to, and agree with, progress, liberalism and civilization."[16] Thus, Catholic-liberalism was a humanistic social philosophy, condemned because of its materialistic bias. There can be little doubt that many of the old *Rouges* had been guilty of Catholic-liberalism. It was natural to believe that the Liberals were equally guilty, for they had compromised with the *Rouges* in politics. This assumption was expressed in a typical political pamphlet entitled "Liberal Tendencies: the *Rouges* are as dangerous as ever."[17] The political effect of this belief may be shown most clearly by a reference to the *Programme Catholique* of 1871. This was a political platform issued by devout Conservatives, after being approved by the ultramontane bishops, Bourget and Laflèche. The intention was to defend the "principles of religion and of nationality."[18] These principles were to be defended by voting for Conservative candidates in all elections. There was only one conceivable qualification to this rule.

In the case where the struggle is between a Conservative rejecting our program and an Opposition representative accepting it, the position is more delicate ..., We advise then the abstention of Catholic electors.[19]

In a joint Pastoral Letter of the bishops of the province in 1875, Catholic-liberalism was denounced as "an unrealistic reconciliation of truth with error."[20] The letter stated that the bishops and priests could intervene in politics if a political party was judged dangerous to the church because of its platform or its previous record.[21] The Liberal party was not denounced by name, but it was obvious that the Pastoral Letter did not refer to the Conservative party. The effect of the Letter was shown in the Charlevoix by-election of January, 1876. The agents of the Conservative candidate, Hector Langevin,[22] presented him as the choice of the clergy.[23] Priests in

---

[16] A. T. Galt, "Church and State," (Montreal, 1876).

[17] (Québec, 1874).

[18] *Mandements*, VIII, 397.

[19] *Ibid.*, 398.

[20] *Ibid.*, VII, 207.

[21] *Ibid.*, 211.

[22] Langevin (1826-1906) was Minister of Public Works 1869-1873 and 1879-1891. In 1876, he was the recognized leader of the French-Canadian Conservatives.

[23] Rumilly. *Histoire*, II, 99.

the constituency declared from the pulpit that the Liberal party had been condemned by the bishops, and that it would be a sin to vote for such a party.[24] Langevin was elected.

The Liberals were forced to resort to desperate measures. It was decided to contest the election in the courts on the grounds of "undue influence." Even legally, the Liberals could not be sure of success. The Elections Act of 1874 was concerned with bribery and violence, but not with spiritual constraint. Nevertheless, the Act did state that a person who "in any manner practises intimidation . . . shall be deemed to have committed the offence of undue influence . . . ."[25] Contesting the election on such grounds might well be politically dangerous. It was not likely to conciliate the clergy. Coming so soon after the Guibord case, it must have seemed yet another attempt to curtail the influence of the church. Bourget's reaction was prompt. In his next Pastoral Letter, Catholic-liberalism had become "a snake which wriggles into all the ranks of Christian society, and steals even into the sanctuary, to spread trouble and desolation."[26] Fortunately for the Liberal party in Quebec, the case was won by them on an appeal to the Supreme Court. Judge Taschereau, brother of the Archbishop of Quebec, read the unanimous decision.[27]

With this decision, more moderate councils within the church had some effect, both in Quebec and at Rome. In Quebec, in a joint Declaration, the Archbishop and bishops criticized the decision on the grounds that it prevented the church from defending itself against anti-clericals, and asked the legislators to amend the Elections Act.[28] But Archbishop Taschereau did not agree that all Liberals were guilty of the sin of Catholic-liberalism. Two prominent Liberals were allowed to continue to lecture in law at the University of Laval in Quebec, even though one of them had been the Liberal advocate in the Charlevoix case.[29] Taschereau exerted some influence at Rome to defend the Liberal party. The result was the despatch of a Papal Delegate, Bishop Conroy, to investigate the situation.

Conroy's instructions made conciliation possible.

It must be added that the Church, while condemning liberalism, did not mean to strike at each and every political party which, by chance, calls itself Liberal, since the decisions of the Church refer

---

[24] "Jugement de Son Honneur le juge Routhier," (Québec, 1876).

[25] *Statutes of Canada*, 37 Vict., c. 9, s. 95.

[26] *Mandements*, VII, 302, 1 Feb, 1867.

[27] Rumilly, *Histoire*, II, 135. Decision dated 23 Feb., 1877.

[28] "Pièces relatives à la question de l'Influence Indue," (Québec, 1881) Declaration dated 26 March, 1877.

[29] Rumilly, *Histoire*, II, 68.

to certain false beliefs opposed to Catholic doctrine, and not to any particular political party.[30]

Conroy's problem was to decide whether Canadian Liberalism meant Catholic-liberalism. The instructions were also a reminder of a fact which the ultramontane bishops were inclined to overlook.

The bishops must be urged to observe the greatest caution in political matters, especially concerning the danger of provoking the Protestants, already uneasy about and angry at the clergy, into a violent battle against the Church, under the pretext of improper influence in elections.[31]

Before Bishop Conroy's visit to Canada, Wilfrid Laurier had not taken a prominent part in the controversy over Catholic-liberalism. In view of his background, Laurier might well have been considered a *Rouge* disguised as a Liberal. His Montreal law-partner, G. Lanctot, had been a *Rouge* who later became a Protestant and a militant anti-Catholic.[32] While in Montreal, Laurier had been an active member of the *Institut Canadien*, and had been Vice-President in 1866.[33] Laurier left Montreal that year for reasons of health, but did not separate himself from the *Rouges*. Instead, he continued the publication of the weekly *Le Défricheur*, founded by Eric Dorion. He appears to have carried on Dorion's feud with *Le Journal des Trois Rivières*, the official organ of the ultramontane Bishop Laflèche,[34] until *Le Défricheur* failed in 1867. After Laurier entered politics, he openly criticized the educational system of the province of Quebec.[35] In his private correspondence, Laurier was even more forthright. He wrote in 1875 that he was not eager for a Cabinet position.

The moment I shall accept office, I will go into it actively and earnestly, & from that moment my quietness & my happiness will be gone. It will be a war with the clergy, a war of every day, of every moment, with the most ignorant, the most bitter, the most prejudiced foes that man ever had to contend with. . . . I will be denounced as Antichrist. You may laugh at that, but it is no laughing matter to us.[36]

[30] *Ibid.*, 141.
[31] *Ibid.*
[32] J. S. Willison, *Sir Wilfrid Laurier and the Liberal Party* (Toronto, 1903), I. 94.
[33] Public Archives of Canada (hereinafter P.A.C.), Laurier Papers (hereinafter LP), 218433, list of officers for that year.
[34] Willison, *Laurier*, I, 113.
[35] *Commons Debates*, 23 March, 1877, 952.
[36] L. P., W. L. to J. Young, 2 Dec., 1875.

As Laurier himself said later, in connection with this and other letters written at this time, this was "forcible language."[37] Nothing could reveal more clearly the strain during these years upon men who believed it possible to be both political Liberals and sincere Roman Catholics.

At the city of Quebec, while Bishop Conroy was still conducting his investigation, Laurier made a speech on the subject of Catholic-liberalism. The speech was a carefully prepared statement of his views on the political situation in the province. Prime Minister Mackenzie had suggested discretion. "The opinion seems to prevail that if you could postpone the lecture until the Legate has finished his Canadian mission it would be the safer course."[38] Laurier does appear to have taken the precaution of submitting his text to a prominent churchman to check its orthodoxy.[39] In spite of the warning and the precaution, the speech was by no means a surrender of political independence. Instead, it was so outspoken that from relative political obscurity, Laurier emerged as the spokesman for French-Canadian Liberals.

Laurier argued that men were either liberal or conservative, depending upon their temperaments. As a result, the two political parties based on the principles of liberalism or conservatism could not be distinguished morally. Laurier defined liberalism as the belief that there were political abuses to be reformed. He was on more controversial grounds when he claimed that the Liberal party in Quebec was the party of Fox, O'Connell, Grey and Russell, rather than the party of European revolutionaries. He admitted that the platform of L'Avenir had been revolutionary. "The only excuse for these Liberals was their youth."[40]

Since that time, the party has received new accessions, calmer and more thoughtful ideas have prevailed in it: and as for the old programme, nothing whatever remains of its social part, while, of the political part, there only remains the principles of the English Liberal party.[41]

Meantime, he argued, the Conservative party had also undergone a transition. George Etienne Cartier had been devoted to the principles of the English constitution; Conservative leaders were now trying to create a Catholic party. Laurier was willing to allow the

[37] Ibid., 4 Dec., 1908.
[38] Ibid., A. Mackenzie to W. L., 21 June, 1877.
[39] Langelier, Souvenirs, I, 39.
[40] U. Barthe, ed., Wilfrid Laurier on the Platform, 1871-1890 (Quebec, 1890), 69.
[41] Ibid., 71.

priests "to say, that if I am elected, the State will be endangered,"[42] but the priest should not use his religious authority to dictate to the elector. Such domination by the clergy could only result in two religious, instead of two political parties, with unfortunate results. The priests, he claimed, were risking the welfare of the church by interfering in politics.

Like all Laurier's major speeches, this speech is almost as effective in print as it was when delivered. Laurier did not rely upon gesticulations or upon emotional appeals. His reasoning has something of the clarity of a geometric theorem. Its impact was nonetheless emotional. There is the impression of an intense conviction held within the bounds of logic and reason. No criticism of his arguments could destroy the impression of sincerity.

Laurier's main argument was not new. He himself had identified the French-Canadian Liberal party with the English Liberal party in the House of Commons in 1874.[43] Nor were able critics of his thesis wanting. L. G. Desjardins pointed out that Laurier had made no attempt to define the program of the present Liberal party in order to contrast it with the *Rouge* program.[44] The speech was important because it was timed to coincide with the visit of the Papal Delegate, who was considering the very issues which Laurier had discussed. At such a time, newspaper editors, Liberal and Conservative, agreed that the speech was newsworthy, and gave it wide publicity. It is worthy of note that the two problems mentioned in Bishop Conroy's instructions, the definition of Canadian Liberalism and the dangers of clerical interference, were the two main points emphasized by Laurier. Conroy's decision may not have been directly influenced by the speech, but had he disagreed with Laurier's conclusions, he would have had to refute them specifically. Laurier's arguments were too widely publicized to be ignored. Indirectly, the speech was important because it made Laurier a prominent figure in the province, and one who was not entirely unknown in culturally remote Toronto.

Whatever the direct effect of Laurier's speech may have been, the result of Conroy's mission was to benefit the Liberal party. In October, a joint Circular of the bishops of the province reminded priests that they were to follow the advice of their bishops in political matters.

When you thus have explained to your flock the principles which ought to guide it in its choice, leave to the conscience of each the

[42] *Ibid.*, 75.
[43] Willison, *Laurier*, I, 143.
[44] "M. Laurier devant l'histoire," (Québec, 1877). Desjardins (1849-1928) was a political pamphleteer and author, and was at this time editor of the ultramontane Québec *Le Canadien*.

*job of applying them to individuals and parties. And when a peni-
tent tells you that he voted in good conscience and in the sight of
God, do not question his good faith. . . .*[45]

This was as great a concession as the Liberals could expect.

This did not end the problem. In 1880, Israel Tarte was still
denouncing "the Liberal-Catholic school."[46] An election in Berthier
county in that same year was annulled by the courts for undue
clerical interference.[47] Bishop Laflèche, in a Memoir to the Vatican,
declared that the Liberal party was only the *Rouge* party in disguise.
He bluntly identified Canadian Liberalism with European liberalism.[48] Archbishop Taschereau replied to this Memoir with a strong
defence of the sincerity of the Liberal leaders. To Laflèche's demand that steps be taken to amend the Elections Act, the Archbishop replied that the time was inopportune in view of the excesses of
the priests in the Berthier county election.[49] The long struggle for
survival of the Liberal party in Quebec may be said to end with an
official letter from Rome, repeating the instructions issued to Bishop
Conroy, and postponing any demand for the amendment of the
Elections Act.[50] The ultramontane group in the church in the province were further humiliated by other decisions from Rome at this
time, decisions which favored Taschereau and the moderate party in
the episcopacy at their expense.[51]

Laurier summarized the results of this decade of controversy in
two letters to Edward Blake. In the first, he explained that the
Liberal party had at least averted the danger of being proscribed by
the clergy in Quebec.

*Clerical influence is not the greatest obstacle we have. It can now
be met and fought: it cannot be overcome, but it is a great advantage to be able to say to conscientious and intelligent Catholics
that by the authority of the Pope they are free.*[52]

But although this had saved the Liberal party from extinction in the
province, the Liberals had not won the confidence of the clergy.

[45] *Mandements*, IX, 128. 11 Oct., 1877.
[46] "Le clergé, ses droits, nos devoirs," (Québec, 1880).
[47] Rumilly, *Histoire*, III, 155.
[48] Archbishop Taschereau, "Rémarques sur le mémoire de l'Evêque
des Trois-Rivières" (Québec, 1882).
[49] "Pièces relatives à la question de l'influence indue," quoting Taschereau to Laflèche, 2 Feb., 1881.
[50] *Mandements*, IX, 383ff. 13 Sept., 1881.
[51] See Rumilly, *Histoire*, IV, 63 and 192 for details on the division of
the diocese of Three Rivers and on the Laval University controversy.
[52] Blake Papers, W. L. to Blake, 7 Dec., 1881.

The colleges with us are a hot bed of conservatism, & this is how it acts. The education which we receive in all our colleges is in the hands of the priests. Very good men they are indeed, but prejudiced, biased, & except upon those branches of knowledge of which they have made a specialty, very ignorant. Very ignorant, especially are they of modern history. The books they have read, all the sources of information to which they have access, are the continental ultramontane books & press. They have there imbibed a horror of the very name of liberalism, which permeates the whole of their teaching.[53]

For the next few elections most of the episcopacy remained Conservative by personal conviction, but were carefully neutral when acting in an official capacity. Thus the Liberal party in Quebec survived, although it was still a puny rival to the Conservative party.

[53] *Ibid.*, 10 July, 1882.

2.
The Castors

The history of Canada in the 1880's is dominated by the momentous challenge of the Canadian Pacific Railway and by the passions evoked by the death of Louis Riel.

In Quebec, this period was one of dissension within the Conservative party which on occasion became an open breach. This factional struggle was never satisfactorily resolved. Divided by incompatible political philosophies, two groups within the party fought an indecisive struggle for supremacy which was only terminated when one was absorbed by the Liberal party in the 1890's. It was this dissension among the Quebec Conservatives, rather than national issues, which was to make possible the emergence of a "solid Liberal" Quebec.

The ultramontane Roman Catholics, clerics and laymen, had not confined their attacks to the Liberals. The *Programme Catholique* had favored the Conservative party, but had added some qualifications.

It is enough to say that by the Conservative Party, we do not mean any collection of men having no other bond but that of gain and personal ambition, but a group of men sincerely ascribing to identical principles of religion and nationality, professing the traditions of the old Conservative Party, summed up in an unshakeable attachment to Catholic doctrines and in a thorough devotion to the national interests of Lower Canada.[1]

On the basis of this definition even Cartier himself was not a true Conservative, and the *Programmistes* were an important factor in Cartier's defeat in Montreal East in 1872.[2] After the death of Cartier, Joseph Adolphe Chapleau soon became the most serious foe of the ultraclericals within the Conservative party.

Chapleau's political interests, like Cartier's, had more affinity with the railways than with the rubric. By 1875, Chapleau was the chief spokesman of the Conservative Boucherville government on railway policy.[3] In 1881, as Premier, Chapleau issued an election manifesto which conveys clearly his political policy.

[1] *Mandements*, VIII, 397.
[2] See Rumilly, *Histoire*, I, 209ff.
[3] *Ibid.*, II, 92.

Our province has entered a new phase; hitherto, we dealt with administration; now, we are obliged to concern ourselves with policy. The subsidies given the railways, the opening up of the North, the projects for new construction of railway tracks, the need to protect against the competition we will have to bear from rival lines, the combinations which would control our financial and commercial affairs, all this will demand new legislation, going far beyond that adopted until now, in importance, in impact and in results to come.[4]

Nowhere in the manifesto is religion mentioned as an issue in the election. The materialistic political philosophy implicit in the pamphlet had little in common with the *Programmiste* definition of "the traditions of the old Conservative Party." Indeed, the open clash between the Chapleau group and the *Programmistes* was precipitated by a decision of Chapleau's in connection with a provincial railway.

One railway dominated Quebec politics – the Quebec, Montreal, Ottawa and Eastern, more often called the North Shore Railway. In the 1870's, companies were organized to build the railway of the *Rive Nord* from Montreal to Quebec, and the railway *du Nord* from Montreal to Ottawa. Both were colonization railways, expected to open up new areas for settlement. Curé Labelle, the "Apostle of Colonization," had strenuously campaigned for the Montreal-Ottawa line, and he had gained the support of Chapleau, who was directly concerned as member for the county of Terrebonne.[5] Unfortunately, neither of the two railway companies could obtain the necessary loans from England because of the depression, and it was widely believed, because of the hostility of the Grand Trunk.[6]

The political importance of the two railways was recognized in the provincial budget of 1875, by which the government assumed the responsibility of purchasing and operating them.[7] For other provincial railways in financial difficulty the government offered only restricted guarantees of interest. This was naturally unsatisfactory to the region south of the St. Lawrence, yet the government remained firm.[8] The political importance of these two railways, now combined to form the North Shore Railway, was again illustrated in 1878 when the government brought in a bill to compel municipalities to pay the subsidies they had pledged.[9] This was the bill

[4] "L'Administration Chapleau," (Montréal, 1881).

[5] Rumilly, *Histoire*, I, 267.

[6] *Ibid.*, 350.

[7] *Ibid.*, II, 89.

[8] *Ibid.*, 102.

[9] *Ibid.*, II, 188.

which Lieutenant Governor Letellier refused to sign, which in turn led to Premier Boucherville's resignation.

The function of the North Shore Railway as a colonization road helps to explain why it was so important politically. Sir Charles Tupper explained to the House of Commons that since the Northwest had no appeal to the French-Canadians, the federal government would be justified in subsidizing colonization lines from Montreal to Ottawa.[10] French-Canadians were very aware that settlement in Western Canada would increase the proportion of English-Canadians in the Dominion. The vision of Archbishop Taché of St. Boniface of a new French Canadian province in the Northwest was already recognized as an illusion. If the French-Canadians were to retain their relative position in the Dominion, new areas of settlement would have to be opened in northern Quebec. With this racial motive was combined a strong religious incentive. The strength of the Roman Catholic church came from the *habitant* in the country parish. As Curé Labelle said of the settlements along the Montreal-Ottawa railway,

This is why, in adopting the parish system as the chief basis of our colonization plan, we have used deliberately a means which is in perfect harmony with the inspirations of the French Canadian.[11]

French-Canadian *nationalisme* is firmly grounded on race and religion, and so the colonization railways had a strong emotional appeal for French Canadians in all areas of the province. No provincial politician could ignore this aspect of the North Shore Railway.

For those actively involved in the North Shore Railway, there were other considerations. If the railway was to be profitable, it would have to handle through-traffic; it had to become the eastern link of the Canadian Pacific Railway. And for those connected with the provincial government, the railway was a political liability which could be best removed by its sale to a private company. Regional ambitions were also involved; both Quebec and Montreal hoped to become the terminus of the Canadian Pacific, and so the major Canadian summer port. And naturally, personal ambitions and profits would not be completely ignored.

The final disposal of the railway could not satisfy all these ambitions. In fact, it precipitated the political crisis. In 1882 Chapleau sold the railway in two sections. The Montreal-Ottawa section was sold to the Canadian Pacific; the Montreal-Quebec section to a

[10] *Commons Debates*, 17 May, 1883, 1253. On this see: A. I. Silver, "French Canada and the Prairie Frontier," *Canadian Historical Review*, L (March, 1969), 11-36.
[11] E. J. Auclair, *Le Curé Labelle* (Montréal, 1930), 131.

company in which Chapleau's friend, L. A. Sénécal, was prominent.[12]

One effect of the sale was regional dissatisfaction. The sale of the western section to the Canadian Pacific meant that Montreal would be the terminus, and hence the summer port. The sale of the eastern section to a provincial syndicate meant that it would become little more than a branch line. Chapleau could argue that he could not sell the entire line to the Canadian Pacific for the very good reason that that company did not choose to buy it.[13] To the disappointed residents of Three Rivers and Quebec somebody was at fault, and the government was the obvious scapegoat. J. J. Ross of Three Rivers resigned from the cabinet.[14] Israel Tarte at Quebec led the Conservative opposition to the railway policy, in the interests of Quebec city.[15] Nor had this regional dissatisfaction been suppressed by 1885. In that year the federal government subsidized the Canadian Pacific Railway "short line", but at the same time authorized the company to buy or lease the Montreal-Quebec railway. The Quebec *L'Electeur* was not appeased. "This line is going to be diverted above Montreal and go to the Atlantic ports through American territory.... The city, the district, the whole French section of the province of Quebec is going to find itself utterly isolated."[16] Later that year the Canadian Pacific did purchase the line, but since Montreal remained the terminus, this gave little satisfaction to the region about Quebec.[17] This regional dissatisfaction was to have some effect on the results of the next federal election.

The most outspoken critics of Chapleau's sale of the railway were the men who became known as the Castors. "Castor" was the pseudonym of the author of a contemporary political pamphlet, entitled *Le Parti, Le Pays et Le Grand Homme*. The pamphlet was probably the most effective political tract ever published in the province. It expressed the point of view of the ultramontane group within the Conservative party, much as the *Programme Catholique* had done in the previous decade. But it was more than a statement of a political philosophy. Couched in a satirical style, with a literary quality unusual in such ephemeral publications, it was a scathing denunciation of Chapleau and the Chapleau faction. From then on, those who belonged to the ultramontane group were known as Castors. And from then on, there was to be no lasting truce between Chapleau and the Castors.

[12] Rumilly, *Histoire*, III, 167.
[13] "Discours de l'Hon. M. Chapleau," (Québec, 1882).
[14] *Ibid.*, 35.
[15] Langelier, *Souvenirs politiques*, I, 179.
[16] *L'Electeur*, 12 June, 1885.
[17] Rumilly, *Histoire*, V, 82.

It seems probable that the sale of the railway on any terms would have been unsatisfactory to the Castors. As has been suggested, many thought of the railway as a racial and religious undertaking. The Castors were of this group. Thus the sale of the railway to a financial syndicate was a betrayal of *nationaliste* interests. "Castor" discussed the widespread indignation at the sale "of that which M. Chapleau himself has called *our greatest! our fairest nationál possession*!!!"[18] But this argument could not be very effective since the provincial government was in such financial straits that the sale of the property was necessary. So "Castor" concentrated on the unprincipled behaviour of "Chapleau, Sénécal, Dansereau & Co." Arthur Dansereau, the editor of the Conservative *La Minerve* of Montreal, and a close friend of Chapleau's, had earned the sobriquet of "Boss" Dansereau because of his activities in connection with political patronage.[19] L. A. Sénécal was a capitalist who had amassed his fortune by speculative investments in railway and steamship companies.[20] According to "Castor," Chapleau controlled and utilized political power for the benefit of the triumvirate, while Dansereau controlled public patronage and Sénécal secured the funds from government subsidies.[21] Of Chapleau he said, "Already the new principle has been stated: the great man first; the party next, and the country – when the interests of the great man permit."[22] The principal charge against Chapleau was political ambition, based on avarice, at the sacrifice of political principles. There was enough truth in the accusation to make it convincing. Certainly the sale of the eastern section of the railway, which Sénécal had built and was administering for the provincial government, to a syndicate which included him, suggested that he and his friends were in no danger of losing money on the transaction.

Chapleau found the challenge too serious to ignore. Not content with defending his policy as logical and necessary, he replied by an attack on the motives of the Castors. He accused them of seeking office under a sham of piety, describing them as "all the ambitious mediocrities who cannot rise by the normal routes, all the disappointed, and a good number of hypocrites who pretend to be religious and conservative. . . ."[23] Such a statement would do little to restore the unity of the party.

[18] "Le parti, le pays et le grand homme," (Montréal, 1882), 73.
[19] See Rumilly, *Histoire*, I, 335 ff.
[20] *Ibid.*, III, 21.
[21] "Le parti, le pays et le grand homme," 94.
[22] *Ibid.*, 20.
[23] "La politique provinciale," (1883), speech of Chapleau, 6 Sept., 1883.

The division was not soon healed. In 1882 Chapleau left for Ottawa to become Secretary of State, but he continued to take an active part in provincial politics. As his successor as Premier, Chapleau had chosen J. A. Mousseau.[24] Mousseau's administration was short-lived. He narrowly escaped defeat at his by-election, and the election of a Liberal at another by-election with the help of the Castors further weakened his government,[25] and he resigned in January, 1884. He was succeeded by J. J. Ross, who included in his government L. O. Taillon. Both these men were *Programmistes* and Castors, and so the formation of the Ross administration marks the victory of the Castor faction in the provincial Conservative party. Yet even this did not end the party schism. Both at Ottawa and at Quebec, the two factions continued their feud. In 1883, Mousseau had complained to Macdonald that two of his cabinet ministers, Langevin and Caron, were giving aid to the Castor group.[26] Three years later, Chapleau was still determined to prevent the Castors from increasing their political influence in the party. To his friend G. A. Nantel, the provincial member for Terrebonne, he wrote: "No Castors! I warn you that if they put one of them into the government, either at Quebec or at Ottawa, I will leave the party the day he comes in."[27] This uncompromising hostility between Chapleau and the Castors was to remain a factor in Quebec politics until the turn of the century.

The Quebec Liberals were directly involved in the dispute between the Chapleau group and the Castors. Chapleau's hatred of the Castors had led to coalition negotiations with some of the Quebec Liberals. These *pourparlers* continued intermittently from 1880 to 1883. Since Chapleau and Mousseau were leaders of the provincial government during these years, the only explanation for their participation in these talks was that Chapleau wished to replace the Castors in his party by securing the support of the moderate section of the Liberal party.

These coalition attempts were not completely unrealistic. They almost succeeded. The discussions involved Chapleau and Mercier as the most prominent figures, with Mousseau, L. O. David and Curé Labelle also involved on occasion.[28] These Conservatives and Liberals shared a desire to emphasize the policy of the economic development of the province, in contrast to the Castor emphasis on

[24] P.A.C., Macdonald Papers, Chapleau to Macdonald, 10 April, 1886.
[25] Rumilly, *Histoire*, IV, 116.
[26] Macdonald Papers, Mousseau to Macdonald, 1 Oct., 1883.
[27] Rumilly, *Histoire*, VII, 59. Letter dated 14 Oct., 1886.
[28] R. Rumilly, *Honoré Mercier* (Montréal, 1936), 121 ff.

religious and racial matters and the *Rouge* policy of social reform. One of the difficulties arose over the policy concerning education. The provincial Education Act of 1875 had eliminated the Minister of Education, and had divided the Council of Public Instruction into two separate Committees. The Catholic Committee was composed of the bishops of the province and an equal number of laymen.[29] This guaranteed clerical control of Catholic education. The Liberals wished to increase political influence in education by restoring the Minister of Education to the cabinet. Another problem concerned the Legislative Council. The Council was a Conservative body, its members having been appointed by successive Conservative governments. As a result, the Liberals demanded its abolition.[30] Nonetheless, these problems might not have proved insurmountable. As Chapleau wrote to Dansereau:

We differ, the Liberal leaders and I, on only a couple of issues: the organization of public education and the Legislative Council. And even on these two points, will it not be better to wait for the first and agree to a reduction of expenditures on the second?[31]

Even Laurier at one time believed that the coalition could not be avoided.[32]

The contemplated coalition failed because party loyalties were too strong. The most outspoken criticisms naturally came from the extremist groups in each party. Castors publicly denounced any agreement with Liberals who wished to secularize education.[33] Doctrinaire Liberals were equally unwilling to compromise Liberal policy in connection with education or the Legislative Council. H. Joly, a French-Canadian Protestant, rigid and austere, resigned as leader of the provincial Liberal party because there seemed to be widespread support for the coalition among Liberals.[34] The *Rouges*, represented by H. Beaugrand and his Montreal newspaper *La Patrie*, were equally uncompromising. In a letter to Laurier, Beaugrand also threatened to retire from politics. "Here, in Montreal, we are uncompromisingly Liberal, and we want to remain clearly Liberal, and we don't want a leader who comes to sing us the old song of coalition."[35] And from Ottawa came protests from French-Canadian politicians of both parties – since provincial coalition

[29] Rumilly, *Histoire*, II, 81.

[30] Ibid., III, 14.

[31] Letter published in "Mémoires sur la coalition," (St. Hyacinthe, 1886). It is dated 18 Oct., 1881.

[32] Blake Papers, W. L. to Blake, 12 Sept., 1882.

[33] J. I. Tarte, "Lettres à l'Hon. H. Langevin," (Québec, 1880).

[34] Blake Papers, W. L. to Blake, 27 Nov., 1882.

[35] L. P. Beaugrand to W. L., 19 Jan., 1883.

would destroy the party organization of the federal parties in the province. It was believed that Langevin used his influence to deter the Conservatives,[36] and certainly the Liberal Senator R. Thibaudeau did his best to rouse Liberal opposition to the coalition.[37] In view of this opposition, a complete merger of the Chapleau group and the moderate Liberals was impossible. Even an alliance could not be arranged, since each group feared domination by the other. Thus the negotiations failed to come to an agreement over the very practical problems of the allocation of portfolios and the choice of a leader in the proposed coalition government.[38]

The Liberals in Quebec derived no immediate benefit from the coalition discussions. The negotiations had widened the breach between Chapleau and the Castors, but their failure left the Conservative party formally united as before. And the contemplated coalition had divided the Liberal as well as the Conservative party. Many Liberals had been eager for a coalition, since this appeared to be the only way to escape the stigma of Catholic-liberalism, and the resultant friction between the Liberal factions was not soon forgotten. For a short interlude, there did seem a possibility that the Liberal party would be strengthened by the support of the Castors. The charge of corruption, raised against the Chapleau administration by the pamphlet of "Castor", was also the main accusation made by the Liberals against the same government. For this reason, Liberals and Castors appeared on the same platform in support of the Liberal candidate opposing Mousseau in his by-election in 1883.[39] But this cooperation could not last for long. Liberals and Castors were opposed on most political issues, and their personal feud over Catholic-liberalism was not yet forgotten. With the formation of the Ross government in 1884, Liberals and Castors were once more in opposite camps.

The incident of the Mousseau by-election was nonetheless significant. One effect was to put an end to the talk of coalition. Too many bitter things were said by Mercier and Chapleau in that campaign to be ignored.[40] Thus, in 1884, Mercier preferred the formation of a government dominated by Castors to the alternative of a coalition with Mousseau.[41] And even the collaboration of the Liberals and Castors at this election, temporary as it was, facilitated the formation of Mercier's *parti national* in 1886.

As far as the Liberal party was concerned, the most significant

[36] Blake Papers, W. L. to Blake, 12 Sept., 1882.
[37] Rumilly, *Histoire*, III, 14 ff.
[38] *Ibid.*, 60.
[39] *Ibid.*, IV, 98.
[40] *Ibid.*, IV, 102 and 104.
[41] *Ibid.*, IV, 123.

result of the coalition discussions was the selection of Mercier as leader of the provincial party when Joly resigned. Mercier was not a *Rouge*. He had left the Conservative party in 1866 on the grounds that Confederation gave inadequate guarantees to the French Canadians.[42] He had been one of the founders of the *Parti National* in 1872. Like Laurier, he had long declared that Liberalism was not a threat to Roman Catholicism.[43] As leader of the party, he went even farther. In his opening speech as leader of the Opposition in 1883, he discussed the problem of education.

We must work harder to assure our children an education which is both practical and moral. Do not forget that atheistic training can produce socialists and revolutionaries, but not honest citizens and faithful patriots. . . . Therefore, let us give our children the nourishment of a moral and Christian education. With that in mind, let us not be afraid to accept respectfully, but without shirking our own responsibilities, the wise and prudent advice of distinguished men who, in the Council of Public Education, can help us carry out for our children the very difficult but very noble mission of training good citizens and proper Christians.[44]

Small wonder, in view of these sentiments, that former *Rouges* like Beaugrand opposed the choice of Mercier as leader. But the *Rouges* remained within the Liberal party since, even under Mercier, the Liberal party was preferable to the Conservative party. Thus, under Mercier's leadership, the Liberal party in Quebec further separated itself from the old *Rouge* traditions, without weakening the party.

During these years of dissension within the provincial parties, Laurier's activities attracted but scant attention. Even Laurier's biographers have almost ignored this phase of his career.[45] Politics was monopolized by the Canadian Pacific Railway during these years, and on this question Laurier had little to say. The railway was not of great moment to the French Canadians, who were more interested in colonization schemes in the Eastern Townships and north of the St. Lawrence than on the remote prairies. Nor did problems of finance greatly interest Laurier – yet this was the only aspect of the Canadian Pacific Railway which the Liberals could safely challenge. Finally, Blake so dominated the Canadian Pacific debates that his lieutenants had little to do but vote for the Opposition amendments. Dafoe's description of Laurier in those years is that of a "deskmate to Blake," handing Blake his references and filling his water-glass, but remaining silent.[46]

Laurier took little part in provincial politics during this period because he was disillusioned with the low moral standards in that sphere. Conservative corruption had been a constant refrain among Liberals, but now Laurier suspected the honesty of some of the Liberals. "The truth is that the (provincial) Conservative party are corrupt to the core, & the Liberal party, these last years have also become greatly contaminated."[47] According to Laurier, it was this contamination which explained the coalition sentiment among provincial Liberals, since these men wished to share in the financial profits available to office-holders. At one time Laurier even implied that coalition would have its compensations.

As to the coalition . . . the pourparlers have been carried so far that I now desire to see the coalition effected at the earliest moment. Our forces now are paralysed. When the coalition is completed, since it cannot be avoided, though we may for the moment be stunned in the scuffle which is sure to ensue, new elements of strength may be gathered, new questions may arise, & new combinations formed. The party cannot be any weaker than it now is . . .[48]

The assumption was that the loss of the coalition Liberals would leave the Liberal party weakened but purified.

Laurier's attitude virtually amounted to a withdrawal from provincial party affairs. It was apparently suggested in 1884 that Laurier might take over the leadership of the party in Quebec. His reply was blunt.

Even if I were free to do so, why should I take upon myself to lead the party, when my views are not those of the party? I know that my conception of the duties of a public man appears to be too rigid and too naive. I am not entering into any controversy on these points for it would be to no purpose; my views are very definite and I could not change them. The clearly defined duty of everyone within our ranks is to make constant opposition to every form of self-interested politics and to adopt a policy of self-abnegation. Our party has not had the courage necessary to follow this self-surrendering course of action. I am not supported in these views

---

[46] J. W. Dafoe, *Laurier: A Study in Canadian Politics* (Toronto, 1922), 16.

[47] Blake Papers, W. L. to Blake, 27 Nov., 1882.

[48] *Ibid.*, 12 Sept., 1882.

and, sensing this, I content myself, when I indulge in politics, to work along my own lines.[49]

With such principles, Laurier had more in common with Joly than with Mercier. In federal politics, he found a kindred spirit in Edward Blake.

Laurier did not confine his criticism of corruption to confidential letters, although in public he contented himself with criticizing Conservative corruption. In 1881, the Liberal *L'Electeur* of Quebec published an article entitled "The Den of Forty Thieves." It was a harsh denunciation of Sénécal's administration of the North Shore Railway, calling it "robbery erected into a system."[50] When a libel suit was brought against the editor, Laurier admitted authorship. Laurier's legal defence was an attempt to prove his accusations. As he wrote to Blake, "If I am successful in this trial, it must help us materially, for if I am successful it will be by showing how perverse the other side is."[51] The jury could not agree, although the majority favored an acquittal.[52] Yet even this indecisive conclusion redounded to the credit of Laurier, and further blackened the reputation of Sénécal.

Although Laurier had little direct influence in provincial politics in this period, his activities at Ottawa were nonetheless important. It was during these years in Opposition that the differentiation between the political philosophies of the two parties was established. Laurier's analysis was probably accepted by most Liberals.

I believe I can also say that it is a matter of history that ever since (Confederation), and especially since the honorable gentleman (John A. Macdonald) returned to power, he has endeavored to forward legislation which is gradually superseding the federative character of this union, and making it a legislative union.[53]

In contrast to this, the Liberals defended provincial rights. The two major issues during these years were the National Policy and the Canadian Pacific. However centralizing in tendency these may have been, the Liberals had admitted in principle the necessity of a tariff and of a transcontinental railway. Thus it was on minor issues that the Liberals defended the principle of a federalism based on provin-

---

[49] L. Pacaud, ed., *Sir Wilfrid Laurier, Letters to My Father* (Toronto, 1935), 15. Letter dated 14 Jan., 1884.

[50] *L'Electeur*, 20 April, 1881.

[51] Blake Papers, W. L. to Blake, 7 Oct., 1881.

[52] Rumilly, *Histoire*, III, 114.

[53] *Commons Debates*, 18 March, 1884, 946.

cial autonomy. And it was Laurier who was the most prominent advocate of provincial rights on these occasions.

The Letellier incident was one of these occasions. The Liberal Lieutenant-Governor Letellier had dismissed the Conservative Boucherville ministry for neglecting to consult the Lieutenant-Governor in the manner established by custom.[54] In private, Laurier expressed the opinion that Letellier was not justified in his action. "We are of the opinion here that Letellier has 'upset the apple-cart'. What he has done is certainly unconstitutional and his action cannot be very well defended."[55] In public, Laurier was less forthright. He argued that it was not the function of the House of Commons to criticize Letellier. "His proper judges were the people of the province of Quebec."[56] Following the provincial elections of 1878, fought on this constitutional issue, the Liberals were able to form a government in the new Assembly.[57] In 1879 at Ottawa, on a motion for Letellier's dismissal, Laurier expressed himself in terms which were blunt, if not extreme. He argued that the question had been settled by the provincial electorate, and that "the Federal power in purely provincial matters is a foreign power."[58]

Laurier expressed a similar opinion when discussing the federal Franchise Act of 1885. This Act was intended to establish a uniform franchise for federal elections. Laurier admitted that it was logical to have uniformity within a community, but "we have not a single community in this country. We have seven different communities."[59]

It should be noted that Laurier mentioned seven different communities and not two. He was not assessing problems from a racial point of view. When discussing the prospect of provincial coalition with Blake, he had suggested that one result would be a solid bloc of Quebec members at Ottawa. He was sure this bloc would demand and probably obtain an additional subsidy for the province. Laurier did not discuss the effect this would have on Quebec; he was more concerned with the "universal clamor of beggary" which this would incite at Ottawa. His solution was national, not narrowly provincial: the assumption of provincial debts and the abolition of all provincial subsidies.[60] On the Ontario boundary dispute of 1882, he defended Ontario's claims on the basis that to

[54] See Rumilly, *Histoire*, II, 191-203.
[55] Pacaud, ed., *Letters*, 9. Letter dated 5 March, 1878.
[56] *Commons Debates*, 11 April, 1878, 1918.
[57] Rumilly, *Histoire*, II, 215.
[58] *Commons Debates*, 12 March, 1879, 325.
[59] *Ibid.*, 17 April, 1885, 1169.
[60] Blake Papers, W. L. to Blake, 12 Sept., 1882.

give justice to Ontario meant no sacrifice to the interests of Quebec.[61] In connection with a federal subsidy to the province of Quebec for the North Shore Railway, Laurier defended Blake's amendment that all other railways built in the national interest should receive similar subsidies. On this occasion he declared that the "peculiar position held in Confederation by our province" was endangered by federal encroachments on provincial authority, but also by granting special favors to one province. Only by a rigid adherence to "justice, equity and fairness" could a minority maintain any constitutional security.[62]

Such a judicial attitude was naturally unpopular among partisan Liberals in Quebec. Laurier defended himself in letters and speeches,[63] but his position might have been more difficult had it not been for Blake. Blake too could find principles of justice and equity where his provincial followers saw only political opportunities. Thus Blake opposed the federal incorporation of the Orange Order, an institution which was powerful in many Ontario ridings. Not content with a silent vote, Blake denounced the Order in a long speech. He gave as one reason the danger to provincial rights, since federal incorporation could give the Order property rights in provinces which had refused provincial incorporation. Of more importance was the danger from a society which was both religious and political. "Our religious opinions should be held entirely separate from our political leanings. No greater calamity can befall a community than when the cleavage of political parties is coincident with the cleavage of religious bodies."[64] Blake illustrated his point by discussing the Catholic-liberalism controversy in Quebec. The speech would have an appeal to all Quebec Liberals; the vote against the Orange Order, to all Roman Catholics.

By 1885 the emphasis on provincial rights had become an established Liberal principle. It was a natural reaction to Macdonald's emphasis on federal authority. The cry of provincial rights, however, could only be politically effective if a province or provinces interpreted this abstract phrase in concrete terms. Only when a sectional group believed it had been discriminated against, would it be influenced by the slogan.

The province of Quebec had some basis for complaint. It was almost bankrupt. In the period 1874 to 1882, $15,000,000 had been borrowed for expenditure on railways.[65] Chapleau had sur-

---

[61] *Commons Debates*, 4 April, 1882, 746.
[62] *Ibid.*, 12 April, 1884, 1542 ff.
[63] Pacaud, ed., *Letters*, 16-17.
[64] *Commons Debates*, 17 March, 1884, 908.
[65] W. Eggleston and C. T. Kraft, *Dominion-Provincial Subsidies or Grants* (Ottawa, 1939), 119.

vived one crisis by the sale of the North Shore Railway, but the problem remained. Both Mousseau and Taillon had appealed to Macdonald for an increase in the provincial subsidy.[66] The North Shore subsidy had been extracted from Macdonald only as a reward for supporting the latter's Pacific Resolutions.[67] The responsibility for the financial chaos in Quebec may not have been that of the federal government. Chapleau's administration had never been described as economical. Direct taxation might have balanced the budget, but no provincial government in Quebec had the courage to adopt this solution. So even the Conservatives were inclined to find the scapegoat at Ottawa. One such argument was that Confederation had meant a government-financed Canadian Pacific west of Quebec, and a government-financed Intercolonial east of Quebec, but Quebec itself had been ignored.[68]

It was easier for the provincial Liberals to use this argument, for it was a criticism of a Conservative government. Mercier had been outspoken in his first speech as leader of the Opposition.

He looked for his financial reform either in the institution of direct taxation or in an increase in the federal subsidy to the province. The latter solution, he stressed, was the best: it was fair as well, since the province, contributing a good deal of the federal budget, was nearly alone in not having seen an increase in its subsidy since Confederation.[69]

Mercier went even farther in his demand for the rights of his province. In 1884 he introduced resolutions to the effect that the provinces were autonomous within the legislative sphere defined by the British North America Act, and "that the frequent encroachments of the federal Parliament on their prerogatives constitute a basic threat."[70] On this issue, the federal and provincial Liberals were as one.

This dissatisfaction in the province of Quebec is important as a background to the Riel agitation. The temporary unanimity of the French-Canadians on that occasion would have been impossible without the previous widespread suspicion that they were being discriminated against by the federal government. There is a danger of exaggerating this emphasis on provincial rights. There is nothing to suggest that the dissatisfaction with the federal government was intense. More important is the fact that the Liberal party had be-

[66] Canada, *Sessional Papers*, 1885, No. 34, 578; No. 34b, 1.
[67] *Commons Debates*, 12 April, 1884, 1542.
[68] Houde, *Commons Debates*, 12 April, 1884, 1539.
[69] Rumilly, *Mercier*, 137ff.
[70] Rumilly, *Histoire*, IV, 145.

come identified with provincial rights. It was perhaps inevitable that Quebec would gravitate towards such a party, for Quebec, more than any other province, had a strong provincial consciousness. The principle of provincial rights could be appealed to by any province on such issues as financial or territorial jurisdiction; the province of Quebec could also appeal to the principle in any conflict of creed, race or language. The next five years were to see these issues become of paramount importance in Quebec.

3.
Mercier

"Since the Conservative government had hanged him [i.e. Riel], Quebec turned against that party, and for most of the next half-century Liberals ruled in a once Conservative stronghold."[1] This generalization has often been accepted uncritically; before Riel's death Quebec was Conservative, after his death, Liberal. This is an oversimplification. It ignores the fact that Quebec elected a Conservative majority in the federal election of 1887, and this in spite of the active support for the Liberals from Mercier and his provincial government. The significance of Riel's execution was that it presented an opportunity for agitation which Mercier used to become premier. The permanent effect on Quebec politics came from Mercier's activities after his election. The Riel incident was important, but it was not decisive.

The actual uprising in the Northwest Territories seems scarcely to have affected provincial politics in Quebec. It is true that Mercier introduced a resolution in the Assembly which held the federal authorities responsible for the uprising,[2] and in the debate there were some expressions of sympathy for "nos frères du Nord-Ouest," but the motion was defeated by forty-one votes to fifteen.[3] Evidently Mercier decided that as a political issue it had little value. Five months later, with the fate of the captured Riel not yet decided, Mercier could make a lengthy political speech which dealt with such local issues as the sale of the North Shore Railway and government extravagance, but which ignored the Northwest entirely.[4]

But only two months later, the execution of Riel roused deep emotions. The execution was a profound shock partly because it was so unexpected. In the past, Riel had become a symbol of *nationalisme*; he had successfully defended the rights of the minority in Manitoba, he had suffered banishment because of Orange prejudices. Now, once more, he had led the minority in a fight for their rights.[5] Many doubtless considered this a proper and appro-

[1] G. M. Wrong, *The Canadians: A Story of a People* (Toronto, 1938), 384.
[2] J. O. Pelland, ed., *L'Hon. Honoré Mercier: biographie, discours, conférences, etc.* (Montréal, 1890), 233.
[3] Rumilly, *Histoire*, v, 28.
[4] H. Mercier, "Discours de l'Hon. M. Mercier," 6 Sept., 1885.
[5] *L'Etendard*, 1 April, 1885.

priate course. Conditions might not quite have justified an appeal to arms, but when the rebellion was over, an amnesty seemed a proper conclusion. The government encouraged such an expectation. Even after the trial, the postponements of the execution suggested that there would be a final reprieve. Conservative as well as Liberal newspapers in Quebec favored clemency. *Le Nord* of St. Jerome, supposedly the mouthpiece of Chapleau, even stated categorically that the execution would not take place. "It is clear Riel will not be executed; that was decided some time ago by our government leaders, and we can now emphasize it. . . . Riel will not be hanged."[6] Naturally when Riel was hanged, there was a reaction all the more violent because of the complacent assumption that it would never happen. It has also been suggested that the violence of the emotional outburst was also affected by a small-pox epidemic in the province at this time.[7] Whatever the reasons, the effect was to unite the French-Canadians as no arguments or logic could ever have done.

On the Champ de Mars in Montreal, a huge protest meeting was held. The resolutions denounced Riel's execution, denounced the French-Canadian ministers who had betrayed their trust, and called upon the people to put aside "all divisions of political parties, of races and of creeds" in order to defeat Macdonald's government.[8] *Rouge* and *Bleu*, Liberal and Castor, French Canadians of every political affiliation addressed the crowd.[9] The formation of a *parti national* was the subject of every speech.

The movement required a leader. The obvious leader was Chapleau. His resignation from the Macdonald cabinet would have been an effective beginning for such a protest movement. Furthermore, Chapleau had the temperament and the oratorical ability. Chapleau was certainly tempted by the opportunity presented. As he wrote on the eve of the meeting on Champ de Mars:

On the night of the 11th instant (of November) . . . I felt the rising of the magnetic wave which has since carried everything before it in Quebec. At the dawn of the day on the 12th I had decided to give up the seat I had in the cabinet and follow the current, but I suddenly glanced in front of me, in the distance such a sight, tumult, fighting, bloodshed, misery and prostration; and a madman looking from the window of a prison and laughing, rubbing his hands and shouting incoherent words of malediction. I was horrified. I then read over my report and the conclusions, which amounted to a resignation with the assumption of the popular

[6] *Le Nord*, early October, 1885, quoted Rumilly, *Histoire*, v, 86.

[7] *Ibid.*, 85.

[8] *Gazette*, 23 Nov., 1885.

[9] *Herald*, 23 Nov., 1885.

movement, and before I could sign it, my resolve was changed and I wrote Sir John asking to inform His Excellency that I was giving my assent to the decision of my colleagues on the question of the execution of Riel.[10]

Behind this dramatized version of Chapleau's decision to abstain from the protest movement, one may postulate the restraining influence of Macdonald. Whatever the ultimate reason for Chapleau's decision, he became ineligible as leader of a *parti national.*

With Chapleau eliminated, Mercier was the logical leader. In order to save Riel, Mercier was willing to efface himself. He had even appealed to Chapleau to resign and had offered to act as Chapleau's lieutenant in the protest movement.[11] After Chapleau's refusal, Mercier no longer hesitated. He became the leader of the *parti national.* It was to be of great significance in the political history of the province that the Liberal Mercier rather than the Conservative Chapleau assumed leadership of the movement.

The fate of the *parti national* depended upon the attitude of the Castors. Most of the prominent Conservatives returned to the party fold when their indignation dissipated.[12] The Castors, with their emphasis on religion and language, were more deeply affected by the affront to *nationalisme.*[13] However, Riel had been an apostate, a religious maniac, and Archbishop Taché of St. Boniface as well as the Quebec bishops had warned against the dangers of a racial conflict, and had reminded their flocks of the respect due to authority.[14] On the other hand, much publicity was given to Riel's death-bed reconciliation with the church,[15] and to Taché's firm denial that the clergy rather than the government were responsible for Riel's death.[16] But even though the Castors might agree that the Conservative party no longer merited their support, it was difficult for them to agree on the alternative of supporting the Liberal party because of its connection with Catholic-liberalism. This dilemma is illustrated by the attitude adopted by two prominent Castors, F. X. Trudel and Bishop Laflèche. Trudel, known as the "Grand Vicar," was the most prominent layman in the Castor group, rigid, intransigent

[10] P. A. C., Chapleau Papers, Chapleau to W. W. Lynch, 21 Nov., 1885.

[11] Mercier to Chapleau, 21 Nov., 1885, quoted, Rumilly, *Mercier*, 252.

[12] Rumilly, *Histoire*, v, 141.

[13] F. X. Trudel in *L'Etendard*, 14 Sept., 1885, quoted, Rumilly, *Histoire*, v, 81.

[14] A. A. Taché, "La situation au Nord-Ouest," (Québec, 1885), 7 and 21, statement of 7 Nov., 1885. See also Rumilly, *Histoire*, v, 142 ff.

[15] "Louis Riel, martyr du Nord-Ouest," (Montréal, 1885).

[16] Taché, "Situation," *op. cit.*

and sincere.[17] Trudel believed that John A. Macdonald must be punished. The ultramontane Bishop Laflèche of Three Rivers, after a decade of denouncing Catholic-liberalism, believed that even a Conservative government was preferable to Liberal government. As Trudel wrote to a friend:

I explained to them [i.e. to Mgr. Laflèche and other clergymen at Three Rivers] as well as I could my point of view, that Sir John had to be overthrown and that, with that in mind, it made no sense to keep an accomplice of that same Sir John in power in Quebec, but they always have that dread fear of Mercier and the Liberals.[18]

Mercier did his best to win the support of the Castors by fanning the flames of resentment and by accentuating his *nationalisme*. In the Assembly in 1886 he appealed to racial and religious emotions.

I believe that the Legislative Assembly of the province of Québec represents above all a French and Catholic population; I believe that the authors of Confederation, those who worked out the federal pact, had at least the wisdom to preserve for us in the new Canada a shelter where sometimes the supporters of our nationality could come together, without danger or threat – a holy sanctuary from which we can, under the protection of the new constitution, speak French and express French sentiments.[19]

Mercier's election manifesto in that year was an appeal for a political union based on *nationaliste* principals. He pledged to "keep all the religious and other guarantees on which our existing education system is based . . ."[20]

Nowhere does the manifesto mention the other controversial issue, the reform of the Legislative Council. There can be no doubt that Mercier was suppressing the old Liberal platform in order to gain the support of the Castors. It seemed possible that the temporary cooperation of Liberals and Castors against Chapleau and Mousseau might be revived.

Even after the provincial election of 1886, the result of Mercier's campaign was in doubt. Castor candidates had run as Nationalist-Conservatives and held the balance of power in the new Assembly. It was not yet clear whether these Castors would support the Ross government or Mercier. Langevin believed that Ross would survive.

[17] See L. O. David, *Mes Contemporains* (Montréal, 1894), 233 ff. for a biographical sketch.
[18] P. A. C., J. I. Tarte Papers, Box 10, F. X. Trudel to P. N. Trudel, 15 Nov., 1886.
[19] Pelland, ed., *Discours*, 234, speech of 7 May, 1886.
[20] Quoted, "Discours de . . . Mercier," (1889).

"Ross's government is much weakened, but I believe it will stand, unless the Nationalist-Conservatives vote with the Liberals to overthrow it, which is not likely. . . . My opinion is that Ross, when the session begins, will have a majority of 7 or 9."[21] Macdonald, however, advised Lieutenant-Governor Masson to allow Ross to resign, and to call upon a Conservative who could be more certain of forming a government which would have the support of the Nationalist-Conservatives. "In my opinion, the best interests of the Dominion would be prejudiced by that discreditable person Mr. Mercier forming a government."[22] L. O. Taillon, former Programmiste and Castor, replaced Ross. Not until the Assembly met in 1887 was the situation clarified. In the Assembly, the Nationalist-Conservatives voted for Mercier's candidate as the Speaker. Mercier was then invited to form an administration.[23]

Mercier had won the election. He had managed to secure the support of the Castors who had broken off relations with the Conservative party. Nonetheless, his position was far from secure. The *parti national* had been founded on passions aroused by Riel's execution, but an emotional protest against such an irrevocable act as an execution is an unstable foundation for a government. Other issues were needed to consolidate the unnatural alliance of Liberal and Castor. Mercier gave himself to the task of consolidation.

Meanwhile, the federal election of 1887 revealed that the Castors were not Liberal. It was the federal government which had hanged Riel, but much time had elapsed since then. The passions roused by the execution in 1885 had subsided by this time. Thus Bishop Laflèche, who had been undecided at the time of the provincial election, now openly returned to the Conservative party. As he wrote to one of his priests; "I find the *mouvement national* dangerous. I am sorry I did not oppose it from the start."[24]

At the same time, the federal Liberal party was not able to capitalize on *nationaliste* emotions as Mercier had done. The attitude of the English Liberals had also to be considered. The result of the provincial elections in Quebec proved that Mercier's platform was unacceptable to English citizens. In the past, Laurier had believed that the struggle over Catholic-liberalism would win all the English Protestants in the province to the Liberal cause.[25] But in the provincial election of 1886 no English Liberal was elected, either in the Eastern Townships or in Montreal.[26] Not until 1888 was

[21] Macdonald Papers, Langevin to Macdonald, 15 Oct., 1886.
[22] *Ibid., Letterbook*, 527, Macdonald to Masson, 8 Dec., 1886.
[23] Rumilly, *Histoire*, v, 214 ff.
[24] Tarte Papers, Laflèche to Curé of Ste. Anne, 19 Feb., 1887.
[25] LP, W. L. To J. Young, 16 Sept., 1874.
[26] Pelland, ed., *Discours*, dated 10 April, 1888.

Mercier able to secure a seat in the Assembly for an English Liberal to whom he could give a portfolio.[27] This had been a calculated risk, even Laurier arguing that it was a tactical necessity to emphasize the Northwest in the provincial campaign. "What ground we have gained and are still gaining, is gained upon that question, & upon that question alone. Were we to suppress it, we would stand exactly as we were before, or nearly so."[28] But in the federal campaign, the English Protestant vote could not be treated so cavalierly.

Nor was Laurier capable of conducting a campaign such as Mercier had done. He did not have the temperament of a demagogue. Laurier had been strongly opposed to Riel's execution. He had never condoned the execution of Scott, but he had maintained that it was a "political offence," the provisional government having been recognized by the federal government.[29] Even in his early years in politics, Laurier was both fair-minded and astute. In 1874, concerning the Manitoba troubles, he had written, "that in both Ontario and Quebec, we have been imprudent in intensifying the feelings of the people as we have done."[30] Now, in 1885, Laurier was convinced that the execution was unjust. Privately he admitted that Riel's conduct could not be defended and that Riel's trial had been fairly conducted. But he believed that "Riel was a monomaniac," and insisted that Riel had been hanged, not for treason, but "for Scott's murder; that is the simple truth of it." Laurier admitted that Quebec had been swept away by "blind prejudices, but the very same passions had caused the execution."[31]

Laurier himself had not been completely devoid of emotion on the Champ de Mars. For years he was to be reminded of his statement on that occasion, that "had I been born on the banks of the Saskatchewan I would myself have shouldered a musket."[32] Like all the speakers at this assembly, Laurier had spoken of the French Canadians uniting.[33] Had he stopped there, it would have been a contradiction of his political philosophy before and after 1885, since it suggested a party based on racial principles. Yet, even on this stirring occasion, Laurier resisted the temptations of demagoguery. He talked of remaining "within constitutional bounds" and of securing "powerful allies in all other provinces." Even the musket he might have shouldered would have been in defence of

[27] Rumilly, *Histoire*, VI, 111.
[28] Blake Papers, W. L. to Blake, 27 July, 1886.
[29] *Commons Debates*, 12 Feb. 1875, 117.
[30] LP, W.L. to J. Young, 16 Sept., 1874.
[31] Blake Papers, W. L. to Blake, 31 Dec., 1885.
[32] *Herald*, 23 Nov., 1885.
[33] *Ibid*.

constitutional rather than religious or racial rights.[34] His lack of passion is best illustrated by the contrast with Mercier.'s opening words on the same occasion: "Our poor brother is dead. He has been sacrificed to the fanaticism of the Orangemen."[35]

In the House of Commons, Laurier was following a difficult path with probable sincerity and undeniable astuteness. The Liberals were embarrassed by a motion introduced by Philippe Landry, a French-Canadian Conservative with Castor principles, which deplored the execution of Riel. [36] All the Liberal members could agree to blame the government for its mismanagement of the Northwest problem, but English Liberals were not willing to criticize the execution of Riel. On this motion, Laurier denounced the execution briefly, and in a dramatic speech went on to indict the cabinet for the shocking blunders which had caused the rebellion.[37] Laurier believed that such a motion of censure for the execution of Riel would ensure a Liberal majority from Quebec at the next elections, but he did not insist upon such a course. "Of course, if our friends in the other provinces cannot support that view, that is an end of it."[38] Thus Laurier was willing to forego a provincial triumph in the interests of the national party.

In the federal election of 1887, the Liberal party did increase its representation from Quebec. Thirty-two Liberals were returned as compared to seventeen in 1882. In view of advantages of the Liberals in this election, this was not a startling gain. For the first time the Liberals had the active support of the provincial government in an election. It has been suggested that Mercier supported Laurier in the hope that Laurier would reward him by conceding an increased federal subsidy if elected.[39] Whatever the explanation, Mercier's vigorous campaigning must have affected the outcome. But for the moderation of the Liberals on the Riel question, it is probable that Quebec would have returned a Liberal majority.

Indeed, it would appear that the railway policy of 1883 and 1885 was as important as the Riel issue in producing an anti-government trend.[40] More surprising than the increase of Liberal members was the regional distribution of the changes. Of the fifteen constituencies

[34] *Ibid.*

[35] *Gazette*, 23 Nov., 1885. [There are several reported versions of this text.]

[36] Rumilly, *Histoire*, v, 158.

[37] *Commons Debates*, 16 March, 1885.

[38] Blake Papers, W. L. to Blake, 31 Dec., 1885.

[39] Langelier, *Souvenirs*, I, 264.

[40] See above, p. 12.

gained by the Liberals, only three were in the Montreal district, [41] whereas eleven were from the districts of Three Rivers and Quebec.[42] The probability that the Liberal gains were regional in nature is illustrated by the fact that one of the Quebec district constituencies had been first won by the Liberals in a by-election which preceded Riel's execution.[43] The Riel execution could explain the increased support for the Liberals in 1887, but it could scarcely explain the regional distribution of these gains. Certainly the agitation over Riel had been more prominent in Montreal than in Three Rivers or Quebec. The defeat of the Conservatives in the eastern districts suggests that the Conservative railway policy was an important factor in the election. The economic historian might cynically dismiss the Riel issue entirely.

In the provincial field for the next few years, Mercier dominated politics as no man had done since Papineau. In part, this was because Mercier's policy was daring and surprisingly successful. But Macdonald's government and the anti-Catholic faction led by Dalton McCarthy have not always received the credit they deserve. Macdonald opposed "that discreditable person Mr. Mercier" whenever it was politically possible to do so. McCarthy waged a campaign which was openly anti-French. Against this opposition, the French Canadians of the province naturally rallied to Mercier's support. Laurier's role in the Liberal party in Quebec for these years was almost secondary. He defended Mercier at Ottawa when possible, and isolated the Mercier group from the rest of the party when it finally became a liability.

Mercier was careful to avoid issues which might alienate the National-Conservatives supporting his government. Nothing was done to implement the Liberal policy in connection with elimination of the Legislative Council. The question of the asylums was also shelved. The Liberals had long advocated state control of the asylums. The Castors had favored control by religious institutions at state expense. Mercier set up a Royal Commission,[44] and when the report was made he postponed any changes until the ten-year contract expired.[45] This left the problem to be dealt with by a subsequent government.

Mercier's emphasis upon colonization had a direct appeal to *nationalisme*. His efforts did not meet with much success in the way

[41] Chambly, Laprairie, L'Assomption.
[42] Beauce, Berthier, Drummond and Arthabaska, Megantic, Dorchester, Kamouraska, Levis, Montmagny, Quebec Centre, Rimouski. The fifteenth was Mississquoi, in the Eastern Townships.
[43] Levis, 14 April, 1885.
[44] Rumilly, *Histoire*, v, 241.
[45] *Ibid.*, vi, 99.

of attracting permanent immigrants,[46] but Mercier did manage to identify himself with an aggressive colonization policy and, politically, nothing more was necessary. Railways, as usual, were expected to open up new areas for settlement.[47] Much more striking was the appointment of Curé Labelle as Deputy-Minister of Colonization. This huge, jovial, energetic priest[48] had none of the asceticism of Bourget or Laflèche, but his popularity did not suffer on that account. His appointment as Deputy-Minster meant that colonization, which had already become linked with this "Apostle of Colonization," would henceforth be connected with the Mercier government.

Mercier's most successful measure, however, was his settlement of the Jesuits' Estates controversy. The problem required careful handling. The Jesuit Order had been despoiled of its property after the conquest. After the suppression of the Order by the Pope, the Roman Catholic church in Canada had continually solicited the government for control of the property.[49] In 1867 the problem became the responsibility of the provincial government. Then in 1871, the Jesuit Order, once more in existence, was authorized by the Pope to negotiate for the property.[50] This was a serious complication. The problem had been one of deciding how much money, if any, was to be paid by the government to the church as compensation for the confiscation. Now there was also the problem of deciding between the claims of the organized church in Canada and the Jesuit Order. This was complicated politically by the support given to the Jesuits by Bourget and the ultramontane group, in opposition to the moderates led by Archbishop Taschereau.[51] The arguments of these groups centred around the problem as to whether the resuscitated Order had any title to estates confiscated from the earlier Order. The real issue was the threat to the educational monopoly of the University of Laval by the Jesuit Order and the ultramontane group.[52] Chapleau and Mousseau had tried and failed to find a solution to the problem.[53]

Mercier took the first important step in 1887. He incorporated the Jesuit Order in the province[54] without any protests. Then he persuaded Rome to take the responsibility of allocating the money

[46] Ibid.
[47] Ibid., 20.
[48] Auclair, Labelle, 187 ff.
[49] Pelland, ed., Discours, 343, 28 June, 1888.
[50] Rumilly, Histoire, I., 225.
[51] Ibid.
[52] Ibid., IV, 65.
[53] Ibid., 66.
[54] Pelland, ed., Discours, 334.

he was about to grant as compensation.[55]After Mercier had persuaded the Jesuits to accept the arbitrary figure of $400,000[56] the political dilemma was resolved. None of the interested parties could refuse to accept the arbitration of Rome, and it was at Rome rather than at Quebec that the difficult decision would be made. The question had been removed from politics. Even the English minority were pacified. The additional sum of $60,000 was granted to the Protestant Committee of Public Instruction. This amount, approximately one-seventh of $400,000, was based on the proportion of the minority to the population of Quebec.[57] Conservatives and English alike accepted this settlement; the bill was passed unanimously.[58]

The Jesuits' Estates Act confirmed many English Canadians' suspicions aroused by the Riel agitation in Quebec. Since the Protestant minority in Quebec had neglected to oppose the measure, some Protestants at Ottawa willingly accepted the responsibility of saving the minority from French-Canadian domination. The acquiescence of the minority was explained as the result of the subservience of their representatives to the French-Canadian majority.[59] In reality, it was hatred of the Jesuit Order which prompted the disinterested attempt to save the English minority in Quebec. O'Brien's motion for the disallowance of the Act describes the Order as a "danger to the civil and religious liberties of the people of Canada."[60] The supporters of the motion quoted freely from criticisms of the Order prior to its suppression in 1774.[61] Since the Jesuits had been quietly incorporated two years before, these criticisms bore little relevance to the Estates Act. Another charge was that the Act gave to a foreign authority, the Pope, the power to interfere in political affairs. Apparently no difficulty was experienced proving that the favorable reply to Mercier's request was "usurpation" of political power by Rome.[62] Only thirteen members voted for the motion.[63]

This did not stop the agitation outside the province of Quebec. The next year D'Alton McCarthy introduced a bill to withdraw the privilege of using the French language in the Assembly of the North-West Territories. Even Laurier stated that he did not object

[55] Cardinal Simeoni to Mercier, 1 March, 1888, quoted in Pelland, ed., *Discours*, 345.
[56] Ibid.,357.
[57] *Ibid.*, 394.
[58] Rumilly, *Histoire*, VI, 27.
[59] D'Alton McCarthy, *Commons Debates,* 27 March, 1889, 853.
[60] *Commons Debates,* 26 March, 1889, 811.
[61] *Ibid.*, 813 ff. (O'Brien); 845 ff. (McCarthy).
[62] *Ibid.*, 811
[63] *Ibid.*, 910.

strongly to the measure, since the French population affected was small.[64] Laurier was not one to tilt at windmills. But the preamble to the bill was more sweeping. "Whereas it is expedient in the interests of the national unity in the Dominion that there should be community of language among the people of Canada . . . "[65] Nor was it difficult to find evidence in McCarthy's speeches to show that he contemplated a campaign against the French Canadians of which this was only a beginning.[66] Sir John Thompson moved an amendment by which the preamble was eliminated and the Assembly authorized to decide the question.[67] Laurier accepted this solution as maintaining the principle of provincial autonomy. As he explained privately, Quebec in its own interests should support the principle even when it appeared to work to the disadvantage of French Canadians.[68]

Although the Protestant agitation had little effect on federal legislation, outside of the House of Commons it received a good deal of publicity. Robert Sellar of the Huntington *Gleaner* provided much of the material. He argued that there was a concerted plan, financed by the Roman Catholic church, to drive the English out of the Eastern Townships. His pamphlet was published by the Equal Rights Association of Toronto.[69] The Toronto *Mail*, which had been the most provocative during the Riel crisis,[70] continued its fulminations.[71] The Protestant Protective Association was organised for the purpose of removing Roman Catholics from jobs and political positions.[72] The Orange Lodges naturally played their accustomed role.[73]

The issue was not a party one. It was natural that the Conservatives would be more outspoken, since Mercier had been a Liberal and still supported Laurier in the federal field. Furthermore, the most militant advocates of Protestantism – McCarthy, the Organgemen and the *Mail* – had all been closely connected with the Conservative party. Nevertheless, in the House, neither the government nor the Opposition supported the McCarthy group. At To-

[64] *Ibid.*, 17 Dec., 1890, 728.
[65] *Ibid.*, 14 Feb., 1890, 674 ff.
[66] *Ibid.*, 17 Feb., 1890, 726 ff.
[67] *Ibid.*, 18 Feb., 1890, 882.
[68] W. L. to E. Pacaud, 22 Feb. 1890, quoted, Pacaud, ed., *Letters*, 52.
[69] H. Mercier, "Réponse au pamphlet de L'Association des 'Equal Rights'," (Quebec, 1890).
[70] *Mail*, 23 Nov., 1885.
[71] Skelton, *Laurier*, I, 385.
[72] Willison, Laurier, II, 207, footnote.
[73] Skelton, *Laurier*, I, 385.

ronto, the *Globe*, as well as the *Mail*, had denounced the Estates Act, and had hoped for its disallowance.[74] The controversy tended to range Catholic against Protestant, Quebec against Ontario, rather than Liberal against Conservative. Laurier's position was a difficult one. Only Mercier could derive political strength from the situation in Quebec. As a leader of a *parti national*, he could pose as the defender of the French Catholics, and could cite the agitation in Ontario as evidence of the need for racial unity.

Our enemies seek to incite prejudices against us, and, uniting awkwardly their hatred of our religion with their hatred of our nationality, they seize the opportunity provided by a great act of justice recently carried out in the name of the state in order to restore properties illegitimately confiscated, to express their rage .... This province of Québec is Catholic and French, and is going to stay Catholic and French. ... To obtain this great result and assure our destiny, we have a pressing, urgent and solemn duty to perform. This duty is to cease our internal battles and unite.[75]

Thus Mercier was appealing to French Canadians regardless of their party affiliations. In this he was successful. Nobody since Papineau had so roused their latent *nationalisme*. Had this been all, the Liberal party would have benefited no more than the Conservative party from Mercier's success, but Mercier's government had been no more successful than its predecessors in balancing the budget. His colonization and railway policy entailed large expenditures, and in all matters the flamboyant Mercier was likely to consider economy measures as belittling the prestige of his province and himself. It was in connection with his financial measures that the Conservatives were openly ranged against Mercier.

Mercier believed that the best way to balance the provincial budget was to increase the federal grant to the province. In 1887 he assembled a Provincial Conference at Quebec to discuss Dominion-Provincial relations. In attendance were Fielding, Blair, Mowat and Norquay.[76] The delegates were unanimous in their desire that the authority of the federal government should be curtailed. Among the resolutions passed was a request that the power of disallowance should be transferred to the Imperial Government, and that the schedule of provincial subsidies should be amended.[77] Sir John ignored the Conference. Mercier had to resort to other means to balance his budget. He hoped to reduce the interest rates on Quebec

[74] *Globe*, 18 Feb., 1889.
[75] Rumilly, *Histoire*, VI, 89 ff.
[76] Rumilly, *Histoire*, V, 273.
[77] *Dominion-Provincial Conferences, 1887-1926*, 20 ff.

bonds from 5 per cent to 4 per cent, but Macdonald advised Tupper in London to arrange for a protest from Imperial bond-holders.[78] Mercier had to agree to make the conversion voluntary.[79] Mercier was forced to resort to a loan, but here again the Conservatives interfered. It was alleged that the Conservatives prevented the negotiation of a loan in New York in 1888, whereupon Mercier successfully borrowed money in France.[80] As Tupper later boasted, he used his influence to prevent a subsequent loan from being negotiated in England,[81] and so Mercier again borrowed money in France. That Mercier and the federal Conservatives were clearly in opposite camps was shown in the provincial election of 1890, when Macdonald used his personal influence to stimulate opposition to Mercier.[82] In this case Macdonald's influence in Quebec was not very effective.[83]

Mercier was no less provocative. Macdonald believed that the preamble to the Jesuits' Estates Act was intentionally objectionable.[84] The District Magistrates Act of 1888 was even more suspect, since it was a threat to appoint two Montreal judges which had "become necessary through the neglect of the federal authorities to appoint the judges authorised by this legislature."[85] Even Chapleau believed that Mercier was "desirous of provoking a conflict" and agreed that the federal government could not condone the "systematic invasion of federal authority."[86] The Act was disallowed.[87]

Mercier's success in Quebec was attested by the results of the election of 1890. His English Minister of Agriculture was defeated, three National-Conservatives were defeated, yet Mercier increased his majority by six.[88] The Riel question had been forgotten[89] and

[78] Macdonald to Tupper, 20 July 1888, quoted, J. H. Pope, ed., *Correspondence of Sir John A. Macdonald* (Toronto, 1921), 417.

[79] Rumilly, *Histoire*, VI, 41.

[80] "Le gouvernement Mercier," (Québec, 1890).

[81] Tupper to McMaster, 21 Oct. 1891, quoted, E. M. Saunders, *The Life and Letters of Sir Charles Tupper* (Toronto, 1916), II, 160.

[82] Macdonald Papers, *Letterbook*, 529, Macdonald to J. J. C. Abbott, 7 June, 1890.

[83] Macdonald Papers, Abbott to Macdonald, 9 June, 1890.

[84] Pope, ed., *Correspondence*, 441.

[85] Canada, *Correspondence, Reports of the Ministers of Justice and Orders in Council upon the subject of Dominion and Provincial Legislation, 1867-1896* (Ottawa, 1896), 344.

[86] P.A.C., Sir John Thompson Papers, Chapleau to Thompson, 5 March, 1889.

[87] *Dominion and Provincial Legislation, 1867-1895*, 344.

[89] Riel is not mentioned in the 354-page campaign booklet *Le gouvernement Mercier*, (Québec, 1890).

the coalition with the National-Conservatives suffered as a result. The election of 1890 showed that the majority of the French-Canadian voters had voted for Mercier rather than against the murderers of Riel.

In some ways, Mercier's success was a handicap to the Liberal party. Among the English Canadians, in Ontario as well as Quebec, his *nationalisme* was resented. There is nothing in the record of Mercier's government which proves discrimination against the provincial minority. Mercier himself insisted on his impartiality.[90] His speeches however left no doubt as to his preferences. Then too, Mercier's success seems to have gone to his head. As one *Rouge* wrote, "There is no government, there is only Mercier."[91] After the election, his arbitrary statement in the Assembly that he would willingly sacrifice his allies in order to obey the popular will[95] was not likely to conciliate his supporters. But most serious of all was his reputation for corruption. To Blake, Laurier admitted that Mercier's methods were "repugnant to my convictions," but he had rationalized his support for Mercier in the provincial election by arguing that his opponents were no better in this regard, and were less "Liberal" in others.[93] Laurier also warned Pacaud and Mercier of the danger to Mercier's government from unsavory railway deals.[94] After the disclosures of the Bay of Chaleurs railway scandal, and Lieutenant-Governor Angers' dismissal of the government,[95] Laurier could no longer restrict his opinions to confidential letters. The details were simple. Pacaud, acting for the provincial government, had arranged a transfer of the Bay of Chaleurs Railway charter from one company to another. The original company was reimbursed to the extent of $175,000. Of this sum, $100,000 was promptly returned to Pacaud.[96] It was never proved that Pacaud or Mercier benefited personally from this money, but not even Mercier's most ardent defenders were able to defend this method of collecting party funds.[97] Laurier could not support Mercier in the elections called by Boucherville in 1892 without losing English

[90] Pelland, ed., *Discours,* speech of 10 April, 1888.
[91] C. Lebeuf to E. Pacaud, 23 April, 1890, quoted, Rumilly, *Histoire,* VI, 134.
[92] *Ibid.,* 168.
[93] Blake Papers, W. L. to Blake, 12 Jan., 1890.
[94] W. L. to E. Pacaud, 20 April 1890, quoted, Pacaud, ed., *Letters,* 54.
[95] P. A. C., J. J. C. Abbott Papers, Box I, Angers-Mercier Correspondence.
[96] Rumilly, *Histoire,* VI, 237.
[97] C. Langelier's *Souvenirs politiques,* II, is an example of a generally pro-Mericer position.

Liberal support. Mercier's promise to reform[98] could not dispel "the widespread belief that Mercier is utterly corrupt."[99] So Laurier adopted the equivocal position of condemning "without hesitation" the Bay of Chaleurs scandal, but not admitting that Mercier's guilt had been proved. However, he continued, "this is not to say that I approve all that has been done by M. Mercier."[100]

After Mercier's rout in this election,[101] the Opposition did its best to eliminate the stigma of corruption. The coalition with the Nationalist Conservatives, weakened by 1890, had come to an end with the revelations of corruption.[102] The name *parti national* was now replaced by the name Liberal; Mercier was replaced as leader of the party by Felix Marchand, whose sober integrity was in sharp contrast to the character of his predecessor.[103] Laurier privately suggested that it would be better if Mercier did not attend the Liberal convention of 1893.[104] Even in 1897 the quarantine was still in effect. Of Marchand's cabinet of that year[105] only one portfolio was given to a former member of Mercier's cabinet.

The Liberal party in Quebec suffered less from Mercier's humiliation than might have been expected. At no time was Laurier or the federal Liberal party linked with the corruption, and the measures taken by the provincial party had some effect. Nor is it irrelevant that the McGreevy scandals had lessened the effect of the charges against the Liberal party. But probably more important was the treatment of Mercier by the provincial Conservatives. Not content with his political defeat, they brought a criminal action against him.[106] Mercier's physical decline was already apparent. Popular sympathy for Mercier developed as the case dragged on, and when the verdict of Not Guilty was announced, Mercier was given a public ovation. It is not too extreme to say that his death from diabetes two years later confirmed the belief that Mercier was a martyr, a victim of Conservative vindictiveness.

Thus the gains made by the Liberal party during Mercier's administration were not irrevocably lost by his political defeat. Laurier believed that Mercier's influence with the French Canadians was such that he could have held the province without resorting to

[98] Blake Papers, W. L. to Blake, 29 Dec., 1891.

[99] LP, Cartwright to W. L., 11 Nov., 1891.

[101] 52 ministerial, 18 opposition, 1 independent.

[102] Rumilly, *Histoire*, VI, 286.

[103] *Ibid.*, 14.

[104] LP, W. L. Fauvel to W. L., 30 May, 1893.

[105] Rumilly, *Histoire*, IX, 9.

[106] Rumilly, *Histoire*, IX, 9; J. I. Tarte, "1892 Procès Mercier,"

undesirable financial arrangements.[107] As we have seen, to the extent that this influence had been channelled along party lines, it had been for the benefit of the Liberals and against the Conservatives. The Riel incident had been important mainly because it made possible Mercier's victory in 1886. By 1890, Mercier had established himself on firmer ground. For the first time since Confederation, the opponents of the Conservatives had played the role of defenders of the French Canadian's race and religion; indeed, no Conservative had ever done it as aggressively as Mercier. In this respect, Mercier was one of the artisans of the "solid Liberal" Quebec. Mercier was not a "Liberal" of the Laurier mold, but he had nonetheless broken the Conservative monopoly as "defenders of the faith," and had made Laurier's political dominance of Quebec possible.

[107] J. S. Willison, *Reminiscences, Political and Personal* (Toronto, 1919), 168.

4.

The Reciprocity Interlude

Two developments in the Liberal party in the late 1880's merit detailed consideration. One was Laurier's succession to Blake as leader of the federal party; the other was the adoption by the party of the policy of Commercial Union, later modified to Unrestricted Reciprocity, with the United States. These two incidents help to explain Laurier's political philosophy. At the same time, these developments may be better understood by an explanation of Laurier's attitude towards them.

Laurier was Blake's choice as his successor as leader of the party. Blake had hoped to broaden the base of the Liberal party by gaining French-Canadian support. To achieve this it was necessary to modify the racial and religious tendencies inherited by the Liberals from the Grits. Hence Blake's criticism of the Orange Order and his refusal to condone the execution of Riel. For this strategy, Blake had found in Laurier an able lieutenant. Like Blake, Laurier was eager to build a party which would attract both English- and French-Canadian support by a political platform which avoided racial and religious appeals. Laurier's moderation during the Riel crisis must have impressed Blake greatly. The two men had reached a common position, acceptable, if not popular, in both Ontario and Quebec. But a moderate platform was not enough. If French Canadians were to become Liberals, it would require something more dramatic to loosen traditional political affiliations. When Blake decided to résign, he saw an opportunity. With Laurier as leader of the party, Blake' strategy would be maintained, and at the same time, Laurier's appointment would be a bold declaration to French Canadians that the Liberal party could be trusted. And so Blake advised his English supporters: "There is only one possible choice – Laurier."[1]

Laurier had a high respect for Blake. On occasion, he was almost fulsome in his praise for him.[2] This feeling was based on more than a respect for Blake's intellect and his legal ability; he was also impressed by his faculty for understanding and appreciating the point of view of the French-Canadian Roman Catholic. Indeed, it

---

[1] Skelton, *Laurier*, I, 341. See also: M. A. Banks, "The Change in the Liberal Party Leadership, 1887," *Canadian Historical Review*, XXXVIII (June, 1957), 109-128.

[2] U. Barthe, ed., *Wilfrid Laurier on the Platform, 1871-1890* (Quebec, 1890), 188.

seems probable that Edward Blake's influence on Laurier has not been fully appreciated. Laurier's lifelong conviction that English and French Canadians could reach a just compromise on controversial issues must have been strengthened by his association with Blake in the 1880's. At any rate, Laurier believed in 1887 that only Blake could retain the confidence of the Liberals in both Ontario and Quebec.[3] His assumption was that Blake would have to be succeeded by an English Canadian, and that no suitable candidate was available.

Laurier was unwilling to become leader because of this racial problem. In a country in which English Canadians were in the majority, he believed a French-Canadian leader would be a handicap. He gave as excuses his health and his poverty – and in fact, his health had never been good and he still depended on his legal practice for his income. But to Blake he explained that he feared that the racial controversies, aroused by Riel and Mercier on one hand, and the *Mail* and McCarthy on the other, would continue to bedevil Canadian politics.

You seem to believe that our party under the actual [actuel?] circumstances will consolidate and crystallize. My anticipations are the very reverse. It is manifest that we must more and more disintegrate. The only redeeming feature – I am selfish enough to use the term redeeming feature – is that the other side are already more disintegrated than we are.[4]

Later, Laurier made his fears more explicit. "A French-Canadian will not get a cheerful support in the English provinces."[5] In 1895, he talked of resigning. "I have always been of the opinion that an English leader would be much stronger than I can ever be, and everything confirms me in that opinion."[6] There is no evidence that Laurier ever changed his mind. In 1907 he still believed that his racial origin was a handicap to the party because of natural racial preferences. "We must take men as they are, and this condition of things has been the cause of more difficulties for me and less success to the party than would have been the case with a leader differently situated."[7] Laurier did not resign in the early years of his leadership only because there seemed no answer to the question he posed to Blake. "The only trouble is, if I give it up, who will assume it since you decline?"[8]

[3] Blake Papers, W.L. to Blake, 16 March, 1887.
[4] *Ibid.*, 16 Jan., 1888.
[5] *Ibid.*, 31 May, 1890.
[6] LP, W. L. to Hyman, 28 March, 1895.
[7] LP, W. L. to J. Kilbourne, 19 Nov., 1907.
[8] Blake Papers, W. L. to Blake, 12 June, 1890.

Laurier's attitude towards the policy of unrestricted reciprocity also seems to have been affected by his concern with the danger of political division along racial lines. A political liberal but not a doctrinaire free-trader, he had little interest in economic questions. As he once said of French Canadians in general: "Tariff and revenue questions are not our chief preoccupations. We rather incline towards the speculative, and have a fondness for theories."[9] There may have been many exceptions to the generalization, but there can be little doubt that it describes Laurier's predilections. He once considered becoming an historian[10] but never a businessman. With this attitude to tariff problems, it was possible for Laurier to adopt unrestricted reciprocity if political conditions seemed to make such a policy desirable.

The political situation in Quebec did not provide any strong incentive for reciprocity. Laurier thought it "would be popular" there.[11] Replies from Quebec to his circular on the subject were not unfavorable. But these replies suggest acquiescence rather than enthusiasm for the measure, and imply that the political effect of demanding great commercial autonomy was as important as the anticipated economic benefits. A typical reply accepted the policy without discussing it.

I am in favour of continuing the struggle to the end;
(1) In favour of Recoprocity.
(2) In favour of the right to make our own commercial treaties.[12]

In this connection, it should be remembered that the province of Quebec was traditionally protectionist. Papineau and Cartier, two of French Canada's political heroes, had favored protection. Among the leading contemporaries, Chapleau could justify his coalition attempt by explaining that, "The Liberal leaders and I . . . we are all *protectionists,* and the country is with us."[13] When both Chapleau and Mercier agreed upon a policy it is presumptive evidence that it was acceptable to the majority of French Canadians. It seems clear that the Quebec Liberals would be willing to accept reciprocity as a party measure only because Ontario Liberals wanted it, and not because they considered it of great political significance in Quebec.

Until 1888, Laurier had never enunciated a personal economic

[9] U. Barthe, ed., *Wilfrid Laurier on the Platform,* 186.
[10] Willison, *Laurier,* II, 372.
[11] Blake Papers, W. L. to Blake, 14 July, 1887.
[12] LP, C. Beausoleil to W. L., 5 Jan., 1889.
[13] Chapleau to Dansereau, 18 Oct., 1881, quoted, "Mémoires sur la coalition," (Ste Hyacinthe, 1886).

philosophy. At Quebec in 1871 he had advocated increased indus-trialization within the province, but had ignored the means by which this should be achieved.[14] At Ottawa, he had defended Mackenzie's revenue tariff, but discussed the inconsistencies of the Opposition statements rather than explaining his own views.[15] In the Opposition under Blake, Laurier criticized aspects of the National Policy without denouncing the policy of protection.[16] Before the election of 1887, Laurier was still trying to reassure businessmen who feared that "a change of administration would bring a radical change in the tariff."[17] After the election of 1887, however, the policy of the Liberal party was drastically altered. There had been a good deal of agitation in Ontario in favor of commercial union with the United States.[18] Cartwright apparently convinced Laurier that the issue had become so important that the party could not ignore it, but must either adopt or reject it.[19]

Nevertheless, Laurier did not immediately come to a decision. In a circular to Liberal members he stated that "there can be no sounder liberal principle than freedom of trade, wherever freedom of trade is possible." But as a practical politician, he suggested that the problem was not so much a question of principle as whether this was the proper time to commit the party.[20] In August, 1887, at least in public Laurier was "not ready to declare that commercial union is an acceptable idea."[21] But a month later, Laurier was asking Blake if it would not be wise to "take our stand at once in favor of the principle."[22] By 1888, Laurier had been converted.

We must try to make a new departure. There is really a deep discontent everywhere. In this province I never knew business as dull as it is now. All classes are in more straitened circumstances than they have ever been within my experience. There is a univer-sal desire for a change. Commercial union would afford relief & commercial union must be popular. It is the general desire that we

[14] Barthe, *op. cit.*, 5.
[15] *Commons Debates*, 22 March, 1877.
[16] *Ibid.*, 30 March, 1882, 622.
[17] Blake Papers, W. L. to Blake, 14 Jan., 1887.
[18] See W. R. Graham, "Sir Richard Cartwright, Wilfrid Laurier, and Liberal Party Trade Policy," *Canadian Historical Review*, XXXIII (March, 1952), 2 ff.
[19] Blake Papers, W. L. to Blake, 14 July, 1887.
[20] *Ibid.*
[21] Skelton, *Laurier*, I, 375.
[22] Blake Papers, W.L. to Blake, 9 Sept., 1887.

*should make it a party issue. The consensus of opinion which I
have received has been singularly unanimous.*[23]

As Laurier soon explained to Blake, the party had adopted unrestricted reciprocity rather than commercial union. "We have nar-
rowed the issue to the mere commercial aspect of the question, &
we intend to keep it strictly on that line. There are political aspects
that will spring up, but for the present it is far better to leave them
out."[24] The "political aspect" was the allegation that commercial
union meant political union. This distinction between commercial
union and unrestricted reciprocity, however, was rather an artificial
one, as this letter of Laurier's suggests. Laurier does not seem to
have thought it of much importance. A year later he favored a
"bold policy," and if a change in policy was to be made it should
be "to move forward."[25] These phrases suggest that Laurier had
little understanding of the economic or financial aspects of the question. To talk of boldness and of moving forward was to represent
the problem in purely political terms.

Nevertheless, there can be no doubt that the Liberal platform of
unrestricted reciprocity was also Laurier's policy. He had not
"stood aloof" as one biographer suggests,[26] but had been readily
converted. There is no simple explanation for this. A new factor to
be taken into account in 1887 was that Laurier had become leader
of the Liberal party. The new policy might be attributed to the
"dictates of expediency."[27] The party had been following a moderate course and had been defeated. What could be more natural than
Laurier, freed from Blake's tutelage, adopting bolder measures?
The difficulty of this explanation is that there is no indication that
Laurier was so eager to prove himself a successful leader, nor even
that he expected this radical departure to be immediately effective.
On the contrary, he genuinely deplored Blake's resignation, and
was continually trying to relieve himself of the burdens of leadership.[28] And of the adoption of the new platform he wrote:

[23] *Ibid.*, 16 Jan. 1888. P. D. Stevens in *Laurier and the Liberal
Party in Ontario, 1887-1911* (unpublished Ph.D. thesis, University
of Toronto, 1966), p 78, cites some evidence that Laurier was
thoroughly "converted" by early August 1887.
[24] *Ibid.*, 29 Mar., 1888.
[25] *Ibid.*, 4 Jan., 1889.
[26] Skelton, *Laurier*, I, 376.
[27] Graham, "Cartwright ... Trade Policy," 17.
[28] Blake Papers, W. L. to Blake, 16 March, 1887 and 4 Jan., 1888;
LP, W. L. to Scriver, 5 June, 1892; LP, W. L. to Hyman, 28
March, 1895.

I do not anticipate an easy nor an early triumph. The power of money & patronage will still be stronger for many years to come, but we will constantly make some progress, and what progress is thus made will be permanent and forever.[29]

It is clear that neither personal ambition nor desire for a quick political victory can account entirely for Laurier's change of heart.

Laurier's attitude to unrestricted reciprocity becomes comprehensible when we remember how conscious he was of the danger of party disintegration for racial reasons. Whereas he had described French Canadians as having a "fondness for theories," he believed that "for the Englishman, politics are a question of business."[30] Believing this, it was not unnatural that he should adopt the striking policy of unrestricted reciprocity which might well distract attention from the racial strife which he feared. Thus he could write to Willison in connection with the French language and separate school question: "My personal opinion would be to keep clear of these irritating questions, and to ring far and loud the trade question."[31] Even after the platform of commercial union had been quietly interred, the trade question continued to be "rung far and loud." A Liberal pamphlet for the anticipated election of 1895, *The Issues of the Campaign*, ignored the school question, and concentrated on flailing the National Policy.

It is difficult to assess the effects of the reciprocity platform in the province of Quebec. It has been noted that Quebec was traditionally protectionist. If we exclude the industrial district centering around Montreal, this attitude does not seem to have been based upon any firmly held economic theory, but rather on a conservative tendency to maintain the policy established by Cartier. And even in Ontario, the election of 1891 was not fought on economic grounds. According to Conservatives, unrestricted reciprocity, whatever its material results, meant annexation. This does not seem to have been decided because of any theory of economic determinism. A simpler explanation is that long years of defending the National Policy had enshrined it as the only truly "national" policy. Reciprocity was thus anti-national, and so annexationist. In Quebec, Chapleau seems to have believed this. He wrote to Macdonald: "Machiavelism [sic] if needed, should be allowed to fight men who publicly profess to surrender our birth-rights to a foreign power."[32] Archbishop Fabre of Montreal also believed that there was a dan-

[29] Blake Papers, W. L. to Blake, 16 Jan., 1888.
[30] Barthe, *op. cit.*, 186, statement on 19 May, 1884.
[31] P. A. C., Sir John Willison Papers, W. L. to Willison, 18 June, 1890.
[32] Macdonald Papers, Chapleau to Macdonald, 11 Aug., 1890.

ger, and issued a Mandement outlining the security of "a national and religious life" within the Empire.[33] But Laurier refused to admit the possibility of reciprocity necessarily leading to annexation.

As for the consequence that Unrestricted Reciprocity would lead us to annexation, if that has any significance whatever, it is that Unrestricted Reciprocity would make two peoples so prosperous that, not satisfied with a commercial alliance, they would wish to vote for political absorption in the American republic. If this is not the true meaning of the charge, and I ask any citizen to judge, it is completely meaningless in any other sense.[34]

Like the Conservatives, Laurier believed that politics could determine economic developments, but he found the converse "completely nonsensical." Outside of Quebec, the annexation charge gained credence because there were some advocates of independence within the Liberal ranks.[35] In Quebec, however, the aspiration for independence was more respectable, and was not identified with annexation, so it seems that the "loyalty cry" was less effective there. It is improbable that party loyalties in the province were affected seriously.

The results of the election in Quebec in 1891 were not decisive. Possibly more important there than the annexation cry was the fact that most of the party funds came from industrialists. Macdonald made clear his belief that a Conservative victory was in the manufacturer's interests.[36] We may assume that he was more convincing than the Liberals among this group. The Liberals in Quebec, on the other hand, had the ardent support of Mercier and his government,[37] and this meant the support of many of the lesser Roman Catholic clergy.[38] And, finally, Tarte's revelations of scandals in the awarding of contracts by the Department of Public Works involved such prominent Conservatives as Langevin and Thomas McGreevy.[39] However we may assess the relative importance of these factors, the results of the elections of 1891 were not startling. The Liberals gained a total of three seats, giving them a majority of the provincial representation at Ottawa.[40]

[33] Rumilly, *Histoire*, VI, 205.
[34] W. Laurier, "Manifeste de Laurier, Réciprocité," (1891).
[35] *Globe*, 27 Feb., 1889 and 20 Feb., 1890, quoted, Skelton, *Laurier*, I, 366. The articles advocated virtual independence.
[36] Macdonald Papers, *Letterbook*, 205, letters to Drummond, Gault and Morrice, 3 Feb., 1891.
[37] Rumilly, *Histoire*, VI, 202.
[38] Macdonald Papers, Chapleau to Macdonald, 11 August, 1890.
[39] *Commons Journals*, 1891, Appendix I.
[40] Thirty-five seats out of sixty-five.

The Liberals did not immediately abandon reciprocity, even after the Conservative ministers had failed to negotiate a treaty with the United States.[41] But by 1893 a tactical withdrawal had clearly begun. "Uniformity of tariffs is not at all essential to reciprocity unless there is a great divergence of tariffs. And if we cannot obtain unrestricted reciprocity we will be willing to accept what reciprocity we can obtain."[42] At the Liberal Convention in June of that year, the distinction between the two parties on the tariff question became even more blurred. "Their ideal is protection, our ideal is free trade. Their immediate object is protection, ours is a tariff for revenue only."[43] By 1894, even a Conservative might have said, "Our policy is to levy duties, not for special interests, but for the general good of the community."[44] The downward revision of the tariff by the Conservatives in 1894 did nothing to clarify the difference between the tariff policies. By 1896 the Liberals had been even more compromising in private than in public. Manufacturers were quietly assured that a Liberal victory would not affect their tariff protection.[45] The National Policy was still criticised, but the emphasis was on the corruption and favoritism resulting from its maladministration rather than on its principle of protection. A letter from Dansereau to Laurier leaves no doubt that this policy bore fruit, and that some of the Conservative manufacturers did support the Liberals in 1896.[46]

The reciprocity interlude had no permanent effect on political affiliations in Quebec. It is more interesting for its revelation of the political beliefs of the new Liberal leader. Some twenty years before, Laurier had been suspicious of Confederation. He had been reconciled to the constitution, and under Blake's leadership his misgivings had disappeared. Laurier had acquired a confidence in the sense of justice of the English Liberals, a faith which survived many crises. Laurier had drawn the logical conclusion from this. As he said at Quebec: "There are some among us . . . who affect to believe that a small French republic or monarchy – I hardly know what they want – should be established on the banks of the St. Lawrence. I cannot accept this idea . . ."[47] Having decided that Confederation

[41] Blake Papers, W. L. to Blake, 9 April, 1892 and 13 April, 1892.
[42] Laurier, *Commons Debates*, 28 Feb., 1893, 1444.
[43] *Official Report of the Liberal Convention, 1893* (Toronto, 1893), Laurier's address, 33.
[44] Laurier, *Commons Debates*, 12 April, 1894, 1239.
[45] F. H. Underhill, "Edward Blake, the Liberal Party and Unrestricted Reciprocity," Canadian Historical Association, *Report*, 1939, 141; Rumilly, Histoire, VIII, 57.
[46] LP, Dansereau to W. L., 19 Dec., 1901.
[47] Willison, *Laurier*, II, 363 ff., statement 4 Jan., 1894.

was irrevocable, Laurier logically believed that national unity should be fostered. Unity did not mean assimilation. "Let us also be true to our double origin."[48] Laurier was painfully aware of the difficulties of the union; he was not deluded into ignoring the bigotry and intolerance present in both races in Canada.[49] His solution was to concentrate attention on national issues which would not rouse these latent prejudices. Unrestricted reciprocity, it was hoped, would absorb the energies which might otherwise be devoted to the Protestant Protective Association. It does not seem to have been a complete failure; in Ontario at least, the election of 1891 was mainly fought on the trade issue. But already, in Manitoba, a religious problem had arisen which could not be ignored, from which attention could not be distracted. The next few years were to provide the first real test of the strength of the federal union of the two races. Laurier's belief that the union must be preserved was to be of supreme importance.

[48] Ibid., 371.
[49] Ibid., 368.

5.
The Manitoba School Question

The Manitoba School Question is a classic example of the danger in Canada of irresponsible appeals to religious prejudices by politicians. The Manitoba school system became a political issue because of the religious problems involved. It remained a disturbing influence in federal politics for five years because the Conservative government evaded its political responsibilities by attempting to shift the responsibilities to the courts. It remained the most prominent federal issue because the Liberal party attempted to derive political benefit from the dilemma of the government.

Laurier, at least, showed some restraint. For five years he refused to express any positive opinion on the question. When finally he did make his policy public, he did not appeal to prejudice but to a spirit of compromise. It would be naive to suggest that the Liberal victory in 1896 was the result of Laurier's moderation. Passions are not so easily repressed. His great achievement was to preserve a semblance of unity in the Liberal party where none existed. He proved himself the most astute political tactician of the day. His tactics resulted in a political victory. They did not solve the Manitoba School Question.

Politically speaking, the "Manitoba School Question," like the negative square root in algebra, could never be satisfactorily solved. The problem involved education and religion, two aspects of social organization on which the two racial communities had incompatible philosophies. The French-Canadian Roman Catholics believed that "separate schools" were essential for their survival. By separate schools they meant a school organization which was completely sectarian, in which the Roman Catholics would have an administration, or Board of Education, composed of Roman Catholics, and in which inspectors, teachers, text-books and the curriculum would all conform to the sectarian principle. The English Protestants advocated "state schools." These schools were to be non-sectarian. The government rather than the church was to control the administration, the appointments and the curriculum. If religion was to be taught at all, it would be a carefully expurgated, non-controversial form of Christianity. The racial factor complicated the situation, since separate schools facilitated the survival of French-Canadian minorities in predominantly English provinces. Protestants believed that separate schools fostered religious prejudice and bigotry, and prevented the social homogeneity essential for democracy. Roman Catholics, on the other hand, believed that state schools, being "godless" or "neutral," were a danger to the religious convictions which were essential to a Christian society. The two groups could agree on one point. Education should be available to all, and so compulsory contributions were necessary to finance education. This meant that the government had to collect and distribute taxes. Thus there could be no complete separation between politics and education. The power of the purse might be used to control education.

In the province of Manitoba a separate school system had been established by the Manitoba Act of 1870. This Act had been passed by Macdonald's government as a compromise. The inhabitants of the region had accepted Canadian sovereignty in exchange for provincial status as determined by the Act. Archbishop Taché of St. Boniface was prominent in the negotiations, and according to him, the concession of separate schools was "an integral part of an agreement or treaty passed between the Dominion of Canada and the settlers of the Red River, previous to the entry of our province into Confederation."[1] This statement was never denied. The Manitoba Act conceded control of education to the province, subject to certain restrictions. There was to be no interference with the rights of "denominational schools which any class of persons have by law or practise in the province at the union." If necessary, "the Parliament of Canada may make remedial laws for the due execution of the provision of this section," in case a provincial law should interfere with these rights.[2] The provincial School Act was in complete accord with the views of the Roman Catholic church. The Board of Education was divided into a Protestant and a Roman Catholic section, each section administering its own schools independently.[3]

Immigration into Manitoba in subsequent years was largely Protestant, with the result that the Roman Catholic minority was proportionately reduced. Nevertheless, there was no significant agitation for a change in the school system until after the Riel execution and the Jesuits' Estates Bill had emphasized racial and religious antagonisms. D'Alton McCarthy provides the link between these issues and the Manitoba school question. He claimed credit for directing attention in Manitoba to the "grievance." Joseph Martin, and then the provincial Liberal party under Greenway, took up the cry.[4] In 1890, Greenway's government passed a Public School Act which abolished state-supported denominational schools. Separate

[1] Archbishop Taché, "Separate Schools," (St. Boniface, 1889).
[2] *Statutes of Canada*, 33 Vict., c. 3, s. 22.
[3] *Manitoba Statutes*, 42 Vict., c. 2, s. 5.
[4] Skelton, *Laurier*, I, 446.

schools could still exist, but would have to rely on voluntary contributions from individuals who would also be paying public school taxes.[5]

The Manitoba school question did not immediately become a political issue at Ottawa. Macdonald had decided to reserve the bill "if it abolishes separate schools," but had later changed his mind.[6] There were petitions and memorials to the federal government for disallowance[7] but these were ignored. The federal power of disallowance had not proved to be effective, and Macdonald probably thought that direct interference would only strengthen the Liberals in Manitoba. A federal election was imminent and at such times controversial issues were better ignored. The Roman Catholics were quietened by promises that their interests would be cared for, both Chapleau and Macdonald approaching "certain parties" to pledge a "certain course of action" in the future.[8] The Liberal party did nothing to prevent the shelving of the question. Indeed, Blake introduced a motion to the effect that the legality of provincial acts should be left to the determination of the courts, regarding it as settled that "there shall be no disallowance of educational acts."[9] Macdonald welcomed the motion, which was passed unanimously.[10] Thus the election of 1891 passed with neither party raising the issue of the school question.

Agitation began in earnest with the decision of the Privy Council on the validity of the Public School Act. The Supreme Court of Canada had unanimously decided that the Act was *ultra vires* since it was "practically depriving them [the Catholics] of their denominational schools."[11] On appeal, the Privy Council reversed this decision. In the judgment it was pointed out that prior to the creation of the province, the Roman Catholics were supporting their own schools. By this legislation they could continue to support them if they so desired. That Roman Catholics would then be forced to support both public and separate schools was admitted: "But what right or privilege is violated or prejudicially affected by the law? It is not the law that is at fault; it is owing to religious

[5] *Manitoba Statutes*, 53 Vict., c. 38, s. 178 ff.
[6] Macdonald Papers, Schultz to Macdonald, 24 March, 1890, 9 April, 1890.
[7] *Sessional Papers*, 1891, No. 63.
[8] Thompson Papers, Chapleau to Thompson, 29 Dec., 1892.
[9] *Commons Debates*, 29 April, 1890, 4086.
[10] *Ibid.*, 4094.
[11] *The Supreme Court of Canada in the Matter of Certain Statutes of the Province of Manitoba relating to Education*, Judgment of Chief Justice Ritchie, 104, 28 Oct., 1891.

conviction. . . ."[12] The decision may have been constitutionally sound in spite of the implication that laws should be for people as they might be, rather than for people as they are, but in practice it could only mean the extinction of separate schools. The province of Quebec was unanimous in its denunciation. Bishop Gravel expressed what many thought in a report to Rome. "That reasoning is so lame that it is impossible to believe that men of such intellectual strength could have advanced it in good faith."[13] Even the English Canadians in the province agreed that the decision was unfortunate.

The first decision, to the effect that the Manitoba school legislation of 1890 is intra vires, came in the nature of a surprise. It was in contradiction to what seemed the clear letter of the Manitoba Constitutional act, in direct conflict with the manifest intention of Parliament in laying down the basis of the union of the province, in reversal of the decision of the majority of Canadian judges who pronounced upon the issue, and an example of poor politics in the largest and best sense of the word, that which concerns the peace and order of the community.[14]

Under these circumstances, the Roman Catholics naturally appealed to the federal Parliament to pass a remedial measure as authorised by the Manitoba Act. It was a difficult situation for the government. A restoration of separate schools would have been unpopular in English-speaking Canada at any time; in the face of the judicial decision it would have been almost impossible. Ignoring the appeal would have meant alienating most of Quebec and many Roman Catholics elsewhere. Sir John Thompson evaded the decision. He went to the courts to determine whether the Canadian Privy Council was legally authorised to entertain the appeal. This merely postponed political action. The Privy Council, on the 19th February, 1895, decided that an appeal was constitutionally admissible. The judgment asserted that "rights and privileges" of the minority had been created by the Schools Acts in Manitoba prior to 1890. The judgment further elaborated that it was not essential that the Act of 1890 be repealed. "All legitimate grounds of complaint would be removed if that system were supplemented by provisions which would remove the grievance upon which the appeal is founded."[15] Constitutionally, this meant that the rights of the mi-

[12] *Ibid.*, Judgment of the Judicial Committee, 151.
[13] Mgr. Gravel, Report, 7 Dec. 1894, quoted, Montreal *Star*, 19 June, 1895.
[14] *Gazette*, Montreal, 31 Jan., 1895.
[15] *Sessional Papers*, 1895, No. 20,12.

nority in Manitoba had been created after the Manitoba Act of 1870; politically, it meant that the days of equivocation were over. The government would have to act.

During the years of indecision, the Liberal party was faced by the same political dilemma as the Conservative party. Any official policy on the school question would have alienated the Protestant or the Roman Catholic Liberals or both. This did not mean that the Liberals remained silent. Many Liberals expressed forthright opinions. *L'Electeur*, edited by Laurier's friend, Ernest Pacaud, and so almost an official organ of the Liberal party in Quebec, warned its readers that the Conservatives planned to betray the Roman Catholics in Manitoba. "Our coreligionists are going to be sacrificed through legal subtleties; the law, which on the face of it is in their favour, will be broken. . . ."[16] On the next day the *Globe*, almost an official organ of the Liberal party in Ontario, made its position clear. "Nothing would please this journal better than to see the Manitoba school question settled in accordance with the judgment of the privy council and the spirit of provincial autonomy, without wounding the conscience of a single Catholic citizen . . ."[17] Desirable as such forthrightness may be, its virtue would have been enhanced by consistency. It would be difficult to evolve a satisfactory policy "in accordance with" these traitorous "legal subtleties."

There can be no doubt that Laurier's personal preference was for the restoration of a separate school system. As a French-Canadian Roman Catholic, and as a Quebec member of Parliament, this was to be expected. Strangely enough, few English Liberals understood this in the 1890's. Thus Willison, a regular correspondent and a personal friend of Laurier's, as late as 1895 could suggest that Laurier adopt the policy of provincial rights – knowing that this would preclude the restoration of separate schools in Manitoba. "It strikes me that on that policy strongly presented, we could very nearly if not certainly carry the country."[18] Laurier was not the man to sacrifice his principles so casually. "How is it possible to talk of Provincial Rights," he asked, "when by the very letter of the constitution, jurisdiction is given to the federal authorities to review and to override provincial legislation." And he frankly explained that, "In this instance, I have not yet made up my mind as to what should be done, though what information I have on the matter inclines me to the side of the minority."[19] Willison was too blinded by his own convictions to realize that Laurier disagreed with him.

[16] *L'Electeur*, 18 Jan. 1893.
[17] *Globe*, 19 Jan., 1893.
[18] LP, Willison to W. L., 22 March, 1895.
[19] Willison Papers, W. L. to J. S. W., 30 March, 1895.

In spite of Laurier's reply, he continued to believe that Laurier was influenced by a devotion to the principle of provincial rights.[20]

Because of the divisions within the party, Laurier made no public statement of his opinions. Just as Thompson had tried to shift the responsibility of determining a policy to the courts, so Laurier tried to shift the responsibility to the government. Only on one point was Laurier blunt. Archbishop Taché had claimed that the Act of 1890 had not destroyed the two systems of education and created a new state school system. Instead, he said, "... it is impossible for me to believe that the public schools of Manitoba are not the continuation of the public Protestant schools ...", established by the province in 1871.[22] Laurier declared that if this statement was true, "the Catholic minority has been subjected to a most infamous tyranny."[22] At Winnipeg, on his western tour in 1894, Laurier repeated this statement, adding that if Roman Catholic children were being forced to attend Protestant schools, it was such an outrage that "no community would permit it."[23] But this was not a statement of policy. Laurier carefully avoided stating whether he believed Taché's statement. Instead, he constantly reiterated that it was the responsibility of the government to investigate the facts.[24] He was willing to denounce the government for acting in a "cowardly way" by evading a decision,[25] but he would not commit himself either as to the facts or a satisfactory solution.

But Laurier's evasions did not mean that Laurier had not formulated a policy. As early as 1893 he had written a private letter to the editor of the Ottawa *Canada* in which he explained that he had "no hesitation on the question of the schools." If the Privy Council decided that no appeal could be entertained by the federal government, "for me, the question will be finally determined." His reason for this is significant.

In the case where the government and the federal authorities have no right to intervene, the only remedy which would remain to the minority would be to request an amendment to the constitution. Such a policy would entail a similar demand on the part of the McCarthy group to abolish the French language in Parliament

[20] Willison to G. Beer, 29 Nov., 1912, quoted in A. H. U. Colquhoun, *Press Politics and People: The Life and Letters of Sir John Willison* (Toronto, 1935), 84.

[21] Archbishop Taché, "Ecoles publiques de Manitoba," (St. Boniface, 1893).

[22] *Commons Debates*, 8 March 1893, 1998.

[23] Montreal *Star*, 4 Sept., 1894.

[24] *Commons Debates*, 8 Mar., 1893, 1998.

[25] *Report of the Liberal Convention*, 37, 20 June, 1893.

*and separate schools in Ontario. Such consequences ought to make
all sensible men reflect.*

Thus Laurier was willing to accept the situation in Manitoba if
agitation on the question would endanger the minority rights secured elsewhere in Canada by the constitution.

On the other hand, he continued, if the judicial decision authorized the appeal of the minority for the restoration of their privileges,
he would demand an investigation of Taché's assertions. "If it were
true that Catholic children were forced to go to Protestant schools,
without a moment's hesitation, I would risk everything to prevent
such a tyranny." And then comes the most revealing passage.

*If, on the contrary, the Catholics actually had their schools as they
have them in New Brunswick and Nova Scotia, the position would
be different, and I believe it would be necessary to accept this state
of affairs.*[26]

The system in New Brunswick was a compromise between state
schools and separate schools. All schools were state-supported and
in theory non-sectarian, but regulations made it possible for Catholic children to be grouped in the same school, for teachers trained in
Roman Catholic teaching Orders to receive teachers' certificates,
and for text-books to be used which were not objectionable on
religious grounds.[27] Among Acadian settlements, the schools were
bilingual.[28] This then was the system which Laurier was willing to
accept in Manitoba. It must be emphasized that this was not a
"separate school" system as understood by the Roman Catholics;
not was it completely non-sectarian, as desired by most English
Protestants. It was a compromise which could be tolerated because
religious or political convictions were not flouted, although, like all
compromises, it was not completely satisfactory to either side.

Few letters could more aptly illustrate Laurier's talents as a politician. He was not blinded by his personal inclinations. Whatever
his opinion of the Manitoba School Act of 1890, he was able to
realize that the decision of the courts that the Act was *intra vires*
had altered the position of the minority in the province. If the
majority in Manitoba refused to consider separate schools as acceptable, it was now useless to insist. And so "it would be necessary" to accept a compromise such as they had in New Brunswick.
If politics is the art of recognizing the possible, this conclusion was
politically justified.

[26] LP, W. L. to O. McDonnell, 14 July, 1893.
[27] K.F.C. MacNaughton, *The Development of the Theory and Practice of Education in New Brunswick, 1784-1900* (Fredericton,
1947), 220.
[28] *Ibid.*, 232.

Even more revealing, the letter was written in 1893, but Laurier did not make his opinions public until 1896. He knew that his policy would not be politically popular. It ignored the Ontario insistence upon "provincial rights" and it also ignored the Quebec appeal to "justice" in the form of separate schools. Not until the government had committed itself to a different policy did Laurier express his opinion. Laurier did not have the temperament of an Edward Blake. He felt no compulsion to write a letter to his electors because he had no horror of being misunderstood. Instead, Laurier had a confidence in himself that could sustain three years of criticism from Protestant and Roman Catholic alike. He took no action until he believed that he could suggest a positive policy which would be endorsed by most of his party. It was not entirely by accident that where Blake had failed, Laurier succeeded in leading the Liberal party to power.

But Laurier's reticence during these years did not prevent the Liberal party from improving its position in the province of Quebec. Other Liberals were less reticent. Of these, Tarte was the most important. Tarte used the school question to sow suspicion of the Conservatives and faith in the Liberals among French-Canadians. As *L'Electeur* wrote: "The position which M. Tarte holds in the party of M. Laurier, for which he is the chief organizer in this province, indicates sufficiently the drift of things."[29] The assumption was that Tarte was speaking for Laurier and the Liberal party. We may well believe that *L'Electeur* would have preferred to base its appeal on the statements of the leader of the party, but since this was difficult in view of Laurier's silence, Tarte's statements would have to suffice.

Joseph Israel Tarte was a remarkable man. He had entered politics as the editor of Langevin's *Le Canadien* at Quebec in 1874.[30] In those days he had been a vigorous opponent of Catholic-liberalism. In 1880 he had written a pamphlet entitled "The Clergy: Its Rights, Its Duties," in which he suggested that it was the right of the clergy to decide how Catholics should vote, and it was the duty of the Catholics to obey.[31] After Riel's death, there had been a temporary aberration. He had spoken in favor of a *parti national* at the meeting on the Champ de Mars,[32] but he was soon back within the Conservative fold.[33] Within the party, however, he shifted from Langevin and the Castor group to the Chapleau group.[34] In 1890

[29] *L'Electeur*, 24 Mar., 1894.

[30] Rumilly, *Histoire*, I, 325.

[31] Tarte, "Le clergé, ses droits, nos devoirs," (1880).

[32] *Herald*, Montreal, 23 Nov., 1885.

[33] Rumilly, *Histoire*, v, 141.

[34] C. Langelier, *Souvenirs*, II, 33.

he had gained possession of the documents revealing the McGreevy scandals, and was soon writing to Laurier that "If the government can be destroyed, it is through this business, believe me."[35] In 1891 Tarte was elected as a Liberal. This was the man who was now acting as spokesman for the Liberal party in Quebec.

It would be wrong to label Tarte as a mere political opportunist. Tarte's chequered career is not easy to explain. He had been a Castor and would soon be challenging the clergy; he was to be an Imperial Federationist who opposed participation in the Boer War; a former protégé of Langevin's, he had ruined Langevin's political career. It may be considered one of Laurier's diplomatic triumphs that he managed to keep Tarte within the Liberal party for a decade! But the political opportunist is devoid of principles, and Tarte had principles. On one occasion, he even argued that political consistency was one of his principles, since he had denounced Letellier's dismissal of Boucherville and denounced Angers' dismissal of Mercier,[36] something which no Quebec politician who had maintained his party loyalty could claim. Tarte's inconsistencies seem to have been the result of conflicting principles. Devoted to the Roman Catholic church, he was also devoted to the interests of the French Canadians. He was a protectionist and an advocate of Canadian automony. But Tarte was a journalist rather than a politician. He was likely to seize upon an obvious aspect of a problem and adopt a position with enthusiasm and even vehemence, only to realize later that the consequences were unexpected. He was a small man, with an impediment in his speech, nervous, impulsive, and sometimes erratic. Unlike Laurier, he was a tactician rather than a strategist.

Tarte was not likely to maintain a discreet silence on any topic; on the Manitoba school question it would have been impossible, since he felt very strongly on the subject. As he told Laurier, he was convinced "that French Canadians have the same rights as other races, in this country, and these rights are being scandalously violated these days, with the connivance of the two political parties of English origin."[37] In another letter he denounced the Ontario Liberals, who were making it impossible for the party to strengthen its position in Quebec, and was especially virulent concerning the *Globe* staff. "They are only miniature George Browns, and have,

[35] LP, Tarte to W.L., 13 May, 1890.
[36] Tarte, "Procès Mercier," (1892). On Tarte see also: L. J. L. La-Pierre, *Politics, Race and Religion in French Canada: Joseph Israel Tarte* (unpublished Ph.D. thesis, University of Toronto, 1962).
[37] LP, Tarte to W. L., 13 Oct., 1893.

thank God, neither his power nor his ability."[38] But in public Tarte concentrated on the sins of the Conservatives. He did not find the topic too restricting.

Tarte's favorite subject was the betrayal of the Manitoba minority by the decision not to disallow the School Act. Tarte stated bluntly that Chapleau had promised Archbishop Taché "that the government was determined to give the Catholics justice, to make sure of the existence of their separate schools, but it would be very difficult to disallow the legislation. . . ."[39] Tarte had many Conservative friends. There can be little doubt that his information was correct.[40] This accusation, however, affected more than the government. To Archbishop Taché, it seemed to be an accusation that he had betrayed his responsibilities. He pointed out that the House of Commons had unanimously voted in favor of Blake's motion against disallowance, and that as a result, there had never been any possibility of disallowance.[41] And so Tarte, the former Castor, was soon engaged in a controversy with the Archbishop. Tarte did nothing with restraint; he repeated his accusations in the House of Commons,[42] at the Liberal Convention,[43] and in *L'Electeur*.[44] It made little difference that the Liberals had opposed disallowance, or that disallowance might not have effectively curbed the Greenway government; Tarte's reiterations were repeated in all the Quebec newspapers and the collusion of the Conservatives and Taché was never formally denied. The government's evasion of the question seemed to substantiate Tarte's charges of betrayal. As was to be expected, Tarte was not satisfied with Laurier's reticence. He tried to convince Laurier "that you are completely wrong in the course you suggest taking concerning the province of Québec. You will excuse my plain talk. But I am so certain that we must agitate and fight, that I want to explain to you all my reasoning." Without party funds, he believed that words and publicity were needed.[45] But Laurier continued to imitate the Sphinx in public. To Tarte belongs the credit of strengthening the position of the Liberal party in Quebec in the days of indecision.

Tarte's success in Quebec was in some respects a serious complication for Laurier. Tarte's aversion to many Ontario Liberals was

[38] LP, Tarte to W. L., 17 Jan., 1894.
[39] *L'Electeur*, 2 June, 1893.
[40] See above, p. 54.
[41] Archbishop Taché, "A Page of the History of the Schools in Manitoba," (St. Boniface, 1893).
[42] *Commons Debates*, 6 March, 1893, 1751 ff.
[43] *Report of the Liberal Convention*, 21 June, 1893, 61.
[44] *L'Electeur*, 25-29 July, 1893.
[45] LP, Tarte to W. L., 30 July, 1894.

reciprocated. In his letters to Laurier, Tarte regularly denounced the "fanatics" of Ontario, and suggested that Laurier should ally himself with men like Oliver Mowat who seemed to have enlightened views. If there were not enough suitable English allies "this Confederation is fit only for breaking up, on the first possible occasion." Tarte went on to make a proposition which has appealed to many French Canadians before and since. "If you were to command fifty M.P.'s from the province of Quebec, you would be well in control of the situation, wouldn't you?"[46] In effect, Tarte was advocating a French-Canadian, Roman Catholic party. It would have destroyed Laurier's goal of a national party in which racial and religious feelings would be respected, but in which political harmony would be achieved by suppressing controversial quarrels. Laurier agreed with Tarte that Mowat was a man of enlightened views,[47] but Laurier's policy with less "enlightened" Liberals was not to read them out of the party but to persuade them to alter their views. He proposed to reassure Ontario that Tarte was less black than he was painted by taking Tarte on an Ontario speaking tour with him. Mulock dared to "venture an observation" that Tarte's presence would do more harm than good,[48] and others were less diplomatic.[49] The tour was given up.

But Laurier defended Tarte's courage in the House[50] and in private he defended Tarte as having "done good and excellent service since he joined us."[51] We may assume that he also used his diplomacy with Tarte, since Tarte confined his criticisms of Liberals to his private correspondence.

We must now return to the quandary of the Conservative party following the Privy Council decision that an appeal to the federal government was permissible. By 1895, Sir John Thompson was dead, and Sir Mackenzie Bowell, an Ontario Orangeman, was Prime Minister. The change of leaders did not change the tactics of the government. Efforts were still made to put the onus of responsibility upon the courts. Instead of introducing remedial legislation,

[46] *Ibid.*, 2 Feb., 1894.
[47] In Ontario Mowat's government had been denounced by the Conman Catholics, but Laurier did not believe, with Tarte, that one should fight fire with fire. Instead he suggested that Mowat should make some small concession to Protestant demands. The minority would derive little benefit if Mowat was unyielding and so lost the election. (LP, W. L. to Mowat, 29 July, 1894).
[48] LP, Mulock to W.L., 5 Sept., 189(3).
[49] *Ibid.*, J. Crerar to W.L., 27 July, 1893.
[50] *Commons Debates*, 28 March, 1893, 3309.
[51] Willison Papers, W.L. to Willison, 3 Nov., 1895.

the Committee of the Queen's Privy Council for Canada, or more simply, the Cabinet, sat as a court and heard the arguments of the Roman Catholic minority and of the Manitoba government once more. The Committee decided that the minority had been deprived of its right to conduct Roman Catholic schools, the right to share proportionately in government grants, and the right of exemption from taxation for other schools. An Order in Council, 19th March, 1895, ordered the provincial government to restore these rights. This decision was described as "a duty devolving upon Your Excellency in Council" because of the decision of the Judicial Committee of the Privy Council in England. In other words there was no discretionary power, but only a duty to enforce the legal decision made in London. The Order in Council further explained that if the Manitoba government refused to obey, Parliament was authorised to enact remedial legislation.[52] The Order in Council might be paraphrased as a command to restore completely separate schools, or remedial legislation would be passed . . . maybe.

In politics, as in poker, a bluff should be a calculated risk. The Remedial Order was a bluff, but it was so transparent that no politician, or poker player, could have been deceived. It was a peremptory request, if such a thing is possible. It demanded the reestablishment of completely separate schools in Manitoba. Conditions in Manitoba should have made it obvious that Greenway could not do this as a favor to the federal government; it is even unlikely that he could have done it under any circumstances without committing political suicide. The provincial government had committed itself in a long series of judicial hearings to the thesis that separate schools were impracticable on grounds of inefficiency and extravagance. Nor had it shown any desire to compromise; an amendment to the provincial School Act in 1894 had even made matters "much worse."[53] And the position of the federal government at this time suggested that the Remedial Order could be ignored with impunity. The Order had not stated that remedial legislation would be passed if the Order was not effective – and Prime Minister Bowell and the Controller of Customs, Clark Wallace, were prominent Orangemen who would find it difficult to restore separate schools.

The Remedial Order may be considered inept, but Bowell's correspondence at this time shows that he was worse than inept. In confidential instructions, Bowell asked Lieutenant-Governor Schultz of Manitoba to suggest to Greenway that some slight con-

[52] *Sessional Papers*, 1895, No. 20, 17ff.
[53] Thompson papers, *Letterbooks*, Thompson to Schultz, 17 Feb., 1894

cession should be made to the minority, "with the probability – you might suggest – of drastic measures being taken . . ." if nothing was done. Bowell went on to make it clear that the government was not formally committed to remedial legislation.[54] Thus the Greenway government was told that the Order was no more than a bluff. After all, in the Remedial Order Bowell's government had recognized the Manitoba Catholic minority's legal right to public support for separate schools; in his letter to Schultz the Prime Minister denied that right.

The Manitoba government's reply to the Order was blunt. After repeating that separate schools were inefficient, it stated that "we cannot accept the responsibility of carrying into effect the terms of the Remedial Order."[55]

Doubts as to the sincerity of the Conservative government were quickly strengthened. Charles Hibbert Tupper temporarily resigned because he feared that Bowell would evade remedial legislation.[56] The three French-Canadian ministers resigned for the same reason. Even Foster's declaration that a special session would be called to enact remedial legislation[57] was not completely reassuring, since the legislation might be inadequate. Caron and Ouimet withdrew their resignations, but Angers was adamant, insisting that legislation should be introduced immediately.[58] The suspicion that the government was insincere was justified. Bowell had again written to Winnipeg to explain that his government had no desire to restore the separate school system. A few concessions "in the way of inspection and qualification of teachers" should be accepted by the minority in their own interests.[59] Such weakness was provocative. The Manitoba government strengthened their position by holding an election on the school issue and winning thirty-three out of forty seats.[60] A settlement was now more difficult than ever.

Laurier had welcomed the judicial decision in London that an appeal was permissible. He believed that the decision meant that the Roman Catholics had certain constitutional rights. But, as he wrote to G. W. Ross of Ontario, the "tactical aspect" in Ontario might

[54] P.A.C., Sir M. Bowell Papers, *Letterbook 124*, Bowell to Schultz, 7 March, 1895.
[55] *Sessional Papers*, 1895, No. 20C, 353, 21 March, 1895.
[56] P. A. C., Sir Charles Tupper Papers, C. H. Tupper to C. Tupper, 29 Jan. 1895; Bowell Papers, C. H. Tupper to Bowell, 29 March, 1895.
[57] *Commons Debates*, 8 July, 1895, 3997.
[58] *Ibid.*, 11 July, 1895, 4188.
[59] Bowell Papers, *Letterbook 124*. Bowell to J. Fisher, 23 April, 1895.
[60] Willison, *Laurier*, II, 228.

make it difficult to declare this too openly.[61] So he continued to wait. "Further steps do not take, I pray, until unavoidable, and then only with such caution as in this instance," he wrote to Willison.[62] *L'Electeur* might write of one of Laurier's speeches that Laurier had "squarely" faced the question,[63] but *L'Electeur* was too partisan to be reliable. Laurier contented himself with criticizing the government as before. Archbishop Langevin, who had succeeded Archbishop Taché at St. Boniface and who was to prove more intransigent than his predecessor, asked Laurier in an interview to approve publicly of the Order in Council. If not, "how can we convince ourselves that you support our Catholic (separate) schools?"[64] But in spite of the temptation to express an opinion, Laurier believed that the wisest course was to remain silent. He analysed his predicament in a letter to Willison.

I fully realize that a good many of our friends are not satisfied with my course on that question. I am not satisfied with it myself. But under existing circumstances it was impossible to make a bold and well defined attitude without breaking the unity of the party. Indeed, such a rupture may be unavoidable in the end. But to exhibit at this moment the spectacle of a divided opposition would have been simply playing the game of the government. My aim therefore was to keep and maintain the party united, whilst the government was hopelessly divided.[65]

Laurier was willing to forgo the personal satisfaction of stating his personal opinion in the hope that the unity of the party might yet be preserved.

After the close of the session, Laurier defended his position while on an Ontario tour. Like Wellington, he had withdrawn behind the lines of the Torres Vedras and was waiting for the enemy to take the initiative. But he had in fact, moved towards a positive policy, although it was not clearly realized at the time. Repeating the fable of the traveller's coat removed by the sun but not by the wind, he said, "If it were in my power, I would try the sunny way."[66] Many Ontario Liberals realized that Laurier was in a difficult position. Cartwright had expected a Remedial Bill in the session of 1895 and had written that "we must make up our minds ... that you and

[61] W. L. to G. W. Ross, 2 March 1895, quoted, Colquhoun, *Press, Politics and People*, 48.

[62] *Willison Papers*, W.L. to Willison, 7 March, 1895.

[63] *L'Electeur*, 7 Feb., 1895.

[64] LP, Langevin to W.L., 11 May, 1895.

[65] Willison Papers, W.L. to J.S.W., 24 July, 1895.

[66] Speech of 8 Oct., 1895, quoted, Skelton, *Laurier*, I, 464.

your friends in Quebec will have to vote for it."[67] It was at least clear to most Liberals that the policy of Laurier and of the party would be determined by developments in Quebec.

In the province of Quebec, the suspicions sowed by Tarte were being nurtured by the delays of the government at Ottawa. The Order in Council was well received. Archbishop Fabre of Montreal warned his priests that they were not to speak of it from the pulpit, but "You are free, nevertheless, outside it, to express the complete satisfaction of the Canadian bishops [episcopate] on the firm and courageous course taken lately by the federal government."[68] The Liberal *L'Electeur*, which had once believed that the Remedial Order "settles nothing at all",[69] was temporarily convinced by the attitude of the clergy, since "it is a question more religious than political."[70] But with the resignation of Angers and the close of the session without any further action, doubts as to the sincerity of the government began to spread even to the Conservative newspapers. *La Presse*, independent Conservative, was especially critical of the delay.[71] So weakened was the government that when Angers did not withdraw his resignation, no Quebec member could be found to take his place. In November, Laurier could say that, "at present in this province, we could sweep everything."[72] In two federal by-elections in December, in constituencies which had been Conservative for almost twenty years, Liberals were elected.[73] As Laurier pointed out, these victories were not because of Liberal policy,

. . . but because the government by their bungling and double-dealing have created an impression of distrust which no efforts on their part have yet been able to dispel, whereas, on the contrary, there is an impression in this province that, were we in office, I personally could do more to settle the question.[74]

Only if the government committed itself to remedial action, did it seem possible that it would regain its support in Quebec. Laurier was certain that the government would make the attempt.[75] When Clark Wallace, an Orange leader, resigned from the government in December 1895, Laurier's suspicions seemed confirmed. The ques-

[67] LP, Cartwright to W. L., 25 March, 1895.
[68] *L'Electeur*, 16 April, 1895; quoting circular, 9 April, 1895.
[69] *L'Electeur*, 26 March, 1895.
[70] *Ibid.*, 16 April, 1895.
[71] *La Presse*, 4 March, 1895.
[72] Willison Papers, W.L. to Willison, 19 Nov., 1895.
[73] In the 1896 election, Jacques Cartier and St. Anne, formerly Montreal Centre, returned Conservatives once again.
[74] Willison Papers, W.L. to J.S.W., 31 Dec., 1895.
[75] LP, W.L. to Fielding, 5 Nov., 1895.

tion was whether even this would regain the confidence of the electors in the province.

Just at the time that the Conservative party seemed to have at last decided to take the responsibility of a political decision, Laurier seems to have decided that a public policy of conciliation would be acceptable. As he wrote to Fielding,

I know for a certainty that the most intelligent and far-seeing among the Roman Catholics – both clergy & laity – dread the action of the government as likely to conduce not to the reestablishment of separate schools in Manitoba, but to an agitation for the abolition of separate schools in all the provinces.[76]

Yet, to Willison, he admitted that his "attitude of conciliation" was criticised in the ministerial press. "I am daily denounced by them as a traitor to my race and religion." And so conciliation, which might not win Ontario could easily lose Quebec. Laurier's conclusion was that "The next session will be the crucial one."[77]

The next session was the crucial one. It did not begin by reassuring the Conservatives in Quebec. The special session was convoked on the second day of January; on the fifth, seven Cabinet Ministers, all Protestants, resigned. The official explanation was Bowell's failure to fill the Cabinet vacancy left by Angers' resignation. The Conservative *La Minerve* suspected an attempt to betray the minority.[78] Whatever the reason, such an incident was not likely to give any assurance of a firm unyielding attitude on the school question. The crisis was settled by a temporary restoration of the Ministers, with Charles Hibbert Tupper replaced by his father Sir Charles Tupper. Even then there was an ominous delay until finally, on February 11, the Remedial Bill received first reading.

The Remedial Bill was intended to re-establish the completely separate school system which had existed before 1890. The Manitoba government was to appoint a Separate School Board composed of Roman Catholics only.[79] This Board was to be responsible for

---

[76] *Ibid.*
[77] Willison Papers, W. L. to Willison, 30 Dec., 1895.
[78] *La Minerve*, 7 Jan., 1896. J. T. Saywell in the "Introduction" to his edition of *The Canadian Journal of Lady Aberdeen, 1893-1898* (Toronto, 1960), LIX-LXIV and L. C. Clark in his *A History of the Conservative Administrations, 1891-1896* (unpublished Ph.d. thesis, University of Toronto, 1968), pp. 439-440 contradict this view of the resigning ministers' motives. Far from wishing to "betray" the minority, Clark argues, most of the "bolters" damned Bowell for his vacillation about bringing in remedial legislation.
[79] *Commons Bills*, 1896, Bill 58, sec. 1.

the administration of the separate schools, for the appointment of teachers and inspectors, and the selection of school books. The provincial government was not completely impotent. In "secular matters" the teachers had to meet the standards set for public schools;[80] inspectors could only be appointed "subject to the approval" of the government;[81] and text-books were to be those authorised for Manitoba public schools or Ontario separate schools. The most controversial aspect of the Bill was the financial settlement. Separate school district trustees could levy school taxes on all Roman Catholics within the school district, with the exception of those Roman Catholics who preferred the public school taxes instead.[82] There was to be no double taxation. The separate schools were given "the right to share proportionately" in any provincial education grant.[83] So, after six years of indecision and even of deceit, the government had decided in favor of the minority.

The determination of the government might still be suspected. While the Bill was being debated in the House, three government Commissioners were trying to negotiate a compromise settlement in Winnipeg. Instead of a separate school system, they favored a system similar to that of New Brunswick. Roman Catholics would attend public schools, but when their numbers warranted it, they would have Roman Catholic teachers and acceptable text-books.[84] However, the Manitoba government was not conciliatory. It objected to the threat implied by the continued debate on the Remedial Bill, and it also objected to some details of the suggested compromise as being too expensive.[85] It is possible that the Greenway government was not sincere in its desire to effect a settlement, being aware that some federal Liberals were not averse to gaining a political advantage by delaying government action.[86] The negotiations were terminated with expressions of regret on both sides. Now that negotiations had failed, the government had no alternative; the Remedial Bill would have to be passed. Charles Tupper, leader of the government in the House of Commons, and leader of the party in the election campaign, could blithely ignore the attempts that had been made to reach a compromise; "the present question is not one of the creation of separate schools at all, but of maintaining the law and Constitution of the country as expounded by the highest tri-

[80] Ibid., sec. 4
[81] Ibid., sec. 69.
[82] Ibid., sec. 28.
[83] Ibid., sec. 74.
[84] Sessional Papers, 1896, No. 39C; 28 Mar., 1896.
[85] Ibid., 30 March, 1896.
[86] J. W. Dafoe, Clifford Sifton in Relation to His Times (Toronto, 1931), 89.

bunal of the Empire."[87] Separate schools had become "the law and the Constitution" only after negotiations had failed. For Tupper, as for Bowell, the Remedial Bill had not been adopted on the principle that completely separate schools were guaranteed by the constitution, but rather because it seemed the most satisfactory solution to a difficult political problem. After the last negotiations had failed, the Conservatives could describe the Bill as representing "justice" in Quebec but "constitutional necessity" in Ontario.

Meanwhile, Wilfrid Laurier and the Liberals had also committed themselves to a policy by which the school question could be settled. On the second reading of the Bill, Laurier moved the six month's hoist. Laurier had pondered and hesitated before making up his mind.[88] It was a bold step. An amendment might have seemed a less drastic challenge. In fact, Laurier's speech was less disruptive for the Liberal party than any amendment could have been. The party was divided between those who opposed any federal interference in provincial matters and those who considered the Bill inadequate. Both groups might be persuaded to vote against the Bill, but no constructive amendment could have satisfied the two sections of the party. Laurier first denounced the dictatorial nature of the Bill. In one of his aptly chosen illustrations, he pointed out that Tupper had chosen compulsion rather than persuasion to bring Nova Scotia into Confederation, and that the result had been dissatisfaction and opposition to union in the province long after 1867. "Experience has taught us that this remedy of interference with local legislation has never been applied and probably never can be applied without friction, disturbance, and discontent. . . ."[89] Such an argument would be most acceptable to the Liberals who considered the question as one of provincial rights. But, as we have seen, Laurier did not believe that that principle was relevant on this issue. He denied that the Privy Council decision ordered interference with the Manitoba legislation, but he did not deny that interference might be permissible.[90] Instead, he argued that the government had not yet investigated to discover the facts, to learn whether the minority were really being mistreated. As for the Bill itself, it was "a half-hearted and faint measure – a measure of compromise and nothing else." More serious, it was a compromise to be "administered by a hostile government."[91] Such an argument would be acceptable to the Liberal defenders of the minority's rights. The specific criti-

[87] Tupper Papers, Tupper to Rev. E. Kelly, 20 April, 1896.
[88] L. O. David, *Laurier et son temps* (Montréal, 1905), 77.
[89] *Commons Debates*, 3 March, 1896, 2742.
[90] *Ibid.*, 2747.
[91] *Ibid.*, 2756.

cisms of the Bill were elaborated by other French-Canadian Liberals. It was pointed out that the Separate School Board members might be Roman Catholics such as Donoghue, who had appeared on behalf of the province of Manitoba before the Privy Council.[92] The most serious weakness was financial. Separate school taxes were likely to be higher, and since Roman Catholics could choose to pay public school taxes, separate schools would be faced with the choice of lower standards and low taxes, or high standards and no taxpayers. More serious still, the promised share of the provincial grant was a delusion. If the provincial government refused to make a grant to schools created against its will, there was nothing in the Bill to compel the payment of the grant, nor any promise to make a federal grant if necessary.[93] Since "nearly a third of the school revenue" came from the provincial grant, according to a Conservative source,[94] this was a serious omission in the Bill.

The result of Laurier's motion was that the Liberal party maintained a semblance of unity. Six Liberals from Quebec refused to vote for Laurier's motion,[95] whereas seventeen Conservatives from Ontario voted for it. It was obvious that Laurier had not succeeded in truly uniting his party, but he had once more postponed an internal crisis. Obstruction in Committee delayed further action on the Bill and the legal life of Parliament ended before the Bill became law. The decision of the Manitoba school question was thus transferred from Parliament to the electorate, the election day being 23 June 1896. Like the Conservatives, the Liberals would defend their policy for one reason in Quebec, and another in Ontario. In Quebec, they would denounce the Remedial Bill as inadequate, in Ontario as an infringement on provincial rights.

It was not enough that Laurier should denounce the method and the details of the Conservative solution to the school question. In Quebec it was necessary to convince voters that he could provide a more satisfactory solution. As a French Canadian it was to be expected that the province of Quebec would have more confidence in his intentions than in the intentions of the Protestant Tupper. To strengthen this attitude, Oliver Mowat was persuaded to agree to enter the Liberal Cabinet if the Liberals won the election. Mowat was known to have been favorable to the rights of the minority in Ontario, and his influence on Ontario Liberals would be very important. So important did Mowat seem that Laurier even offered him the Premiership if necessary. J. S. Ewart, Mowat's nephew and advocate for the Manitoba minority in the various judicial proceed-

[92] F. Langelier, *Commons Debates*, 5 March, 1896, 2984.

[93] C. S. Geoffrion, *Commons Debates*, 4 March, 1896, 2847ff.

[94] Montreal *Gazette*, 12 Feb., 1896.

[95] C. Angers, Beausoleil, Delisle, Devlin, Fremont, Vaillancourt.

ings, acted as intermediary in the negotiations. To him, Laurier explained why he was willing to efface himself. "The interest which I take in the Manitoba School question and my desire to see it settled in a way that will give satisfaction to the minority, are so great that it would be a pleasure for me to make any sacrifice in order to induce Sir Oliver into Federal politics."[96]

In Quebec, Laurier could also promise that "justice will be given to the Manitoba minority without prejudice to the majority,"[97] but he could make no guarantee of this. He could only appeal to the confidence of the electorate. In fact, Laurier did have some assurance that the Liberal government in Manitoba would not be uncompromising if he was in power. J. D. Cameron, Provincial Secretary, had hinted in correspondence that: "if any injustice has been done the local authorities will remedy that far more speedily of their own free will than under the threat of coercion." Cameron had also suggested that the New Brunswick solution might be possible.[98] The Manitoba government may have been more specific in personal interviews. Nevertheless, Laurier's policy of a negotiated agreement depended on the goodwill of the Manitoba government, and of this he had no absolute guarantee. He could not explain to the electorate in Quebec what terms he would obtain for the Manitoba minority. "Sunny ways" might be less effective than bluster.

The attitude of the Roman Catholic clergy was of vital importance. They had approved of the Remedial Order, but had not officially intervened to influence the political attitude of their flock.[99] But even before Laurier's speech on the Bill, it was obvious that the clergy would not remain neutral. In January, before the Remedial Bill had been made public, Laurier had received a letter from Father Lacombe, speaking "in the name of our bishops, of the hierarchy and the Catholics of Canada," and appealing to Laurier to vote for the Remedial Bill.

If, which may God not grant, you do not believe it to be your duty to accede to our just demands, and if the government, which is anxious to give us the promised law, is beaten and overthrown while keeping firm to the end of the struggle, I inform you, with regret, that the episcopacy, like one man, united with the clergy, will rise to support those who may have fallen in defending us.[100]

[96] LP, W. L. to Ewart, 20 April, 1896.
[97] *La Presse*, 7 May, 1896.
[98] LP, Cameron to W. L., 9 April and 26 July, 1895.
[99] See above, p. 110.
[100] Skelton, *Laurier*, I, 470, letter dated 20 Jan., 1896. The letter was published in *L'Electeur*, 21 Feb., 1896. Skelton suggests it was made public through ecclesiastical channels. Dafoe says it was a "calculated indiscretion" by some Liberals. (Dafoe, *Laurier*, 46).

Archbishop Langevin was as decisive after the Bill had been opposed and as the session ended. In April he wired to Tupper.

*In the name of the Catholic minority of Manitoba that I represent
officially I ask the House of Commons to pass the whole Remedial
Act as it is now amended. It will be satisfactory to the said Catholic minority, that will consider it as a substantial, workable and
final settlement of the school question according to the Constitution.*[101]

In view of the Liberal criticisms of the Bill, it was a sharp reproof
to have the Archbishop of St. Boniface welcome it as a "final
settlement."

It is not easy to understand why Langevin was willing to commit
himself so completely. It would have been more logical for him to
argue that the Remedial Bill was preferable to the vague compromise promise by Laurier. He might well have supported his position
by referring to the refusal of the Liberal government in Manitoba to
accept the compromise suggested by the federal government. But
why should he accept it as final, and even state in Quebec; "I
approve of not only the principles in the remedial bill, but also the
details."[102] It seems unlikely that Langevin was impartial. He apparently believed that all Liberals were really guilty of Catholic-
liberalism and so were to be feared and detested. Of the Conservatives he had written; "Assuredly, I do believe that the Conservative
party is the only one to include within itself the elements of national
life and prosperity. . . .", although he unwillingly admitted later that
"We should not think that every Conservative is a true Catholic."[103] These statements might well have been written by a Castor –
or by Bishop Bourget. With this conviction, Langevin was not
likely to content himself with stating a mere preference for the
Conservative solution of the school question. Any doubts concerning the Remedial Bill would be forgotten in the desire to prevent a
dreaded Liberal victory.

The attitude of Father Lacombe and Archbishop Langevin could
not but influence the Roman Catholic episcopacy in the rest of
Canada. These two men had a direct responsibility for the welfare
of the minority in Manitoba. And if the bishops of Quebec accepted Langevin's interpretation of the Bill, the Liberal party would be
in serious difficulty in the province. As Laurier wrote to Willison:

[101] Tupper Papers, Langevin to Tupper, 13 April, 1896.
[102] Rumilly, *Histoire*, VIII, 58, sermon at Joliette, 5 May, 1896.
[103] Letters dated 21 Dec., 1893 and 14 Feb., 1896, quoted in L.
    Groulx, ed., "Correspondance Langevin-Audet," *Revue d'histoire
    de l'Amerique française* (1947), 274-276.

You can see by the letter of Father Lacombe the fight which we will have in Quebec. It will tell heavily against us, though the great bulk of the Liberals will not abandon me. As to my own course, it is plainer yet to me perhaps than it ever was. If we are to have a country at all, we must put down the threats of all factions, and appeal with greater courage than ever to the nobler sentiments of all Canadians. I fully expect that the active hostility of the Church may crush us just now; it will very soon make us stronger. I do not disguise (from) you however, that I am passing through a very severe ordeal. The thought that my action is to cost the political life of many of the noble fellows who support me so loyally is rather painful and even distressing – but there is only one way open, and it is very plain.[104]

In the House of Commons, Laurier bluntly stated that his position was based, "not upon grounds of Roman Catholicism, not upon grounds of Protestantism, but upon grounds which can appeal to the consciences of all men. . ."[105]

Nevertheless, Laurier had no intention of fighting the episcopacy if it could be avoided. In private he wrote to Mgr. Bégin, coadjutor of Quebec, explaining that he believed his solution would be more satisfactory than that of the government, and asked that the clergy would not interfere.[106] Other Liberals asked Bégin to conform to Archbishop Taschereau's Circular in connection with the dispute over the New Brunswick schools in the 1870's. Taschereau had stated that all Catholics must approve of separate schools. "A Catholic is nevertheless free to choose to reach this very desirable goal by means which he judges, to the best of his knowledge, to be the most appropriate, with the least possible danger for the religious peace of the country."[107] For the Liberals it would be an achievement if the episcopacy could be persuaded to adopt a position of official neutrality.

Bégin was not neutral. He heartily endorsed Langevin's preference for a solution by means of remedial legislation. "No one has doubted – for quite a while – that all the bishops of Canada alike have appreciated the remedial legislation proposed in the federal Parliament, and have desired keenly that it be adopted, while yet improved as much as possible."[108] Bégin's faith in the adequacy of

---

[104] Willison Papers, W.L. to J.S.W., 22 Feb., 1896.

[105] Commons Debates, 3 March, 1896, 2759.

[106] LP, W.L. to Bégin, 24 Feb., 1896.

[107] Tarte Papers, Box I, unsigned copy of letter dated 18 Feb., 1896; quoting Circular, 18 July, 1872.

[108] LP Microfilm, C 371, Bégin to D. C. Rinfret, 29 April, 1896.

the Remedial Bill was not as complete as Langevin's, but his attitude to the Liberal policy was just as uncompromising.

It is significant that only the French-Canadian members of the episcopacy took this attitude. Separate schools were important to the church but compromises with the public school system had proved possible elsewhere. The French bishops were undoubtedly sincere in their use of religious arguments against compromise – but we must assume that the English bishops were as devoted to the interests of the church. Other factors help to explain the intensity of the opposition to the Liberals by the French-Canadian episcopacy. One reason was that compromise with the public school system was a threat to French-Canadian survival. Completely separate schools might preserve French as the language of instruction, since the French Canadians would be proportionately stronger in such an organization, whereas public schools were likely to insist upon English as the language of instruction. Another reason for the difference between the French and the English bishops on this occasion was suggested by Laurier in a letter to an Apostolic Delegate some years later.

The bishops have authority in a province where Catholics are in a great majority and where, as a result, their rights in the field of education are absolutely sheltered from all attack. In all the other provinces, on the contrary, Protestants make up the great majority: Catholics, however, either by virtue of the law or through tolerance, enjoy considerable rights and privileges in the area of education, and the Catholic bishops in these provinces do not want to foment an agitation whose result could endanger these rights and privileges.[109]

Nevertheless, when the mandement on the Remedial Bill was published it was not as critical as many Liberals had feared. It was signed by all the French-Canadian bishops. It stated that Catholics ought to vote for candidates who would pledge themselves to vote "in favour of a law restoring to the Catholic minority of Manitoba the school rights which have been recognized by the honourable Privy Council of England", but referred only to candidates and not to any political party.[110] At least it was not a condemnation of the Liberal party. As a joint declaration of the bishops, it could only express the views of the most moderate of its signers, in this case Bishop Emard of Valleyfield.[111] That many of the bishops felt more strongly, we may infer from their sermons. Bishop Laflèche de-

[109] *Ibid.*, W.L. to Sbaretti, 30 May, 1903.
[110] *La Presse,* 18 May, 1896.
[111] Rumilly, *Histoire,* VIII, 68.

nounced Laurier's attitude of compromise as "the affirmation of the liberalism condemned by the Church."[112] Others were no less forthright.[113] Among the lesser clergy there was less unanimity, some priests even supporting the Liberal party openly.[114] But the mandement was the most important statement by the clergy on the school question, and it was not decisive. There was no doubt that it favored the Conservatives, but the pledge it demanded might even be taken by Liberal candidates on the assumption that if Laurier could not obtain a satisfactory compromise, he would pass a remedial bill.[115] As Tarte wrote to Willison, "it is not as wicked as it might have been although it is doubtless directed against us."[116]

The election has sometimes been over-simplified into a contest between Laurier and certain wilfully intransigent bishops in Quebec. This explanation scarcely does justice to the motives of the bishops. The election issue which most interested the province of Quebec was one with which the bishops were directly concerned. But the bishops also became directly involved because of the weakness of Conservative leadership in the province. Just as military heroines may emerge because the natural leaders fail to meet the challenge, so the bishops became prominent because the Conservative politicians were found wanting. If the interests of the church were to be adequately defended, the bishops had to intervene. The bishops were at a disadvantage in a political contest with men who made a career of fighting elections. In the cynical phrase attributed to Tarte, "elections are not made with prayers." The bishops were also at a disadvantage because their opponents evaded a direct challenge to the church. But if the bishops believed that a Conservative victory was essential to the church, the bishops had to enter the political campaign. None of the Conservative leaders were capable of winning the election in Quebec.

In the re-organisation of the Cabinet by Sir Charles Tupper at the close of the session, the Quebec representation was once more complete. Angers was persuaded to return, and with him were associated Desjardins, Ross and Taillon.[117] These four men had

---

[112] *Ibid.*, 62.

[113] *Ibid.*, 66ff.

[114] C. Lepatrie, "Le libéralisme Catholique et les Elections 23 juin, 1896," (Québec, 1896), II, 2159.

[115] "Justitia" in "La campagne politico-religieuse de 1896-1897," (Québec, 1897) quotes some of the pledges taken, and states that most of the French-Canadian Liberal candidates made such a pledge.

[116] Willison Papers, Tarte to Willison, 17 May, 1896.

[117] Ives represented the Eastern Townships.

much in common. They were men of firm principles, but they lacked oratorical ability and flamboyance. They were administrators rather than political leaders. Alphonse Desjardins had represented a Montreal constituency for almost twenty years, but not until 1896 did he become a Minister. His lack of personal magnetism is suggested by his defeat in the general election of this year; his impersonal attitude to politics by his retirement from active politics after his defeat. J. J. Ross had succeeded Mousseau as Prime Minister of Quebec in 1884. A Legislative Councillor and then a Senator, we may deduce that he was not of a crusading temperament. L. O. Taillon was also a former Prime Minister of Quebec although, like Ross, he had never won a provincial election as leader of the party. He had succeeded Ross in 1887 and Boucherville in 1893. In 1896 he resigned to contest a federal seat. Like Ross, he was defeated in the general election and retired to private life. Indeed, he had considered retirement from politics even before 1896. In 1892 he had sought a judgeship,[118] and in 1894 he informed Thompson that "I am in politics contrary to my tastes and my interests."[119] A. R. Angers was the strongest of the French Canadian Ministers, and was the acknowledged leader of the Conservative party in Quebec. Angers' firmness had been a handicap in his political career. He had once proposed to "take the municipalities by the throat,"[120] and the resulting unpopularity had led to his personal defeat in the election of 1878. As Lieutenant-Governor, he had dismissed Mercier, a bold step but again, not a popular one. Angers had been a judge, and had only accepted the Lieutenant-Governorship in 1887 on condition that he would be protected "against an uncertain future."[121] He entered Thompson's Cabinet in 1892 on the understanding that he would be given a judgeship.[122] His courage and sincerity cannot be questioned; in spite of his desire for security, he had remained out of the Cabinet for a year as a protest against the delay in the school settlement. Nevertheless, courage and austerity were not enough, without enthusiasm. Angers too was defeated in 1896 and retired to private life.

These ministers had more than temperament in common. Politically, they all belonged to the Castor section of the Conservative party. Desjardins, Ross and Taillon had all been adherents to the *Programme Catholique* of 1871[123] and a decade later they had all

[118] Thompson Papers, Angers to Thompson, 20 Oct., 1892.
[119] *Ibid.*, Taillon to Thompson, 25 Jan., 1894.
[120] Rumilly, *Histoire*, II, 188.
[121] Macdonald Papers, Macdonald to Angers, 21 Oct., 1887.
[122] Bowell Papers, Bowell Letterbook, 124, Bowell to T.C. Casgrain, 5 April, 1895.
[123] Rumilly, *Histoire*, I, 176, 178.

been Castors. Angers, being out of politics in the 1880's, was not directly affiliated to the Castor group, but he had been responsible for the separate school legislation in Quebec,[124] and his hostility to the Chapleau group had been no secret.[125] It was not surprising that these four should be wholehearted in their support of the Remedial Bill, which conformed so closely to the racial and religious emphasis of the Castors.

This uniformity, both in temperament and principle, was a great disadvantage in the election of 1896. By temperament, they were incapable of arousing emotional support from their followers. As Castors, they represented only a minority of the Conservatives within the province – and a minority which could be depended upon to vote Conservative in any case, in 1896.

One man might have saved the party in 1896 – Chapleau. Chapleau might have won the support of the non-Castor Conservatives in the province, and he was certainly capable of arousing more enthusiasm than the actual ministers. Chapleau's importance was clearly realised at the time. Even Archbishop Langevin wrote of the party in Quebec, that "Chapleau will strengthen it politically, but it is not he who will unite it from the doctrinal point of view."[126] Tupper appealed to Chapleau to re-enter the cabinet, but Chapleau bluntly declined. "The grave reasons which induced me to quit active political life are still sufficient to keep me away from it now."[127] To understand what these "grave reasons" were, we must recall Chapleau's feud with the Castors in the 1880's.

The feud had not ended with Chapleau's departure for Ottawa. Macdonald had found it difficult to keep the peace.[128] In the election of 1887, Chapleau felt his position vindicated since the Montreal district had been more loyal to the Conservatives than the Quebec district under Hector Langevin. Chapleau arranged to have Sénécal appointed Senator. Sénécal was virulently hated by the Castors, and his appointment was an intentional affront. "I needed a striking proof of the power that I claim in the region which I had to and wanted to run. I made it as dazzling as possible....", he wrote to Tarte.[129] But Chapleau failed to oust the Castor wing. Macdonald's tact postponed the crisis, but after his death it could not long be avoided. Chapleau continued to complain that he had "neither the influence nor position in the ministry his services and

[124] *Ibid.*, II, 81.
[185] *Ibid.*, 284.
[126] Groulx, "Langevin-Audet Correspondance," 276, letter dated 14 Feb., 1896.
[127] Tupper Papers, Chapleau to Tupper, 29 April, 1896, telegram.
[128] Macdonald Papers, Macdonald to Chapleau, 21 Jan., 1887.
[129] Tarte Papers, Box 13, 4 Mar., 1887.

ability entitle him to, and rather than remain muzzled he prefers recuperating his powers in the repose of a Lieutenant-Governorship."[130] Cynical men might suggest that Chapleau resigned because he did not become Minister of Railways,[131] but this only illustrates how principles and personalities had merged in the Chapleau-Castor feud. If Chapleau had not obtained the position he sought, it must be because Castor influence had prevented it. If further evidence is needed to show how bitter the struggle had become, we need only cite the resignation of the Castor Premier, Boucherville, when Chapleau became his Lieutenant-Governor.[132]

In 1896, had Chapleau returned to the federal government, it would have been as a colleague of the Castors. According to G. A. Nantel, a close friend of Chapleau's, Chapleau believed that the Castors were hypocrites who wished to exploit his talents and then discard him.[133] Dansereau had a similar explanation.[134] Hence Chapleau's refusal.

The result was to restrict the representation in the Cabinet to the Castor group. As Dansereau wrote, if Chapleau did not accept, Angers would choose his colleagues, and the anomalous result would be that the Orangemen in the Cabinet, those "mangeurs de prêtres", would impose three Castors on Quebec.[135] The effect of Chapleau's abstention was to prevent the full recovery of the Conservative party from its parlous position of the year before. As *La Presse* observed, even Chapleau and Angers, with the help of the bishops, would have difficulty in winning the election when allied to such Orangemen as MacLean, Sproule and Wallace.[136] The official reason given for Chapleau's refusal was ill-health,[137] and certainly his health was not good. But if his refusal to accept a portfolio did not make public the party schism, it did nothing to overcome it. Without the confidence which Chapleau could inspire, the future for the party was black indeed. Dansereau may have been exaggerating, but he was not completely mistaken when he wrote: "The people who needed an idol turned to Laurier in 1896."[138]

The Manitoba school question reflects little credit upon Canadian politics, judged from the point of view of decisiveness and con-

[130] Thompson Papers, R. S. White to Thompson, 19 Sep., 1892.
[131] *La Patrie*, 13 Dec., 1894, R. Dandurand.
[132] Rumilly, *Histoire*, VII, 60ff.
[133] *La Presse*, 14 Dec., 1901.
[134] *Ibid.*, 30 Nov., 1901.
[135] P.A.C., R. Lemieux Papers, Dansereau to Chapleau, undated (circa. 1 May, 1896).
[136] *La Presse*, 27 April, 1896.
[137] *Gazette*, 30 April, 1896.
[138] *La Presse*, 30 Nov., 1901.

sistency. The Conservative government had constantly evaded the responsibility of settling the question. For five years it sought some judicial decision which would be decisive, whether it restored separate schools or not. After the final decision of the English Privy Council, the government's indecision led them to deceit. The Remedial Order and the Remedial Bill were explained as merely putting into effect the judicial decision, yet at the same time negotiations were being conducted, secretly and then openly, for a compromise settlement which would have been the negation of the judicial decision as the government interpreted it. In the province of Quebec, the equivocation destroyed the party. Not one French-Canadian member of Macdonald's last Cabinet survived the changes to become a member of Tupper's Cabinet in 1896. For almost a year the Conservatives had been unable to fill the Cabinet vacancy left by Angers. And then in 1896, the French-Canadian ministers were chosen from a numerically small group of doctrinaires, who must be credited with sincerity but not with popularity. The Remedial Bill and the agreement of the bishops would have won their support; it was the support of the Chapleau group that should most have concerned the party. Small wonder that not one French-Canadian Minister and only sixteen Conservatives were elected in Quebec.

The Liberal party in Quebec was not much more decisive in its attitude. Tarte had done much to undermine confidence in the Conservative government by his criticisms of its refusal to disallow the School Act of 1890, yet the Liberal party had opposed disallowance at the time. And while criticising the indecision of the government, the Liberals had offered no constructive advice. Laurier had suggested no solution, with the avowed intention of avoiding the division in the Liberal ranks which any positive policy would have disclosed. Some Quebec Liberals had even pledged to obey the *mandement* which asked for remedial legislation, when common sense should have shown them that Laurier's policy of compromise had committed the party so completely that unsuccessful negotiations could never be reversed by legislation. Neither party could boast of its consistency.

This was not entirely the fault of the politicians. The parties were inconsistent because the nation was divided on the issue of separate schools. If the parties were to be national parties they could not declare for or against separate schools. It was the recognition of this fact, and the early realization that this made a compromise essential, that establishes Laurier's reputation as a national statesman. Laurier was no more sincere than Angers or Bishop Laflèche or than D'Alton McCarthy, but his analysis of the political situation was more sound. His policy of compromise was acceptable to the opponents of separate schools and to the advocates of provincial autonomy, and in New Brunswick at least, had been acceptable to the advocates of separate schools. The alternative of coercive legislation was unworkable. The Manitoba government was likely to administer a Remedial Act in a manner unfair to the separate schools, convinced as they were that the system was impracticable. Neither party was so united in its determination to restore separate schools that it could have passed subsequent, more stringent remedial acts to coerce the provincial government, or could have accepted the alternative of federal grants to the separate schools. It might be argued that Laurier was thinking only of the unity of his party and not of the interests of the nation. This criticism is based on a form of political cynicism which ignores the national function of political parties. In the Canadian federation, national political life is based upon national political parties; they alone are capable of determining national policies. Hence national political unity is dependent upon the unity of national parties.

Laurier's policy was a national policy. If it was to be successful it had to be accepted in Quebec. It was accepted there, as the election proved; the Liberals increasing their representation from thirty-five to forty-nine seats. The weakness of Conservative leadership could not be compensated for by the religious influence of the bishops. Nevertheless, the Liberals were able to take full advantage of the situation only because of Wilfrid Laurier. His influence in Quebec was in part the result of the *nationalisme* fostered by the agitation over the Jesuits' Estates Act and the school question. Laurier made no direct appeal to *nationalisme*, but it was not necessary. He was a French Canadian; if elected he would be Prime Minister. Laurier's political career, his defence of his language and religion at Ottawa and even at Toronto, had established confidence in him. There was no need to draft the terms of the settlement he would obtain because the electors had confidence in him.

The bold reliance on these tactics in Quebec has been credited to Tarte.[139] Years before, Tarte had written to Laurier that; "with your eloquence and your unblemished reputation, we can stir up many things."[140] But nevertheless, the credit for the victory belongs to Laurier. It was his personal reputation that was being used as the gambling stake, and it must have been he who had made the final decision to stake it.

The victory in Quebec in 1896 was not decisive proof that Quebec had become a Liberal province. The Conservatives had failed to satisfy the French Canadians by their policy, and the

Liberals were now to be given an opportunity. Laurier was aware of his responsibility. He had hesitated to commit himself, but now the die was cast. The fate of the minority in Manitoba and the fate of the Liberal party in Quebec depended upon the results of his negotiations with the Manitoba government.

6.
The Manitoba School Settlement

Winning the election had not solved Laurier's problems. There could be no security of tenure for the Liberal government until a satisfactory solution of the Manitoba school question had been found. A compromise had first to be agreed upon with the Greenway government in Manitoba; then it would be necessary to persuade the Roman Catholic authorities to accept the terms as adequate, if not completely satisfactory. Laurier wasted no time. Clifford Sifton, Solicitor-General in Greenway's government, had been selected as the Cabinet representative from the west,[1] but to provide him with an incentive, the appointment was not confirmed until a compromise had been arranged with the Greenway government. After preliminary correspondence with Sifton as to desirable terms,[2] Tarte and Henri Bourassa were sent out to complete the negotiations.[3] Terms were agreed upon in November, 1896.[4]

The terms were similar to the suggested compromise which the Manitoba government had rejected in 1895. In some respects they were even more advantageous for the minority, as for example the clause that entitled forty Roman Catholic pupils in urban areas to be taught by a Roman Catholic teacher, as compared to fifty in 1895.[5] Religious teaching was relegated to a half-hour period at the end of the school day; during "secular school work" there was to be no denominational segregation. An important concession to the minority was that when ten students were French-speaking, their language of instruction would be French.[6] The explanation for Manitoba's more conciliatory attitude cannot be positively determined. Laurier and his negotiators deserve some credit. Sifton, for instance had insisted that "the number of pupils to each Protestant

[1] Dafoe, *Sifton*, 96.
[2] LP, Sifton to W.L., 28 Aug., 1896.
[3] Rumilly, *Histoire*, VIII, 124.
[4] LP, Sifton to W.L., 9 Nov., 1896.
[5] *Sessional Papers*, 1896, No. 39c; 1897, No. 35.
[6] W. L. to Abbé Proulx, 23 Nov. 1896 and Fitzpatrick, "Les écoles du Manitoba," speech of 15 Dec. 1896, quoted, Rumilly, *Histoire*, VIII, 137.

and Catholic teacher will have to be placed at fifty ...",[7] whereas Laurier had asked to have the number set at thirty.[8] Also, as a Liberal, Greenway might be expected to be less uncompromising with Laurier than he had been with Bowell. Probably of some importance too, was the fact that the Conservative party had done well in the federal elections in Manitoba, which must have suggested to Greenway that a settlement of the question was desirable.

The attitude adopted by Archbishop Langevin was once again a matter of grave importance. Laurier had taken some precautions to gain his support. Judge Routhier, a former Castor who now favored a compromise, was sent out to Manitoba to influence the clergy.[9] Tarte and Bourassa, also, must have been re-assuring delegates from the point of view of the Church, and certainly Tarte had been careful to interview Langevin during his negotiations.[10] The Archbishop, however, refused to consider anything short of completely separate schools, and publicly denounced the compromise as a betrayal of the minority and unacceptable to the Church.[11] Greenway made a conciliatory speech in Montreal, promising further concessions if necessary.[12] These would have been administrative concessions, such as Catholic representation on the Board of Education, Catholic school inspectors, and the selection of textbooks acceptable to the Church.[13] Without the cooperation of Langevin and the minority, these administrative arrangements were impossible. The difficulty of a settlement under these conditions may be illustrated by the problem of selecting a Roman Catholic school inspector. Attorney-General Cameron of Manitoba asked Laurier's advice as to a suitable inspector.[14] T. Rochon was selected, Rochon having been a successful teacher in Ontario, acceptable to the clergy of the Archbishopric of Ottawa, and a fellow-student of Langevin himself.[15] Rochon visited Langevin in Montreal before going to Manitoba, but Langevin bluntly told him he would receive Rochon as a friend but not as one of Greenway's school inspectors.[16] Langevin finally ordered Catholic teachers to refuse Rochon admission

[7] LP, Sifton to W.L., 3 Sept., 1896.
[8] Ibid., 28 Aug., 1896.
[9] Ibid., Fitzpatrick to W.L., 17 July, 1896.
[10] Tarte, Commons Debates, 30 March, 1897, 243.
[11] Rumilly, Histoire, VIII, 130.
[12] Ibid., 142.
[13] LP, W.L. to J. D. Edgar, 9 Dec., 1896.
[14] Ibid., Cameron to W.L., 19 Jan., 1897.
[15] Ibid., Rochon to R. Scott, no date.
[16] Ibid., Rochon to W.L., 9 Feb., 1897.

to their schools.[17] In the face of such an uncompromising attitude, no settlement was possible.

The Archbishop of St. Boniface could rely upon the support of both the Conservatives and the Church of Quebec. The Conservatives may have been influenced by partisan motives. Conservative newspapers had favored the terms proposed in 1895,[18] but the concessions in 1896 were "insignificant crumbs".[19] Such newspapers could be answered by Liberal newspapers, and Laurier made certain that the settlement was defended in the province.[20] The Quebec bishops, however, were certain to be influenced by Langevin's attitude, and Laurier found it more difficult to reply to them. Efforts by the episcopacy to make clerical opposition to the settlement unanimous failed because Archbishop Walsh of Toronto and the other English bishops refused to intervene.[21] Even among the French-Canadian clergy there was not complete unanimity, since individuals such as Mgr. Laflamme and Mgr. Mathieu of Laval University, Quebec, favored a compromise settlement.[22] Officially, however, the "so-called settlement" was denounced by Mgr. Bégin of Quebec as an "unjustifiable abandonment of the best established and most sacred rights of the Catholic minority,"[23] and criticized by other bishops in a similar vein.[24] Laurier's only hope of a satisfactory conclusion to the school question was to appeal to an authority which could quell the opposition of the episcopacy.

Even before the settlement had been published, Laurier had two emissaries in Rome, the Abbé Proulx and a former Papal Zouave, G. Drolet. Laurier publicly denied that there was an "official mission" sent to Rome[25] but, official or not, these two had been sent by Laurier to present his side of the question in Rome, carrying with them a confidential letter from Laurier.[26] Nor were these two the only Canadians who arrived at Rome at this time – Archbishop Langevin and the Bishops of Quebec, Nicolet and Chicoutimi undertaking a similar pilgrimage.[27] As the Abbé Proulx wrote: "Almost all Canada is going to travel to Rome; it would be very much

[17] *Ibid.*, Tarte to W.L., 16 July, 1897.

[18] *La Minerve* and *L'Evénement*, 4 April, 1895.

[19] *La Minerve*, 18 Nov., 1896.

[20] LP, L.P. Brodeur to W.L., 20 Nov., 1896.

[21] *Ibid.*, H. MacMahon to Fitzpatrick, 11 Jan., 1897, copy

[22] LP, Fitzpatrick to W.L., quoted, Rumilly, *Histoire*, VIII, 152.

[23] Circular to the clergy, quoted, Rumilly, *Histoire*, VIII, 152.

[24] *Ibid.*, 152.

[25] *Commons Debates*, 17 Sept., 1896, 1371.

[26] LP, Proulx to W.L., 5 Oct., 1896.

[27] Rumilly, *Histoire*, VIII, 135.

[28] LP, Proulx to W.L., 12 Sept., 1896.

simpler if a single person, in Rome's name, travelled to Canada."[28]
This was indeed what Laurier wanted. A Papal Delegate in Canada
might see the danger of racial and religious strife, and would be able
to order the bishops to accept the settlement. The confidential letter
carried by the Abbé Proulx was that signed by the Liberal Roman
Catholic members of the Senate and the House of Commons, complaining of clerical interference in politics and requesting the appointment of a Delegate.[29]

At this time a book appeared, written by Laurier's friend, L. O.
David. David had written an historical survey of the clergy and
Canadian politics, and in connection with the school question had
said:

*Thus, according to Mgr. Laflèche, in order to be a good Catholic,
an M.P. should vote for a law he believed bad from a national or
constitutional point of view, once a bishop found it to be good.
That is the denial of all political freedom, the overturning of the
basic principles of the constitution, it is a heresy as dangerous for
the Church as for the State.*[30]

The book was put on the Index. This added fuel to the flames. The
bishops in Rome were reported to be saying that Laurier was a false
Catholic, a free-thinker and an anti-clerical.[31] David's book was
used to confirm these statements.[32] Drolet cabled from Rome advising David's immediate submission to the decision of the church[33] –
which was promptly forthcoming.[34] At the same time however,
L'Electeur, edited by Laurier's friend, Pacaud, was formally forbid-
den to Catholic readers by the episcopacy for having published
excerpts from David's book and for other articles of a similar
nature.[35] The Pastoral Letter was read in the churches on Sunday;
on Monday, Pacaud's newspaper came out under the name of *Le
Soleil*.[36] Bishop Labrecque of Chicoutimi promptly banned *Le Soleil* in his diocese,[37] although the other bishops took no further
action. With the bishops and the Liberals fighting openly in
Quebec, it is small wonder that Laurier's emissaries had trouble

[29] Tarte, *Commons Debates*, 30 March, 1897, quotes letter dated Oct
1896.
[30] L. O. David, "Le clergé canadien, sa mission, son oeuvre," (Montréal, 1896), 89.
[31] LP, Drolet to W.L., 2 Dec., 1896.
[32] *Ibid.*, 30 Dec., 1896.
[33] *Ibid.*, 21 Dec., 1896.
[34] Skelton, *Laurier*, II, 27.
[35] Pastoral Letter, 22 Dec., 1896, quoted, *La Minerve*, 28 Dec. 1896.
[36] Rumilly, *Histoire*, VIII, 141.
[37] *Ibid.*, 169.

convincing Rome of Laurier's sincere interest in the welfare of the church. Laurier recalled them.[38]

It was then that the inexperienced Laurier revealed his talent as a diplomatist. Rome had to be made to listen to his arguments if his government was to survive. One hope was that Bishop Emard of Valleyfield would go to Rome to plead his cause. Emard was the only French-Canadian bishop who favored the compromise, but he was not eager to make war on his colleagues. Tarte reported that Emard "is altogether with us, but will go to Rome only if invited by Rome."[39] Laurier meanwhile had decided to send Fitzpatrick, his Solicitor-General.

Laurier was careful to strengthen Fitzpatrick's diplomatic position as much as possible. As Laurier wrote to the Governor-General, Lord Aberdeen, "I fully realize this is a matter in which the British authorities cannot in any way interfere. . ." yet nevertheless it would be well that Rome should learn that the "British authorities deem it advisable and prudent. . ." that this settlement be accepted.[40] Fitzpatrick was able to write from England that he was leaving for Rome with letters from Cardinal Vaughan and the Duke of Norfolk, Joseph Chamberlain and Chief Justice Russell, and with a constitutional opinion from Edward Blake, "so that I go well-armed."[41] Helping Fitzpatrick in Rome was Charles Russell, the son of the Chief Justice. Fitzpatrick's argument was that Canada was not a Roman Catholic country, and so discretion was necessary. He was able to point out that only six of the twenty-nine bishops in Canada had protested against the settlement,[42] a fact which was too easily ignored in Catholic Quebec. Indeed, this fact shows how religious and *nationaliste* sentiments had merged to make the school question of special significance to French-Canadian bishops. Fitzpatrick was in a difficult position. The story is told that he had to spend so much time at his devotions in order to prove that a Liberal could be a sincere Catholic, that he had little time for diplomatic negotiations. But his mission was successful. It was finally decided in Rome to send a Papal Delegate to restore religious peace in Canada.[43]

Mgr. Merry del Val arrived as Papal Delegate in March 1897. Del Val already knew something of the problem. Charles Russell had informed his father that "my friend Mgr. Merry del Val, who, as you know, is the Pope's companion and attendant. . ." was

[38] *Ibid.*, 144.
[39] LP, Tarte to W.L., 14 Jan., 1897, decoded telegram.
[40] *Ibid.*, W.L. to Aberdeen, 23 Dec., 1896.
[41] *Ibid.*, Fitzpatrick to W.L., 21 Jan., 1897.
[42] *Ibid.*, 3 Feb., 1897.
[43] *Ibid.*, 28 Feb., 1897.

being of invaluable assistance to them in their negotiations in Rome.[44] Fitzpatrick had hoped for "an Englishman with some knowledge of the constitution" as Delegate,[45] but we may assume that he made no protest when the actual appointment was announced. Del Val was not sent as a diplomat to arrange a satisfactory settlement of the school question. In his own words; "*I have not been invited to discuss or to approve of the accords which have been reached between the Federal Government and the Government of Manitoba. I have been called to verify, not to discuss, the facts.*"[46]

Nevertheless, del Val's task was a very delicate and a very important one. He could not be a detached observer. There was first of all, a disagreement among the episcopacy. The French-Canadian bishops presented their point of view,[47] but a different analysis of the situation was given by the Archbishops of Kingston and Toronto, who feared that the re-opening of the Manitoba school question would endanger separate schools in Ontario.[48] But the real difficulty was in Manitoba, where del Val had to decide whether Greenway was offering adequate concessions in good faith, or whether Langevin's intransigence was justified. To decide this, del Val found it necessary to send Laurier a "memorandum of administrative concessions which will help to make the settlement more acceptable."[49] This memorandum dealt with the appointment of a member of the Board of Education and a school inspector acceptable to the Archbishop, the authorization of acceptable text-books, and the certification of teachers from religious communities. "These concessions guaranteed in the manner suggested pending the possibility of legislative measures entirely satisfactory to Catholic claims and leaving full freedom of action are calculated to determine a less hostile attitude on the part of the Catholics."[50] This memorandum might be considered an ultimatum from del Val. Elsewhere, del Val had pointed out the necessity of an acceptable solution. The alternative was the uniting of the Vatican and "the Episcopacy *all together*" against Laurier.[51] On the other hand, if the concessions were made, del Val was almost committed to defending the settlement at Rome.

[44] *Ibid.*, 30 Jan., 1897, copy.

[45] *Ibid.*, Fitzpatrick to W.L., 21 June, 1897.

[46] *Ibid.*, del Val to W.L., 16 June, 1897.

[47] Rumilly, *Histoire*, VIII, 165 ff.

[48] LP, G. W. Ross to W.L., 11 May, 1897.

[49] *Ibid.*, W. L. to Cardinal Rampolla, no date. Rampolla was Secretary of State at the Vatican.

[50] LP, page 14127, no date. This memorandum is in del Val's distinctive handwriting.

[51] LP, del Val to W.L., 19 May, 1897.

Thus Laurier's difficulties did not end with the appointment of the Papal Delegate. It was still necessary to obtain administrative concessions for the minority in Manitoba. And Laurier was not in a strong bargaining position where Greenway was concerned. The greater the concessions Laurier exacted, the greater the political benefits he would derive; it was Greenway who was taking all the political risk by yielding to the demands of the minority. Greenway was persuaded to adopt a satisfactory Order in Council under pressure from Laurier and Sifton,[52] but he failed to enforce the Order. "The Government of Manitoba has been seized by fright and perhaps also by a lack of good faith", wrote Tarte to Laurier.[53]

However, Laurier had a trump card to play. By the Dominion Lands Act the federal government was responsible for selling the school lands in the province of Manitoba and paying the provincial government the interest from the sums realized, the money to be used for provincial education requirements. In this period of expansion, Manitoba's capital expenditures were high, and the province badly needed a grant from the principal of the fund.[54] A resolution was introduced in the federal House to grant $300,000 from the school fund, but was not adopted; "the Catholic M.P.'s opposed it absolutely".[55] Laurier was informed that del Val accepted this gesture as "some evidence of our earnest desire to secure the modification of the Agreement."[56] Del Val left with the negotiations not yet completed and returned to Rome.

In Rome, del Val set about convincing the papal authorities that Laurier was in the right. Opposing this interpretation was Mgr. Bruchési, recently appointed Archbishop of Montreal. Del Val was reported to have remarked on Bruchési's extreme violence,[57] but he was confident of success. The arguments he used were the arguments on which Laurier had relied.

The worst of all is that these good bishops are perfectly right in all their arguments. The Catholics of Manitoba have been done out of their rights. The central Parliament has the power under the constitution to pass remedial laws. The church does not sanction mixed schools when the faith of the children may be lost, but the bishops seem incapable of grasping the situation as it is, that as a matter of practical politics the central Parliament cannot pass (no matter which side is in power) a remedial law, and that the Church

[52] *Ibid.*, 30 May, 1897.
[53] *Ibid.*, Tarte to W.L., 1 July, 1897.
[54] C. Martin, *Dominion Lands Policy* (Toronto, 1938), 339 ff.
[55] LP, Tarte to W.L., 1 July, 1897.
[56] *Ibid.*, R. W. Scott to W.L., 12 July, 1897.
[57] *Ibid.*, C. Russell to W.L., 22 Oct., 1898.

cannot allow generation after generation of children to grow up without any education at all, waiting until there is a Catholic majority in Manitoba which may never be.[58]

Del Val won the argument. The Papal Encyclical *Affari Vos* in December of 1897 stated that the School Act of 1890 was unjust, and that the Laurier settlement was inadequate, but that this partial satisfaction should be accepted and people should work with good-will and moderation to make the best of the situation.[59] It was as much as the Liberals had hoped for. The method of compromise, if not the results, had received the official sanction of Rome.

Even the authority of Rome could not placate Archbishop Langevin. He did not protest in public against the Encyclical.

I do not cling to protecting souls more than the Pope himself, and if the road of concessions, after having made things easier for us for a time, leads us to the abyss, I would not be at all responsible before God and before my conscience. I am ready to continue to struggle in poverty, in humiliation and without the least encouragement from Rome; but I do not want to say a word nor take a step against the will of our supreme head.[60]

But this grudging acceptance of the Encyclical did not prevent Langevin from interfering in school matters. For example, the federal Liberals considered it essential that arrangements should be completed so that the Catholic schools could open in 1898 in conformity to the provincial law. One of the requirements was a formal declaration by all teachers that there would be no religious exercises prior to half-past three o'clock. Without this declaration there would be no school grant. Laurier persuaded Greenway to make a verbal modification in the declaration to make it more acceptable to the Roman Catholics,[61] and Langevin accepted it in the new form.[62] A *modus vivendi* seemed established which some Protestants deplored as the re-establishment of separate schools,[63] but which del Val acclaimed as a practical solution.[64] Yet a few months later,

[58] *Ibid.*, C. Russell to W.L., 27 November, 1897, quoting del Val in Rome.
[59] Commons Debates, 5335 ff., 11 May, 1898, Encyclical quoted by McDougall.
[60] Langevin to Bégin, 22 Jan., 1898.
[61] LP 25993, copy of Blumhart's report to Langevin of an interview with Laurier, 24 Aug., 1898.
[62] LP, Dansereau to W.L., 8 Sept., 1898.
[63] Tarte Papers, Box 11, clipping from Winnipeg *Tribune*, 28 Dec., 1898.
[64] LP, del Val to W.L., 7 Nov., 1898.

Langevin changed his mind and forbade Catholic teachers to sign the declaration until Rome had been consulted.[65] Fortunately Rome accepted the form of the declaration as satisfactory.[66] Even so, two years later in a Circular to the clergy, Langevin again deplored the "odious restriction" imposed by this declaration.[67] In the city of Winnipeg, the Catholic schools had still not accepted the settlement. Laurier informed Rome that he believed that Langevin was retarding an amicable settlement. "With all the respect due to His Grace, I am bound to say that in my opinion, he has neither the tact, the prudence nor the coolness which the delicacy of the task had demanded."[68]

In Manitoba, the political tension was eased by the Conservative victory over Greenway in 1900. As Laurier remarked, it would no longer be possible to blame the Liberal party for the situation with the Conservatives in power in the province.[69] Correspondence concerning the Winnipeg schools continued for many years,[70] but the Manitoba school question was no longer of any political significance.

For the national Conservative party, the school question had been answered by the Quebec voters in 1896. Sir Charles Tupper expressed this opinion in an interview with del Val. "I discussed the Manitoba school question with him, and told him frankly that the French Catholics having supported Mr. Laurier, I must leave the case in his hands."[71] This was a betrayal of the Quebec wing of the Conservative party. Some of the Conservatives from Quebec were not willing to surrender so readily the principle on which they had fought the campaign of 1896, even after *Affari Vos*. In the House of Commons[72] and in the Senate,[73] French-Canadian Conservatives introduced the question, but with no support from their English colleagues. Liberals such as Tarte took pleasure in pointing out the realities of politics to the French-Canadian Conservatives. "If it suits the honorable gentlemen opposite to fight over again the battle of the Manitoba school question ... " in the next election campaign, Tarte expressed his readiness to "repeat the dose."[74] Even Bourassa hoped that "this is the last time this question will come

[65] *Ibid.*, W.L. to Bertrand, 27 Jan., 1899.
[66] *Ibid.*, Langevin to W. L., 2 Feb. 1899.
[67] *Ibid.*, 43517, copy of circular, 29 March, 1900.
[68] LP, W.L. to Cardinal Rampolla, 22 April, 1901.
[69] LP, W.L. to D'Hellencourt, 4 June, 1900.
[70] LP, W.L. to G. Bryce, 5 March, 1909.
[71] E. M. Saunders, *Life and Letters of Sir Charles Tupper*, II, 224.
[72] Bergeron, *Commons Debates*, 12 May, 1898, 5416.
[73] Landry, *Senate Debates*, 17 May, 1898, 809; 15 May, 1900, 544.
[74] *Commons Debates*, 30 March, 1897, 236.

before us as a political question."[75] As far as the national political parties were concerned, the school question was settled and the long controversy was at an end.

In the province of Quebec, the effects of the controversy lived on. The conflict between the episcopacy and the Liberal party in 1896 was not soon forgotten. *Affari Vos* had restrained the bishops but it had not altered their suspicions of the Liberal party. The hostility of the Church was further aggravated by the policy of the provincial Liberal party in the next few years. In his own interests, Laurier found it necessary to intervene in provincial politics in order to conciliate the Church.

The provincial Conservative government was affected by the disaster of the 23rd of June 1896. J. Flynn, successor to Taillon as Premier of the province, was a former Liberal who had joined Chapleau's administration in 1879.[76] The Castors had long memories. As Chapleau wrote to Laurier, "I am told that there has been quite serious trouble between the Conservative element and the 'castor' group."[77] Nevertheless an election could not be avoided because the statutory five years had almost elapsed. The problem was to unite the two wings of the party. The Castors were believed to be anxious to fight the provincial election by denouncing the Laurier-Greenway compromise,[78] whereas Flynn preferred to concentrate on provincial issues.[79] The arrival of the Papal Delegate solved this problem, since it forced a truce on politico-religious questions. As del Val's secretary wrote to *Le Soleil*: "All His Excellency wishes to say for the moment is that in an election concerning purely administrative issues every one is free in conscience to vote for the candidate he favours."[80]

.Once more, Chapleau's political influence affected the results of the election. Chapleau, with his interest in the material side of politics and his dislike for Castors, could not be impartial.

If the result of the provincial election is what I anticipate, not to say prepare for, I believe that the question of Manitoba Schools will become soon, from the political point of view, a thing of the past. ... The Castors lost in the battle of June 23, their heads and their tails; they have old claws and teeth; they even are short of breath for becoming excited and for shrieking, and I hope that before the date of the Queen's Jubilee, we shall be able to say that

[75] *Ibid.*, 12 May, 1898, 5425.
[76] Rumilly, *Histoire*, II, 281.
[77] LP, Chapleau to W.L., 16 Nov., 1896.
[78] *Le Soleil*, 4 March, 1897.
[79] LP, Chapleau to W.L., 21 Feb., 1897.
[80] *Le Soleil*, 8 May, 1897.

*this race of rodents is extinct and is numbered only in the cata-
logue of vanished species!*[81]

A man of Chapleau's temperament was not likely to be satisfied
with mere hoping, even when Lieutenant-Governor. His solution
was to eliminate the dissension within the Conservative party by
forming a coalition with the moderate Liberals – and so eliminating
the Castors.[82] Dansereau later defended his chief against the charge
that he had supported the Liberals in the election. According to
Dansereau, Chapleau had foreseen Flynn's defeat and had proposed a coalition on the grounds that "half a loaf is better than
none."[83] Whatever Chapleau's intentions, the effect of his intervention was to weaken the Conservatives even more. The Liberals,
staunchly supported by the federal Liberals in the campaign, gained
fifty-nine seats out of seventy-four in May, 1897. It seems unlikely
that Archbishop Langevin would have agreed with the explanatory
headline in *Le Soleil* after the Liberal victory; "Vox populi, vox
Dei!"[84]

The Liberal victory in Quebec affected Laurier's relations with
the bishops because F. G. Marchand, now Premier of the province,
was determined to effect the venerable Liberal policy of educational
reform. Marchand did not advocate "Godless schools", but he
wanted an increased emphasis on practical subjects, "so that our
youth can acquire all the training necessary to put it on the level of
the youth of our sister provinces."[85] In his Speech from the Throne,
Marchand promised to introduce a bill which would create a Minister of Education and would establish uniformity in school text
books, although he also promised to be guided by the advice of the
Council of Public Instruction.[86] Archbishop Bruchési, already opposing the federal Liberal school settlement at the Vatican, wired
from Rome that the Pope requested that the bill be postponed.[87]
Marchand agreed to postpone the bill but not to suspend it. He
argued that to do so was politically impossible because he had made
a formal promise to the electorate before the election.[88] Subsequently he explained that he believed the bill had been made acceptable

[81] LP, Chapleau to W.L., 21 Feb., 1897.
[82] La Presse, 14 Dec., 1901. G. A. Nantel started a controversy in
the press at this time by defending his mentor Chapleau from the
charge that Chapleau had supported the Liberals in 1897.
[83] *La Presse*, 2 Dec., 1901.
[84] *Le Soleil*, 12 May, 1897.
[85] "Discours sur l'instruction primaire." (Québec, 1896).
[86] Rumilly, *Histoire*, IX, 23.
[87] LP, Bruchési to Marchand, 22 Nov., 1897, copy.
[88] *Ibid.*, Marchand to Bruchési, 11 Dec., 1897, copy.

to the church, "while leaving to the Catholic Committee the full and complete direction of instruction and while giving to the ministers only purely administrative functions which do not impinge at all in that sphere."[89] The bill was not withdrawn, but it was defeated in the Legislative Council.[90] The bishops must have been further convinced by this episode that the Liberals wished to secularize all education,

The epilogue to this education bill may have reassured the episcopacy to some extent. Before the next session, Tarte interviewed Archbishop Bruchési, and reported to Laurier that the Archbishop was opposed to the re-introduction of the bill. "I admit to you that I am somewhat of the Archbishop's opinion."[91] Whether Laurier influenced Marchand or not, the bill introduced and passed in 1899 conformed to the wishes of the bishops. There was to be more uniformity in provincial schools but there was no mention of a Minister of Education.[92]

This educational issue involved Laurier in a minor political crisis which involved Chapleau. Laurier could not remain detached from the problem. Even the clergy favorable to Laurier's school settlement in Manitoba wanted Laurier to persuade Marchand to withdraw his original bill, arguing that his political future depended upon confidence at Rome in the Liberal policy.[93] Laurier turned to Chapleau. As Lieutenant-Governor of the province, and as the leading figure among French-Canadian Conservatives, Chapleau's support for Marchand's policy would be useful. Chapleau had already explained that in his opinion, "there must be reforms, and radical reforms, not so much perhaps in instruction itself as in the organization of the 'educational' machine" and he expressed his willingness to help Laurier in every way.[94] Chapleau's term as Lieutenant-Governor was almost terminated, but that might be arranged. A second term was discussed, Chapleau stressing the importance of the decision because he was certain that the expected educational reforms would be opposed by the ultramontanes.[95] The renewal of his term of office was agreed upon.[96] Chapleau did his part by writing a letter to Bruchési which denied that Marchand's bill was an infringement on the Church's control of education, and

[89] Marchand to Bruchési, 8 Jan. 1898, quoted, Rumilly, *Histoire*, IX, 40.

[90] *Ibid.*, 41.

[91] LP, Tarte to W.L., 3 Dec., 1898.

[92] Rumilly, *Histoire*, IX, 89.

[93] LP, Fitzpatrick to W.L., 4 Jan., 1898.

[94] Tarte Papers, Chapleau to Tarte, 17 May, 1897.

[95] LP, Chapleau to W.L., 25 Sept., 1897.

[96] *Ibid.*, 15 Nov., 1897.

argued that the clergy would endanger their authority more by suppressing the bill since it would strengthen the opposition of the anti-clericals to the Church.[97]

On this occasion there was some danger that the Quebec Liberals would rebel against Laurier's tactics. The Liberals had been in opposition for a long time, and many of them were hungry for office. Coming after a partiality shown to Conservatives by Laurier's Cabinet appointments, a second term for Chapleau seemed the complete betrayal of the "old Liberals". Beginning in September, 1897, letters were sent to Laurier complaining of the rumored renewal. Senator Pelletier, a prominent Quebec City Liberal, believed that the suggestion had caused an "alarming discontent" in the province.[98] There was no official second term granted, but Chapleau remained in office after the 7th of December, when his first term elapsed. Even this temporizing solution was too extreme for one Liberal who had a personal interest in the question. François Langelier, long a faithful Liberal and a friend of Laurier's, had received a written promise from Laurier that he would succeed Chapleau at Spencer Wood.[99] Langelier publicly denounced the agreement with Chapleau as a betrayal of the "old Liberals." Even *Le Soleil* agreed with him, stating that the real leaders of the "old Liberals" had been ignored by the government – although Pacaud somehow absolved Laurier from all blame, Tarte presumably being the culprit.[100] It was almost a revolt. The situation was complicated by the fact that Langelier might not be too acceptable to the episcopacy on educational matters, since he had actively favored educational reform while in the provincial Assembly.[101] Laurier's solution was to replace Chapleau by L. A. Jetté and to appoint Langelier as a judge. Jetté's appointment would be welcome to the bishops since he had never been tainted with *rougisme*.[102] In spite of his insubordination, Langelier was forgiven by Laurier, who explained that "I cannot forget an old friendship."[103]

Langelier was given promotions on the Bench and finally became Lieutenant-Governor in 1911. Even Chapleau bore no grudge. He loved the comforts of Spencer Wood but he assured Laurier that he understood the political predicament.[104] The dissident Liberals were thus appeased.

[97] Rumilly, *Histoire*, IX, 28; no date.
[98] LP, C. A. Pelletier to W.L., 4 Oct., 1897.
[99] Willison Papers, Tarte to Willison, 16 Dec., 1897.
[100] *Le Soleil*, 11 Dec., 1897.
[101] Rumilly, *Histoire*, VII, 36.
[102] *Ibid.*, I, 193.
[103] LP, W.L. to P. A. Choquette, 24 Oct., 1901.

For the next few years Laurier was concerned with the problem of conciliating the Roman Catholic episcopacy in Quebec. If the Liberal party was to secure its political victory in Quebec, clerical hostility had to be modified. But the clerical suspicion of the Liberal party was deeply rooted. The Manitoba school controversy had strengthened it.

The situation was especially serious in the archdiocese of Quebec. As Tarte wrote to Laurier, the Liberals could not expect much cooperation from Mgr. Bégin and the personnel of the Archbishopric.[105] Bégin, who became Archbishop in 1898, and Mgr. Marois, Vicar-general of Quebec, had been unalterably opposed to any compromise in Manitoba. As a priest in the diocese wrote to Laurier, "as long as Mgr. Marois occupies his position, it is useless to think of religious peace in Canada."[106] Laurier was not without friends in the diocese, Fitzpatrick regularly conferring with what he called his "oecumenical Council" at Laval.[107] Prominent in this group were Mgr. Mathieu, the Rector, and Mgr. Laflamme, his successor. These men however, were in a difficult position. They hesitated to express their opinions, even in private correspondence. In a letter to Fitzpatrick explaining that "we admire the cautious and dignified manner in which you pursue your cause . . .", they concluded, "Pardon anonymity, we cannot sign."[108] Tarte argued that Montreal was the key to the situation. "If we could secure for ourselves some of the religious power in this city, we would have done something eminently worthwhile."[109] Bruchési, the new Archbishop there, had not adopted an encouraging attitude in connection with del Val's mission or with Marchand's bill. His great interest in Catholic education may explain this. Yet on Bruchési's return from Rome and after the promulgation of *Affari Vos*, Bruchési became much more conciliatory. Tarte believed that he was ambitious and that he hoped with Laurier's aid to win a Cardinal's hat[110] – but one must make allowances for Tarte's tendency to assume that everyone believed that he and Laurier were omnipotent. Bruchési's explanation to Laurier would not be as appealing to a romantic schemer such as Tarte, but it is more convincing.

I pray with all my heart that the question of the schools soon receives the solution which Catholic conscience demands and the

[104] *Ibid.*, Chapleau to W.L., 21 Jan., 1898.
[105] *Ibid.*, Tarte to W.L., 21 July, 1898.
[106] *Ibid.*, Abbé Marquis to W.L., 20 Jan., 1898.
[107] *Ibid.*, Fitzpatrick to W.L., 31 Dec., 1897.
[108] *Ibid.*, letter to Fitzpatrick, 24 March, 1891.
[109] *Ibid.*, Tarte to W.L. 2 July, 1898.
[110] *Ibid.*, Tarte to W. L., 2 July, 1898.

Holy See desires. You wish this also, Mr. Minister, I am sure. For the whole country it will be a deliverance. . . . Leo XIII asked me to work with all my strength to obtain it: I shall so labour.[111]

Thus *Affari Vos* accounts for Bruchési's change of heart.

Bruchési soon became Laurier's most important link with the episcopacy in Quebec. He, rather than Archbishop Langevin, carried on the negotiations in connection with the Manitoba schools, even to such specific details as changes in text-books.[112] From Winnipeg, Laurier was informed that the "Catholic Father will take no responsibility without conferring with Montreal Archbishop."[113] For all his being "wise and discreet,"[114] Bruchési could not always suppress Archbishop Langevin. In spite of Bruchési, Langevin had appealed to Rome against the statutory declaration with reference to religious instruction in the Manitoba schools.[115] But there can be no doubt that he did restrain the Archbishop of St. Boniface. The official liaison between Laurier and Bruchési developed into a personal friendship which helped to smooth over many minor frictions.[116] The amicable relationship may be illustrated by a note from Bruchési in 1899. Bruchési sent Laurier a review in *La Minerve* of an article which accused Laurier of having become a Conservative and having surrendered to the Church on important occasions. Bruchési appended an ironical note. "Poor Sir Wilfrid! How guilty you are! And to think that I am responsible for your greatest sins.'"[117] There is even a suggestion in one of Bruchési's letters that this friendship had helped to strengthen Laurier's religious faith.[118] Laurier, in turn, defended Bruchési against the criticisms of many Liberals.[119] Whatever doubts Bruchési may have had, he was soon convinced of Laurier's sincerity.

Even the influence of the Archbishop of Montreal could not

111 *Ibid.*, Bruchési to W.L., 27 Jan., 1898.
112 *Ibid.*, Bruchési to W.L., 9 June, 1898.
113 *Ibid.*, S. A. D. Bertrand to W.L., 3 June, 1898, telegram. "Catholic Father" meant Abbé Cherrier, acting for Langevin at this time.
114 *Ibid.*, W.L. to Sen. Power, 27 Oct., 1898.
115 *Ibid.*, Bruchési to W.L., 29 Jan., 1899.
116 *Ibid.*, Bruchési to W.L., 29 Oct., 1898, telegram. Bruchési asks Laurier to prevent a conflict in timing between a religious ceremony and a political demonstration which some of the faithful saw as a deliberate affront to the Church. In a subsequent letter, 2 Nov., 1898, Bruchési thanks Laurier and Tarte for their co-operation.
117 LP, Bruchési to W.L., 11 Jan., 1899.
118 LP, Bruchési to W.L., 7 June, 1899. This may be what Willison meant when he wrote that by 1905 Laurier "was no longer estranged from the Catholic church." (Willison, *Laurier* [1926 edn.], II, 371.
119 *Ibid.*, W.L. to Sen. Power, 27 Oct., 1898.

restore peace in the Archbishopric of Quebec. As Laurier explained to del Val, who continued to be Laurier's confidant at Rome:

Mgr. Bruchési, with whom I have had the most satisfactory relations, had made me hope that a new era was going to dawn. I regret to have to note that he had expected too much. Nothing has changed in the dioceses of Québec, Rimouski and Chicoutimi. The warfare which went on there, goes on still, with this difference, that it has become undercover in place of open.[120]

Of the Quebec diocese in particular, he wrote, "He is absolutely certain that the clergy who show sympathy for the present government are subjected to more or less open, more or less serious, persecution, which makes their position more than difficult . . . "[121]

Laurier's solution was once more an appeal to Rome, this time for a permanent Apostolic Delegate. He had once hoped that del Val would be appointed; now that Bruchési had failed to influence his colleagues, he would be satisfied with anyone.[122] Again Laurier exerted pressure in Rome. In addition to del Val, Charles Russell had returned to Rome to request a permanent Delegate,[123] and at Laurier's request, Marchand wrote to the Vatican for the same purpose.[124] Laurier himself explained that del Val's mission had accomplished a great deal, and "if these happy results are to remain permanent and effective . . ." a prolonged delegation was necessary.[125] After the delay caused by Bruchési's intervention, the request was repeated.[126] Finally, in June of 1899, Archbishop Falconio was appointed as a permanent delegate to Canada.[127]

Laurier took steps to convince the Papal Delegate of his determination to reach a final settlement of the school question in Manitoba which would be satisfactory to the minority. He had already used the federal lands fund as a bribe for further concessions in the administration of the School Act.[128] He now disclosed to the representatives of the Church that this was his firm policy. As Falconio wrote;

I learned with great pleasure that, in the meeting of the Archbishops which took place yesterday, you really wanted to point out

[120] *Ibid.*, W.L. to del Val, 25 Nov., 1898.
[121] *Ibid.*, 26217, 5 Sept., 1898.
[122] *Ibid.*, 28347, 5 Sept., 1898.
[123] *Commons Debates*, 5 May, 1898, 4924.
[124] LP, Marchand to Cardinal Rampolla, 30 Oct., 1898.
[125] LP, W.L. to Cardinal Rampolla, 24 Nov., 1898.
[126] *Ibid.*, 5 June, 1899.
[127] *Ibid.*, Rampolla to W.L., 5 June, 1899.
[128] *Ibid.*, W.L. to Greenway, 7 March, 1898.

the possibility that an equitable solution of the Manitoba Schools question could be arrived at, by taking advantage of the cession of school lands, and that you declared yourself determined to make use of this means of reaching so desirable an end."[129]

This might be described as political blackmail, since there was no real connection between the school lands fund and the separate school question. To a protest from Manitoba, Laurier offered the euphemistic explanation that "it is always more easy to govern men if, besides appealing to their best nature, we can also show them some substantial advantage."[130] The "best nature" of the Greenway government was apparently not considered sufficient without this stimulus. Laurier nevertheless made it clear to Falconio that separate schools in Manitoba to the extent of dual administration would never be possible.[131] Apparently he succeeded in gaining the confidence of the Delegate and the Delegate in turn had some influence within the church. Mgr. Mathieu later wrote that "the old prejudices disappear. Your friends have spoken well of you, while saying the truth; you are better known and consequently better understood in quarters where hitherto slander had done its wicked work in good and simple souls."[132] So satisfactory was the appointment of a permanent Delegate that Laurier was worried that Falconio was to be recalled.[133] Instead, Falconio was replaced by Mgr. Sbarretti, and there has been an Apostolic Delegate in Canada ever since.

Even in Rome, Laurier had succeeded in convincing the authorities that his political analysis of the situation had been correct, and that he was sincere in his wish to secure concessions for the minority. A few years after the crucial time when Rome had seemed unwilling even to send a Delegate to investigate the situation, del Val could send Laurier a flattering account of his prestige there. "It is undeniable that in finally settling the question you have won the gratitude of the Holy See, and strengthened by that support it will be a great deal easier for you to carry out other plans in your program for the moral, material and political advantage of your country."[134]

The settlement of the Manitoba school question was a vindication of Laurier's policy of compromise. He had settled a political

[129] *Ibid.*, Falconio to W.L., 31 Jan., 1900.
[130] *Ibid.*, W.L. to Bryce, 10 March, 1898.
[131] *Ibid.*, W.L. to Falconio, 5 Feb., 1901.
[132] *Ibid.*, Mathieu to W.L., 2 March, 1902.
[133] *Ibid.*, del Val to W.L., 3 May, 1902.
[134] *Ibid.*, 1 April, 1904.

dispute which had disrupted the country for most of a decade by removing it from national politics. Nor can there be any doubt that by the Laurier-Greenway compromise, the position of the minority had been improved in Manitoba.

Yet it was in the province of Quebec that Laurier achieved the most signal results. Because of his successful appeal to Rome for a Delegate, and because of the Encyclical *Affari Vos*, the episcopate had been forced to accept the settlement. Much more important for the future, Laurier had won the confidence of the authorities at the Vatican. In the province, active hostility had been modified to passive hostility, and in some cases this passive hostility had become political neutrality. In the important instance of the Archbishop of Montreal, Laurier's personality had transformed neutrality into friendship.

Reputations fade slowly if they fade at all. The Liberal party was still looked on with suspicion by most clericals. But at least it was tolerated. This was essential if Laurier was to retain the political support his party had received in 1896 and 1897. To achieve his goal, Laurier was willing to modify the Liberal platform in connection with provincial education, and to collaborate with former Conservatives. Objections to this might be raised by Liberals of *Rouge* traditions, but only an insignificant minority would withdraw their support from the Liberal party so long as it remained less clerical than the Conservative party. With the school question removed from politics and with the clergy pacified, it would be possible to consolidate the Liberal victories. Laurier could now turn his attention to the more traditional rivalry between Liberals and Conservatives.

7.
Imperialism

Like the problem of religious education in Canada, the problem of Imperialism was a challenge to national unity because the two racial groups disagreed as to what the problem involved. Many French Canadians believed they could dispassionately consider the various aspects of Imperialism and that their conclusions would be based on the simple criterion of what would be of most benefit to Canada. As Bourassa wrote of the typical French Canadian in 1902, "sentimental arguments in favor of British Imperialism cannot have any hold upon him. To his reason alone must appeals on this ground be made."[1] As early as 1888, Laurier had stated in the House of Commons that "if I have to choose between the duty I owe to England and the duty I owe to my native land, I stand by my native land."[2] However, it is suggestive that French Canadians were almost unanimous in deciding that it was in the interests of Canada to avoid more intimate relations with the rest of the Empire, either political, military or economic. This is the more surprising since many English Canadians, who likewise believed that they were dispassionately basing their decision on the interests of Canada, decided in favor of one or more of these forms of Imperial integration. The explanation for this division along racial lines must be that Imperialism, like religion, is not a subject which is easily dealt with objectively or rationally. French Canadians with their desire for survival as a racial group could not but be aware that any form of Imperial unity would so reduce their influence as to endanger this survival. When we remember that some extreme *nationalistes* of this period looked forward to the creation of a French Canadian nation in North America,[3] we can understand that anyone who took pride in being a French Canadian would be suspicious of a movement which threatened to destroy what political influence they had within the Dominion. English Canadians on the other hand, seem also to have been influenced by emotional factors. The Imperialism of the late nineteenth century was never free from racial appeals. Chamberlain, for example, could talk of "that proud, per-

[1] Bourassa, *The French Canadian in the British Empire*, (London, 1902), 25.

[2] *Commons Debates*, 5 Apr., 1888, 563.

[3] J.-P. Tardivel, *La Vérité*, 1 Jan., 1905.

sistent, self-asserting and resolute stock that no change of climate or condition can alter, and which is infallibly destined to be the predominating force in the future history and civilisation of the world."[4] This vision of a militant Anglo-Saxondom converting the lesser breeds to civilization had an appeal to many English Canadians to whom a united Empire seemed preferable to the relative insignificance of an isolated colony. Arguments for a co-ordinated Imperial defence system or for an Imperial Zollverein were often no more than rationalizations of this racial appeal. Thus George Parkin, a prominent Canadian Imperial Federationist of the 1890's, explicitly based his political theories on an assumption of racial superiority.[5] Small wonder then that Imperialism had an emotional appeal for many English Canadians which was absent among French Canadians.

As leader of the Opposition, Laurier had stated his attitutde towards Imperialism. He stated his belief that "Canada is not always to remain a colony" but went on to deny that the next stage in Canadian constitutional development would be any form of Imperial Federation. "I do not believe in imperial federation." He rejected the three forms of Imperialism most commonly discussed. Political federation was impracticable because the British Parliament would not be willing to modify its traditions to the extent necessary; economic imperialism based on preferential tariffs was impossible because England could not be expected to revoke her free trade policy; a co-ordinated system of imperial defence was impossible because Canadians were not willing to assume the financial burden of constant Imperial warfare.[6] Instead of a united Empire, Laurier looked forward to eventual independence for Canada, although he had no immediate desire for this. "Even with those, who, like myself, look to independence as the supreme goal, there remains a love for the Motherland and a desire to remain in connection with it."[7] It was at this time, however, that the Liberal party was campaigning for unrestricted reciprocity with the United States. As the next step towards independence, Laurier thought "that the time has come when we must ask the power to negotiate our own (commercial) treaties and decide for ourselves what is best for us."[8] Privately to Rodolphe Lemieux, then a young advocate of independence, Laurier expressed himself more explicitly.

[4] J. Buchan, *Lord Minto* (London, 1924), 162. The quote is from a Chamberlain speech in Canada in 1887.

[5] G. R. Parkin, *Imperial Federation* (London, 1892), Chapter I.

[6] *Commons Debates*, 7 April, 1892, 1136ff.

[7] *Ibid.*, 1137.

[8] *Ibid.*, 1143.

You think that the time has come to put independence at the head of our program. I am thinking about this constantly, for I am convinced that the colonial bond, at this time, however light it may be, is a cause of atrophy. The colonial tie has become an obstacle to the development of the country; it stifles initiative, it subordinates all our aspirations to the consideration of the interests of the metropolis. But believe me, the hour has not yet come, although it cannot be, I think, very far off.

If there were only French Canadians in Confederation, I would not hesitate a single instant, but the idea is not yet ripe enough for the English population, and I contend that before commencing this change, we must have strong support from friends of both races. Without this previous condition we will put the two races in conflict - instead of hastening the change, we will put it back.[9]

It is instructive that even in 1892 Laurier gave precedence to racial harmony.

The conviction that Canada would ultimately become independent did not prevent Laurier from recognizing that Imperial Federation had a strong emotional appeal: "there is a grandeur in the idea of a galaxy of nations acknowledging the same allegiance and all bound together by the ties of free trade."[10] But as a practical politician he continued to deny its feasibility. In London, at the Colonial Conference of 1897, he orated on the possibility of a Canadian of French descent attending a Parliament of Greater Britain, but few people noted his qualification that "he could not hope to live long enough to see it, but some of those who were in Canada that day might live to see it."[11] And at this Colonial Conference it was Laurier himself who drafted the Resolution that "the present political relations are generally satisfactory under existing conditions."[12] Chapleau had been justified in writing to Laurier before his departure for England, "You are less of a democrat than I, but you are not courtier enough to lose your head while bowing before the Royal Majesty."[13] Chapleau thought of himself as a "man of the people" and had even acted as a political spokesman for the Knights of Labor – hence the claim to be more democratic. Laurier was more "patrician" in outlook. The statement by Armand Lavergne that Laurier was an Imperialist in 1897 and that "since my tender youth, I have known him as an out and out imperialist and a convinced Anglomaniac" is no more than an illustration of the self-

[9] Lemieux Papers, W.L. to Lemieux, 1 Dec., 1892.
[10] *Commons Debates*, 4 Feb., 1894, 90.
[11] London *Times*, 5 July, 1897.
[12] L. Pacaud, ed., *Letters*, 117.
[13] LP, Chapleau to Laurier, 31 May, 1897.

deception of many *nationalistes*. It is probable that Laurier in 1897 no longer believed that Canadian independence was immediately desirable, since "the colonial tie" at that time was not restricting the Canadian government in any way. But there seems to be no doubt that Laurier still believed independence to be Canada's eventual fate. If Imperialism became a political issue, his solution would be based on autonomist rather than Imperialist predilections. Meanwhile the issue was dormant and was expected to remain so. His rhetoric on Imperial Federation must have seemed as innocuous as a discussion of world federation.

With the Boer War, Imperialism became a disconcertingly practical issue in Canadian politics. Noncommittal phrases such as conditions being "generally satisfactory" were no longer acceptable. Canada must either send troops to South Africa or she must not. It is significant that Laurier never again talked of Imperial Federation as an appealing vision. For the next two decades, Imperialism was a controversial political topic. It was no longer a subject for oratorical flourishes.

The question of Canadian participation in an Imperial war had never been seriously considered before. In connection with the Sudan War of 1885, Macdonald had written that "the time has not arrived, nor the occasion, for our volunteering military aid to the Mother Country. . . . Why should we waste money and men in this wretched business?"[14] Conditions had so changed by 1899 that many Canadians believed that the time and the occasion had arrived. "Gladstone and Co." had been replaced by Chamberlain; and the Spanish-American War suggested that Imperialism could flourish on either side of the Atlantic.

From the beginning Laurier was convinced that the crisis in the Transvaal was no concern of Canada's. He had often stated that "if the day should ever come" when England was in danger, British subjects would rally to her aid whatever their origin,[15] but the Boers did not seem to him to be a serious threat to England. Imperialists, however, had a different conception of Imperial responsibilities; they believed that the Transvaal incident provided an opportunity to display to the rest of the world a united Empire. The Imperialist South African Association distributed pamphlets and tracts to prove that the demands of the British subjects in the Transvaal were amply justified,[16] and the Association tried to persuade Canadian

[14] Macdonald to Tupper, 12 March, 1885, quoted, Pope, ed., *Correspondence of Macdonald*, 337.

[15] *Commons Debates*, 5 Feb. 1896, 1216; *Times*, London, 19 June, 1897.

[16] LP, J. Davis Allen to W.L., 17 July, 1899.

Imperialists to obtain a Resolution of sympathy for the Uitlanders in the House of Commons.[17] Minto expressed the opinion of many Imperialists when he wrote to Laurier that a resolution of sympathy and a promise of military aid, if necessary, would "strengthen enormously the Empire generally," and so would indirectly benefit each colony, although at the same time Minto admitted that a colony "deeply interested in its own development" might not always be in a position to assist the Mother Country.[18] Laurier at first refused to consider any resolution of sympathy. "Personally I feel very strongly with them (Uitlanders) but it would be more than questionable wisdom to pretend to have a word to say on such a question. I told those who approached me very flatly that 'we might leave the matter in the hands of Lord Salisbury'."[19] Laurier was instinctively thinking as a Canadian rather than as a citizen of the British Empire. A few months later, however, at Tupper's request,[20] Laurier moved Resolutions which "viewed with regret" the developments in the Transvaal, and desired "to express its sympathy" with the efforts to obtain "justice and political recognition" for the British subjects there.[21] As Laurier said, the object of the Resolutions was the hope that this mark of sympathy might cause more humane councils to prevail in the Transvaal.[22] It might be argued that a promise of military aid to Great Britain if necessary, would have had more influence on the Boers, but Laurier had no intention of making such a promise. As he wrote to Minto:

The present case does not seem to be one in which England, if there is a war, ought to ask us, or even to expect us to take a part, nor do I believe that it would add to the strength of the Imperial sentiment to assert at this juncture that the colonies should assume the burdens of military expenditure, except – which God forbid – in the case of pressing danger.[23]

In the House of Commons, however, the reception of the Resolutions suggested that many members had a different opinion as to the responsibilities of Canada. The Resolutions were passed unani-

---

[17] P.A.C., Earl of Minto Papers, Vol. 20, 8, anonymous memorandum on South African War, 23 Sept., 1902. Hereafter cited as South African Memo.

[18] LP, Minto to W.L., 19 July, 1899.

[19] Minto Papers, W.L. to Minto, 2 May, 1899.

[20] *Ibid.*, South African Memo.

[21] *Commons Debates*, 31 July, 1899, 8994.

[22] *Ibid.*

[23] *Minto Papers*, v.7, 100; Laurier to Minto, 30 July, 1899.

mously, and since a mere vote seemed inadequate, the members then rose and sang the National Anthem.[24]

When war finally became inevitable, Resolutions of sympathy could no longer satisfy sincere Imperialists. Laurier gave an interview to the Toronto *Globe* which was intended to prevent any agitation for the sending of troops but at the same time to allay any suspicions that he lacked Imperialist sympathies.

As I understand the Militia Act, and I may say that I have given it some study of late, our volunteers are enrolled to be used in the defence of the Dominion. They are Canada's troops to be used to fight in Canada's defence. Perhaps the most widespread misapprehension is that they cannot be sent out of Canada. To my mind it is clear that cases might arise when they might be sent to a foreign land to fight ... Sometimes the best method of defending oneself is to attack ... The case of the South African Republic is not analogous. There is no menace to Canada, and although we are willing to contribute troops, I do not see how we can do so. Then again, how could we do so without Parliament's granting us the money? We simply could not do anything. In other words, we would have to summon Parliament.[25]

This was only a pretext. As Laurier wrote to Willison, whose sympathies were Imperialist; "I doubt the wisdom of Canada going into military expenditure. ... I am not prepared to think it is a wise policy, even from an Imperial point of view, to take a share in all the secondary wars in which England is always engaged."[26] The constitutional argument presented publicly was used because it was likely to be more effective in English-speaking Canada than Laurier's fear of becoming involved in military expenditures in what were to him foreign countries. Apparently convinced that his statement had settled the question, Laurier left for Chicago.

Laurier was wrong. During his absence, Imperialist sympathies in favor of active participation in the war were so roused that the question had to be reconsidered. According to one account, "it is no exaggeration to say that it was a newspaper which saved the honor of Canada."[27] This newspaper was Hugh Graham's Montreal *Star*. The *Star* was tardy in beginning the campaign for Canadian honor. Only passing mention was made of the Transvaal Resolutions,[28] and even in September the *Star* believed that "our active

[24] *Commons Debates*, 31 July, 1899, 8999.
[25] *Globe*, 4 Oct., 1899.
[26] Willison Papers, W.L. to J.S.W., 5 Oct., 1899.
[27] Minto Papers, South African memo.
[28] *Star*, 3 Aug., 1899.

militia are not enrolled for foreign service" – although it did favor Sam Hughes' idea of a volunteer regiment.[29] Not until early October did the *Star* begin to campaign in earnest for wholehearted Canadian participation in the war, the assumption being that "it is our fight that is going to be fought by British troops."[30] Laurier's statement to the *Globe* seems to have confirmed the *Star's* Imperialism. "It is not constitutional authority that the Government lacks to send Canadian troops to the Transvaal, it is moral courage to do its duty as the risk of offending a disloyal element which objects to any action that tends to strengthen the bonds which unite England and Canada."[31] The *Star* pretended to prove the widespread desire for Canadian participation by publishing favorable statements made by Canadian mayors, statements which were really replies to leading questions submitted to them by the *Star*.[32]

It may be doubted whether the *Star* was as influential as some believed, but there can be little doubt that it was expressing sentiments acceptable to many English Canadians. Chamberlain had cabled his high appreciation of Canadian offers to serve in South Africa and had included details as to how a contingent should be organized.[33] The contents of the telegram had been published in the British press,[34] inadvertently or otherwise, and this had strengthened Canadian demands for participation. Even the *Globe* agreed that troops should be sent and indeed, stated that they would be sent.[35]

Laurier left Chicago on the eleventh of October and went directly to Ottawa, where the Cabinet was assembled. The motives of the British government had been explained by Chamberlain. "We do not intend to accept any offer from volunteers. We do not want the men, and the whole point of the offer would be lost unless it was endorsed by the Government of the Colony."[36] That is, Chamberlain wanted a concrete illustration of Imperial unity. That English Canadians favored official participation also seemed clear. Judging by the French-Canadian newspapers, however, French Canadians agreed with Laurier that the Boer War meant nothing to Canada. Most of these newspapers ignored the problem of Canadian participation during Laurier's visit to Chicago, apparently assuming that the statement to the *Globe* was decisive. "We congratulate M.

[29] *Ibid.*, 26 Sept., 1899.
[30] *Ibid.*, 3 Oct., 1899.
[31] *Ibid.*, 4 Oct., 1899.
[32] *Ibid.*, 7 Oct., 1899, and subsequent issues.
[33] Minto Papers. Chamberlain to Minto, 3 Oct., 1899.
[34] J. Buchan, *Lord Minto*, 139.
[35] *Globe*, Toronto, 11 Oct., 1899.
[36] Minto Papers, Chamberlain to Minto, 7 Oct., 1899.

Laurier on having at last muted his jingoism, his imperialism and his Toryism," said an unfriendly weekly in Quebec.[37] The exception to this silent acquiescence was *La Patrie*, by this time under the management of the sons of J. Israel Tarte. Like Tarte, *La Patrie* found it difficult magnanimously to ignore a victory: "What business do we have in African affairs?"[38] It added:

For our part, we have no hesitation in declaring that if the Laurier cabinet had taken on itself the responsibility of committing Canada, by sending a military contingent to the Transvaal at the expense of the State, we would have condemned its policy.[39]

Tarte himself is said to have declared in public, "not a man, not a cent for South Africa."[40] Laurier is also reported to have been "reluctant, unconvinced and rebellious" at this time.[41] Under these conditions the Cabinet meetings must have been stormy ones. The final decision was to some extent a compromise. The official announcement, released on the thirteenth of October, stated that there had never been any question as to the desirability of "co-operating" with the Imperial government, but that the sending of troops and the authorizing of large expenditures without the sanction of Parliament had seemed a dangerous precedent. However, in view of the Imperial plan by which Canada would recruit, equip and transport volunteers to South Africa, with the Imperial government assuming all subsequent expenses, the constitutional difficulty was minimized, and it had been decided to send one thousand men.[42] The Order in Council stated that the action taken was not to be "construed as a precedent for future action."[43] But none of this talk of Parliaments or precedents could conceal the fact that the Laurier government had acceded to the demand in English Canada for participation in a remote Imperial war.

Laurier's attitude seems inconsistent with his conviction that the Boer War was no immediate concern of Canada. Nevertheless it must be remembered that Laurier believed that the Imperial government was fighting a just war. "To me it is clearly and manifestly a war for religious liberty, political equality and civil rights."[44] In a speech after Parliament had assembled, he went so far as to state

[37] *La Vérité*, 14 Oct., 1899.
[38] *La Patrie*, 9 Oct., 1899.
[39] *Ibid.*, 11 Oct., 1899.
[40] Dafoe, *Laurier*, 114.
[41] Willison, *Reminiscences*, 304.
[42] *Globe*, 14 Oct., 1899.
[43] W. S. Evans, *The Canadian Contingents and Canadian Imperialism* (London, 1901), 66.
[44] LP, W.L. to L. Gabriel, 6 Jan., 1900.

that he believed "that there never was a juster war on the part of England."[45] Believing this, the decision to send troops could be determined by a consideration of Canadian interests. In spite of his unwillingness to participate, Laurier understood that English Canadians sincerely disagreed with him. He believed that the important question was no longer the abstract issue as to whether Canada should engage in Imperial wars, but how the dangers of racial division in Canada on the question could best be evaded. As Willison says, his conclusion had been "that public feeling in the English Provinces was too strong to be opposed and that under all the circumstances the Government could not afford to challenge the sentiment of the country."[46] To Laurier the principle of national unity was the primary consideration, and to that end personal convictions would be adapted if necessary.

If national unity was to be maintained, the province of Quebec had to be persuaded to accede to participation in the Boer War. Not all French Canadians were opposed to the sending of troops. Raymond Préfontaine, Mayor of Montreal and Liberal member in the Commons, had joined the Imperial South African Association,[47] and believed that the Transvaal Resolutions were a formal commitment to send troops in case of war.[48] Ernest Pacaud of *Le Soleil* had regularly published pro-British cartoons[49] and he approved "energetically" of Laurier's decision.[50] And from the beginning, *La Presse* accepted Laurier's policy as satisfactory.

The French Canadian element was certainly opposed to the sending of a force armed and maintained by us, but there was not in that any disloyalty. The recently formulated doctrine that all the wars of England are ours, must be, like the thousands of other rational questions, subject to the rules of prudence and moderation. We French Canadians, more than our other compatriots, are in a position to gauge the consequence of a violent movement which threatens to become a stampede.

If England were in danger, that would be something else. . . .

Happily the English government was confronted with this false situation; and with the practical spirit that it displays in all things,

[45] *Commons Debates*, 13 Mar., 1900, 1842.
[46] J. Willison, *Reminiscences*, 304.
[47] Minto Papers, South African Memo.
[48] *Star*, 13 Oct., 1899.
[49] *Le Soleil*, 7 Oct., 1899.
[50] LP, Pacaud to W.L., 21 Oct., 1899.

it cut short the difficulties. To come and look for recruits here is quite another matter; let him go who wants to.[51]

Thus even *La Presse* tolerated the policy only because it interpreted it as a policy of non-participation. There can be no doubt that most French Canadians were of like mind, and that they were opposed to participation and were not enthusiastic about the compromise. As Laurier wrote to Willison:

I must pay some attention to the province of Quebec, where our action in sending troops to South Africa is not popular. I am hopeful that I may carry it with me yet (in the coming election) as solidly as I did last time, but if I do I will have to accept the victory as one of which I shall have personal reason to be proud.[52]

Israel Tarte was the immediate problem. His outspoken opposition to the sending of troops made it difficult for him to accept the decision. According to Laurier, he threatened to resign during the Cabinet discussions,[53] and Tarte's opinions were so well known that rumors of his actual resignation were widespread.[54] Tarte finally submitted, *La Patrie* defending the reversal of policy. "We say openly and firmly that the departure of volunteers, in the circumstances and on the conditions in question, was not at all nor will be a precedent."[55] Laurier's influence over Tarte was certainly great, and there can be no doubt that it was Laurier who persuaded Tarte to yield. Certainly Tarte made no more public protests against Canadian participation. According to Minto, "Sir Wilfrid tells me he is now doing all he can to persuade Mr. Tarte to do away with the harm he has already created by his utterances and he hopes that with this view he will shortly visit Ontario and speak in public."[56] This may explain *La Patrie's* conciliatory attitude. "Whatever may be our opinion on the subject of the causes and the behaviour which led to the present conflict, our duty as British citizens is to hope for the success of British arms."[57] The acquiescence of Tarte meant that the most serious political danger to the Liberal party in Quebec had been averted.

Nevertheless, there was one Liberal from the province who was more intransigent than the Minister of Public Works. Henri Bourassa resigned his seat in protest. Bourassa was the most prominent

[51] *La Presse*, 14 Oct., 1899.
[52] Willison Papers, W.L. to Willison, 25 Dec., 1899.
[53] Minto Papers, Vol. 1, 33, memorandum of a conversation, 16 Nov., 1899.
[54] LP, Strathcona to W.L., 16 Oct., 1899.
[55] *La Patrie*, 21 Oct., 1899.
[56] Minto Papers, Vol. 1, 33, memo of conversation, 15 Nov. 1899.
[57] *La Patrie*, 27 Dec., 1899.

young Liberal in the province. According to Tarte, he had been "one of my favorites since 1891" and Laurier had "treated him as his child."[58] And, like many French-Canadian Liberals, Bourassa had come under the spell of Laurier's personality. But Bourassa was an independent thinker who had the courage to disagree with his leader. His resignation could not affect Laurier's political control of the province of Quebec. The important fact is that the disagreement between Bourassa and Laurier contained the seeds of future political crises in the province over the problem of Imperialism.

Bourassa was in agreement with Laurier on the constitutional question of participation in Imperial wars. As his open letter of resignation stated, he completely agreed with Laurier's statement in the *Globe*.[59] Bourassa, however, argued that sending troops was a constitutional precedent which would involve Canada in future wars regardless of Orders in Council which denied that this precedent was a precedent. "I say and I repeat that I have resigned not because the government sent soldiers to the Transvaal, but because this act constitutes a radical change in our relations with England."[60] In an assembly held in his constituency, Bourassa proposed resolutions to the following effect: "We are opposed to all effort at military federation of the Empire and to the participation of Canada in the wars of the Empire without right of representation in the councils of the Empire."[61] Laurier denied that Canada was now committed to participation in Imperial wars, but otherwise expressed agreement with Bourassa's arguments.

If we were to be compelled to take part in all the wars of Great Britain, I have no hesitation in saying that I agree with my hon. friend (Bourassa) that, sharing the burden we should also share the responsibilities. Under that condition of things which does not exist, we should have the right to say to Great Britain: If you want us to help you, call us to your councils.[62]

But this talk of attending Imperial Councils was mere verbiage. As Bourassa wrote to a periodical, "Please note that I have never argued in favour of any sort of imperial federation," and went on to explain that he was satisfied with the present position of Canada as a colony, but that if constitutional changes became necessary he was

[58] Willison Papers, Tarte to Willison, 20 Oct., 1899.
[59] *La Patrie,* 20 Oct., 1899.
[60] Rumilly, *Histoire,* IX, 132.
[61] *Ibid.*
[62] *Commons Debates,* 13 March, 1900, 1846.

willing to consider propositions for federation on their merit.[63] This coincides almost exactly with Laurier's position at the Colonial Conference of 1897; satisfaction with the present colonial status, a willingness to discuss Imperial Federation as an intellectual problem, but a firm conviction that Canada's real future was independence.

The real difference of opinion between Bourassa and Laurier was that Bourassa did not believe that the British policy towards the Boers was justified. Laurier, a Gladstonian Liberal who had great respect for the moral right of the individual, was easily convinced that the war was a struggle for the political and religious liberty of the Uitlanders. Not so Bourassa. In a thoughtful political essay Bourassa analysed the historical background, emphasizing the decline of British industrial supremacy with the consequent development of commercial imperialism.[64] British Imperialism was described as "a lust for land-grabbing and military dominion ... In short, *military contributions from the colonies to Great Britain* in men and treasure, but mainly in men, constitutes British Imperialism."[65] With this conviction, it is hardly surprising that Bourassa could not view with equanimity Laurier's decision to become involved in this Imperial war. To Laurier the war was an isolated incident; to Bourassa it was the first of many such Imperial wars. Possibly more fundamental was Laurier's confidence that the British government could be relied upon to act from such honorable motives as the desire to maintain political justice, whereas Bourassa suspected the British government of acting from motives of material self-interest. To this extent it was true that Laurier was more of an Imperialist than Bourassa.

It seems probable that the identity of their views as to the undesirability of being involved in Imperial wars actually widened the breach between Laurier and Bourassa. Neither could comprehend the attitude of the other without assuming a more serious divergence of political principles than was really the case. From Laurier's point of view, helping volunteers to arrive in South Africa was such a minor concession that opposition to it seemed almost a challenge to the compromise of Confederation itself. What other explanation could there be for Bourassa's objection to a policy demanded by the majority of Canadians? Thus Laurier at one time even suggested that Bourassa was advocating an independent French-Canadian nation along the St. Lawrence.[66] Bourassa, knowing that Laurier did

[63] *La Vérité*, 18 Nov., 1899, letter dated 11 Nov., 1899.

[64] "Great Britain and Canada," (Montréal, 1901), 27.

[65] *Ibid.*, 4.

[66] Minto Papers, Vol. 1, 44, memo of conversation, 23 March, 1900.

not favor participation, and taking a serious view of this precedent, could only explain Laurier's action by assuming that Laurier had betrayed his principles to conciliate a vocal minority of Imperialists.[67] It is important to notice that Bourassa did not yet believe that Laurier himself was an Imperialist; he considered Laurier to be weak but not subversive.

Bourassa's suspicions of British motives in the Transvaal were not unique. As *La Presse* pointed out after Bourassa's resignation, Englishmen such as Morley and Labouchere had denounced economic Imperialism as the true cause of the war.[68] Nor was Bourassa's conviction the result of a sudden conversion. He declared that had he been in the House in July he would have voted against the Transvaal Resolutions,[69] and Laurier believed that it was he who had influenced Tarte to oppose the sending of a contingent in early October.[70] Nevertheless, Bourassa had no desire for an open breach with Laurier. At the time of his resignation he wrote to Laurier, "I remain the personal admirer of all your high qualities of spirit and of your nobility of heart. But I shall regret always what I consider an act of weakness on your part." At the same time, Bourassa explained that he intended to support the government in its general policy.[71] Laurier replied that Bourassa was deluding himself; that his constitutional arguments were only a pretext to justify his opposition to sending troops, and that French Canadians had to choose between isolation or co-operation with the rest of Canada.[72] Bourassa thereupon denied that he had ever intended to isolate the province of Quebec, and hopefully suggested that "perhaps, basically, we are less divided than you may believe."[73] Thus Bourassa's opposition was still restricted to the single issue of Imperialism; he still considered himself a Liberal.

Nor did Laurier want to alienate Bourassa. He was not willing to allow Bourassa's arguments to go unanswered. From the beginning he had influenced the Liberal press in Quebec to support his policy,[74] and after Bourassa's resignation he wrote to Pacaud; "It is absolutely false that I prefer silence on this question of Bourassa's letter. I do not want to make any more fuss about it, but, on the other hand, I mean to be supported by my party in the attitude I

[67] "Great Britain and Canada," 43ff.
[68] *La Presse*, 24 Oct., 1899. 13 Mar., 1900, 1796.
[69] *Commons Debates*.
[70] Minto Papers, Vol. 1, 32, memo. of conversation, 16 Nov., 1899.
[71] LP, Bourassa to W.L., 27 Oct., 1899.
[72] *Ibid.*, W. L. to Bourassa, 2 Nov., 1899.
[73] *Ibid.*, Bourassa to W. L., 4 Nov., 1899.
[74] W. L. to E. Pacaud, 14 Oct., 1899, in L. Pacaud, ed., *Letters*, 112.

have taken."[75] *Le Soleil* had certainly conformed to Laurier's wishes. Its reply to Bourassa's letter had flattered Bourassa as "the personification of honour and integrity" but had gone on to argue that Bourassa's mistake had been to ignore the fact that Laurier could not ignore: "the aspirations of the great majority in this country."[76] Laurier made it clear to his supporters that he had no intention of opposing Bourassa in the by-election following his resignation. "The government does not believe it desirable to intervene in the election which must take place, and to give more importance to what is regrettable incident."[77] Laurier's assumption was that Bourassa would soon realize that Laurier had been right, and that would be an end of it.[78]

For the duration of the Boer War, Bourassa made reconciliation impossible by challenging the spectre of Imperialism at every possible occasion. Even before the debate on the Speech from the Throne in 1900, Bourassa asked to have tabled the correspondence with the Imperial authorities on participation in the war.[79] Later in the session he ably presented his views of the war and moved that the House declare that the sending of troops was not to be a precedent for any change in the constitutional relations between Canada and Great Britain without parliamentary consent.[80] Laurier's response was not likely to reassure Bourassa. He declared that "I do not find fault with the principles involved in the motion", but he opposed the motion nonetheless, as being inopportune and because Bourassa's arguments were unnecessarily harsh.[81] Nine other members, five Liberals and four Conservatives, but all French-Canadians, voted for Bourassa's motion.[82] Bourassa also opposed a resolution moved by Laurier and seconded by Tupper congratulating the Queen on the "approaching termination of the war."[83] Bourassa would not accept the implication that it was a just war, and declared that he was expressing the views "of a large proportion if not the majority of the Canadian people and not only of the French Canadians but of all the nationalities and creeds."[84] To a practical politician, such an attitude, which even Bourassa admitted

[75] LP, W. L. to E. Pacaud, 27 Oct., 1899.

[76] *Le Soleil*, 21 Oct., 1899.

[77] LP, W. L. to F. Mackay, 3 Dec., 1899.

[78] *Ibid.*, W. L. to Bourassa, 2 Nov., 1899.

[79] *Commons Debates*, 5 Feb., 1900, 5

[80] *Ibid.*, 13 Mar., 1900, 1837.

[81] *Ibid.*, 1838.

[82] *Ibid.*, 1875.

[83] *Ibid.*, 7 June, 1900, 6900.

[84] *Ibid.*, 6906.

was "not in accord with the feelings of this House,"[85] was worse than foolhardy since it accentuated racial antagonism with no hope of accomplishing anything. The reaction of the English Canadians seems to justify Laurier's attitude. Mr. Montague's reply to Bourassa on this occasion deserves some attention. "I think that the best answer we can make to the hon. gentleman is to give three cheers for Her Majesty the Queen." Whereupon three cheers were duly given, followed by God Save the Queen.[86] When Imperialist emotions were so roused that such patriotic effusions were considered an answer to carefully reasoned arguments, however mistaken they may have been, Laurier could hardly be blamed for trying to evade a discussion of the subject. On the other hand, Bourassa was not likely to be convinced or even placated if this was the "best answer" that could be made. In the next session Bourassa continued his criticisms, still isolated from both of the major parties. In March he recommended that the House should recommend peace terms which would concede Boer independence.[87] Laurier insisted that the "enlightened power of England" was preferable to the "semi-barbaric civilization of the Dutch."[88] Two French-Canadian Liberals supported Bourassa's motion.[89] In May Bourassa objected to the recruiting of Imperial Army officers in Canada.[90] In the following year he seconded a motion by John Charlton which recommended a peace based on British supremacy but with generous terms for the Boers.[91] Once more he argued that although there was a probability that Great Britain would offer generous terms, in view of Chamberlain's conduct of the negotiations before the war it was well to make this recommendation.[92] Once more Laurier agreed with the terms of the Resolution, but considered it inadvisable to interfere without any knowledge of the details of the negotiation; and he was confident that the British would concede just peace terms.[93] Not until the war had ended and the problem of Imperialism could once more be discussed in terms of general principles could Laurier and Bourassa meet on common ground.

While the war was being fought, a general election was held. Since even Laurier admitted that participation in the South African War was not popular in his province, it might have been expected

[85] *Ibid.*
[86] *Ibid.*, 6909.
[87] *Commons Debates*, 12 March, 1901, 1326.
[88] *Ibid.*, 1336.
[89] *Ibid.*, 1366.
[90] *Ibid.*, 22 May, 1901, 5886.
[91] *Ibid.*, 23 April, 1902, 3316.
[92] *Ibid.*, 3331.
[93] *Ibid.*, 3334.

that the Liberals would lose some seats in Quebec. Instead, the Conservatives lost nine seats, reducing their representation to seven out of sixty-five. This is easily explained. Voters who thought that the Liberal policy was too Imperialist could not support the Conservatives because they appeared to be more Imperialist than the Liberals. Sir Charles Tupper had long opposed a constitutional form of Imperial Federation, but there could be no mistaking his Imperialist sympathies. In connection with the Sudan in 1885, he "would have been glad if Canada had taken the matter up more warmly."[94] In connection with the Boer War, Tupper believed prompt participation would be "interpreting the sentiments of the people of Canada."[95] From the beginning, he criticised the government policy of allowing Canadian troops in South Africa to be paid by Great Britain, arguing that the Dominion should willingly accept the burden.[96] According to the *Star*, Tupper virtually believed in the voluntary military union of the Empire. "Sir Charles Tupper takes the ground that the Canadian people, acting through their own government and their own Parliament at Ottawa, will always be willing to support Great Britain in her wars."[97] Outside of Quebec, Tupper's Imperialist sympathies were surpassed by the Conservative press. On some occasions, Imperialism became no more than a pretext for anti-French propaganda. An extreme example of this was quoted by *La Patrie*.

Unless the British Canadians of this Province are cravens, they will not tolerate a condition of subjection to the French Canadians, and if through the ballot boxes there is no redress, they will find other means of emancipating themselves from the dominance of an inferior people that peculiar circumstances have placed in authority in the Dominion.[98]

Lord Minto wrote to his brother that this was a widespread attitude.

The writing of the leading Opposition papers in Ontario has been positively wicked, simply aiming at stirring up hatred of French Canada. At home you do not call a man disloyal if he disapproves

[94] Tupper to Macdonald, 18 Feb., 1885, quoted, J. Pope, ed., *Correspondence of Macdonald*, 334.
[95] Minto Papers, Vol. 20, 16, South African memo, quoting Tupper speech of 27 Sept., 1899.
[96] Tupper to W. L. 14 Oct., 1899, quoted, *Star*, 16 Oct., 1899.
[97] *Star*, Montreal, 6 Apr., 1900.
[98] *La Partrie*, 24 Oct., 1899, quoting *News*, no date.

of the war. Here, if he is only lukewarm, and is a French Canadian, he must be a rebel! That is the British bull-dog argument![99]

In the province of Quebec, the Imperialism of the Conservatives was more attenuated but nonetheless apparent. Tupper was on intimate terms with the arch-Imperialist Hugh Graham of the *Star*. Indeed, it was Graham who had offered the financial backing for an offer made by Tupper to insure the members of the Canadian contingent.[100] Henry Dalby, on the staff of the *Star*, was appointed English Conservative organiser for the province of Quebec.[101] As Tupper explained, "the diversity of opinion" among French-Canadian Conservatives made it impossible to select a single French-Canadian organiser, so that three were finally chosen on a regional basis.[102] The three selected were all in favor of active participation in the war, Bergeron of the Montreal district and T. C. Casgrain of the Quebec district being described in the *Gazette*, as having "followed the lines of their chief, Sir Charles Tupper,"[103] and Sir Adolphe Caron of the district of Three Rivers having publicly expressed his approval of the war.[104]

Nevertheless, some effort was made by the Conservatives in Quebec to appeal to the anti-Imperial sentiment there. Sir Charles Tupper, in a speech at Quebec, described his own opposition to the Imperial Federation League, at the same time representing Laurier as an advocate of Imperial Federation.[105] In an interview in Montreal, Tupper again appealed to anti-Imperial sentiment: "As far as Sir Wilfrid Laurier is concerned, you can say in effect that he is too English for me, with his program of imperial federation."[106] In a Conservative pamphlet, written in French, it was stated of Imperial Federation, "Laurier approves of it; Tupper condemns it," and the pamphlet went on to quote from Laurier's speeches at the Colonial Conference. The pamphlet described Laurier as promising to take part in other British wars if necessary.[107]

A survey of the French-Canadian press in the province suggests that this argument against Laurier was ineffective. The Liberal newspapers naturally denounced the Conservatives as being more Impe-

[99] Minto to A. Elliot, Nov. 1900, quoted, Buchan, Minto, 161.

[100] Saunders, *Tupper*, II, 238.

[101] Tupper Papers, *Letterbook*, Tupper to Dalby, 6 Feb., 1899.

[102] *Ibid.*, Tupper to F. Bisaillon, 15 Apr., 1899.

[103] *Gazette*, Montreal, 26 Oct., 1899.

[104] *Star*, Montreal, 10 Nov., 1899

[105] 31 March, 1900, quoted, Willison, *Laurier*, II 330.

[106] *La Presse*, 18 Aug., 1900.

[107] "No. 6: 'La fédération imperiale'," published by the Liberals as "Notorious Tory No. 6" (1902).

rial than the Liberals,[108] but even non-Liberal papers made similar statements.[109] One periodical stated the predicament of the anti-Imperialist. "Imperial federation is an impossible dream, and, consequently, without danger. It is the project of a few visionaries, including Sir Wilfrid Laurier." The real threat was to be found in the movement towards military Imperialism.

To approve the policy of the government is to approve military imperialism, the participation of Canada in the wars of the Empire. Practically, however, how can one attack this ministerial policy without throwing oneself into the arms of the Tory opposition which criticizes the government for not having gone far enough nor blithely enough on the wrong road?[110]

If the anti-Imperialist sentiment was to weaken the support for the Liberal party in the election it could only be done by the creation of a third party. If such a party had been organised, the leader seemed obvious. Henri Bourassa might have rallied Liberal and Conservative anti-Imperialist alike. Opposition newspapers in Quebec had openly applauded his stand.[111] *La Presse* not only suggested that such a third party was possible, but that Bourassa might have a prominent recruit. According to *La Presse*, it was rumored that Tarte would support Bourassa in an anti-Imperialist third-party movement, which, it was hoped, would get support from both French and English Canadians.[112] It appears unlikely that the rumor had any foundation. Tarte and Bourassa had both opposed participation, but Tarte had accepted Laurier's decision, and from the beginning had tried to moderate Bourassa's intransigence.[113] Nor is there any suggestion that Bourassa had ever intended to do any more than define his position. His admission that he would get little support in the House of Commons is more reminiscent of a voice crying in the wilderness than of a leader expecting to be followed to the Promised Land. His declaration that he supported all the Liberal policies apart from this issue does not suggest any intention to found a third party.

The attitude of the Roman Catholic Church to the Boer War is not irrelevant. It is probable that there were many priests as well as

[108] *Le Soleil,* 17 Oct., 1899; *La Patrie,* 14 Oct., 1899.
[109] Montreal *Monde Canadien,* 19 Oct., 1899; Trois-Rivières *Triflurien,* 7 Nov., 1899.
[110] *La Vérité,* 16 Dec., 1899.
[111] Québec *Courrier du Canada,* 27 Oct., 1899; *La Vérité,* 28 Oct., 1899.
[112] *La Presse,* 17 Aug., 1900.
[113] LP, Tarte to W. L., decoded telegram, 19 Oct., 1899.

laymen who believed that the war was no concern of Canada. In a religious periodical published under the auspices of the Archbishopric of Quebec an article described England as having invaded islands and continents with mercenaries for centuries, and suggested that retribution was at hand.[114] Next week however, the editor repudiated the article;[115] Archbishop Bégin publicly denied his responsibility;[116] and Archbishop Bruchési publicly vouched for the loyalty to the Queen of himself, all his clergy, and all the Catholics in his diocese.[117] Since no third party based on French Canadian *nationalisme* could be successful without the support or at least the benevolent neutrality of the church, these official pronouncements were not unimportant.

Nevertheless, the Liberal victory in the province of Quebec in 1900 was a vote of confidence in Laurier as much as it was a vote against the Conservatives. Laurier himself had been confident that he could retain Quebec support. He had not ignored the difficulties but had made efforts "with a view to enlightening the population on Imperial questions."[118] Years later Laurier maintained that during the Boer War, he had successfully assumed the responsibility of rallying the French-Canadians to his policy. "In 1899 we had the responsibility, we shouldered it bravely, publicly; and privately, I asked our compatriots to uphold the honour of our race."[119] An observer in Montreal analysed the political results for Laurier. "The participation in the South African War is not popular among French Canadians, but they excuse the Government, whose hand has been forced by the English element and circumstances."[120] There can be little doubt that the government was more readily excused because of the anti-French sentiments expressed by many English-Canadian newspapers. The French-Canadian Liberals did not hesitate to reply to this campaign by appealing to *nationaliste* sentiments, one campaign pamphlet for example quoting at length from Conservative speeches to show that Conservatives were anti-French. The conclusion was "It is not a question today of protection or free trade, of purely material concern; the very future of the Canadian nation is at stake."[121] Thus a vote for Laurier became a vote for *nationalisme*. To many, this was the major issue of the campaign. After the election, one judge wrote to Laurier "I am pleased with my race which realized

[114] *La Semaine Réligieuse de Quebec*, 5 Jan. 1900.

[115] *Ibid.*, 13 Jan., 1900.

[116] Bégin to Bruchési, quoted in "No. 6: La fédération imperiale."

[117] *Star*, 11 Jan., 1900

[118] Minto Papers, Vol 1, 44, memo of conversation, 23 March, 1900.

[119] LP 190759, Laurier to R. Lemieux, 14 Aug., 1914.

[120] LP, Z. Mayrand to W. L., 1 Aug., 1900.

[121] "Le toryisme; voilà l'ennemi," (1900).

that in the present circumstances it had to unite around you. It is Ontario which placed the battle on this ground, and Québec has responded eloquently."[122] Dansereau explained the election result with similar arguments.[123] The French Canadians had supported Laurier just as a decade before a similar situation had ensured their support for Mercier.

The Imperial Conference of 1902 interred Imperialism as a political issue in the province of Quebec. In 1901, *La Presse* had quoted a leading Chapleau-Conservative on the subject of Imperialism.

Let us not delude ourselves. Laurier, unacceptable to many people because of his imperialist and British tendencies, will gain lasting support from the great majority of his compatriots on the day when, realizing that he has gone too far, he reverts to being completely Canadian, repudiates imperialism in all its forms, and returns to the great traditions of Lafontaine, Cartier and Chapleau.[124]

In 1902 Laurier again showed himself "completely" Canadian.

Chamberlain had hoped to use the Imperial sentiments engendered by the war to create some form of permanent Imperial Council which would discuss and advise on questions concerning Imperial defence, "and gradually it might assume more and more importance and in time might be given greater powers."[125] From the beginning, Laurier opposed any overt changes in the constitutional relations within the Empire,[126] and argued that voluntary assistance in case of need was a satisfactory arrangement.[127] Minto wrote that it was "almost impossible sufficiently to impress Sir Wilfrid with the need for efficiency" in the Canadian forces – "efficiency" to an Imperialist meaning integration with Imperial forces.[128] In reply to the invitation to attend the Imperial Conference the Government replied that "we see little advantage in discussing the political situation or the military situation."[129] As in 1897, political relations between Canada and Great Britain seemed satisfactory, and as for Imperial defence, Canada's major interest should be in developing her natural resources while at the same time taking measures to look after home defence. It would be "suicidal" to become involved in the

[122] LP, A. B. Routhier to W. L., 8 Nov., 1900.
[123] *La Presse*, 30 Nov., 1901.
[124] *Ibid.*, 19 Dec., 1901, quoting a letter from G. A. Nantel.
[125] Minto Papers, Chamberlain to Minto, 2 March, 1900.
[126] *Ibid.*, Vol. 1, 41, memo of conversation, 16 March, 1900.
[127] *Ibid.*, Vol. 1, 47, 9 April, 1900.
[128] *Ibid.*, Vol. 2, 11, memo of conversation, 3 June, 1902.
[129] Laurier, *Commons Debates*, 15 Apr., 1902, 2740.

vortex of European militarism.[130] To Willison, Laurier wrote of his opposition to entering any scheme of military expenditures.

At all events, it is absolutely repugnant to the convictions of all my life, and that is one of the questions to which I will not give in, and as to which, so far as I am personally concerned, I am quite ready to take the consequences. I believe, however, that reasonable people, both in England and Canada, will look at the question in the light of common sense.[131]

In London, on this occasion Laurier made no rhetorical flourishes concerning Parliaments of Greater Britain; instead, he said it seemed "evident that no condition exists for any organic changes. . . ."[132] Other incidents on his return pointed to a Canadian as opposed to an Imperial policy by Laurier. Lord Dundonald was dismissed from his position as General Officer Commanding the Canadian Militia for criticising Canadian administrative policy,[133] and in the Militia Act of 1904, a phrase was interpolated which definitely restricted the use of the Militia to the defence of Canada only.[134]

In the province of Quebec there were no dissident voices raised. On his attitude at the Conference, even the Castor *La Vérité* felicitated him.[135] In the Quebec Assembly, a motion protesting against the dangerous tendencies of Imperialism was withdrawn on the grounds that Laurier's recent pronouncements had removed any present danger.[136] Even Bourassa was reassured. He applauded the negative results of the Conference,[137] and later stated that "after the Conference of 1902, my reconciliation with Mr. Laurier was complete."[138] If in the election of 1900, Laurier found himself with an almost "solid Quebec" in the House of Commons, after 1902 his position must have been unassailable.

Nevertheless, Laurier's policy during the Boer War was not forgotten by those who were disillusioned by his surrender to Imperialist fanatics. The former confidence in Laurier as the personification of French-Canadian beliefs was never restored. Even after 1902 young French-Canadian *nationalistes* thought it was necessary to conduct an educational campaign against Imperialism to ensure

[130] *Ibid.*, 2741.
[131] Willison Papers, W.L. to Willison, 12 June, 1902.
[132] *Canadian Annual Review*, 1902, 118; speech of 11 July, 1902.
[133] *Commons Debates*, 24 June, 1904, 5531.
[134] *Statutes of Canada*, 4 Edw. VII, c.23, s.70. Compare to 46 V., c.11, s.61.
[135] *La Vérité*, 6 Sept., 1902.
[136] *Canadian Annual Review*, 1902, 56.
[137] *Commons Debates*, 13 Mar., 1903, 75.
[138] *Le Devoir*, 27 June, 1911.

that Canada would never again be involved in Imperial wars. The *Ligue Nationaliste* was defined by one of its founders as "a gathering of young men of all parties and of independents who came together for the defence of certain common ideas and for the study of political problems, purely from a perspective of the public interest."[139] According to Bourassa himself, this *nationaliste* association was the direct result of Canadian participation in the South African War.[140] The platform of the *Ligue*, published in October 1903, advocated political, commercial and military autonomy for Canada without going so far as to demand complete independence.[141] Bourassa was not a member of the *Ligue* but in the House of Commons[142] and in *Ligue* assemblies in the province, he expounded its platform and became its acknowledged spokesman.[143] In the weekly *Nationaliste*, founded as the organ of the *Ligue* in March 1904, the campaign was continued, with Bourassa contributing frequent articles.[144] In view of this we may well doubt whether Bourassa's reconciliation with Laurier was complete. His first speech under *Ligue* auspices had applauded Laurier's attitude at the Imperial Conference,[145] but the *Ligue* platform was by implication a criticism of Laurier's former policy. Furthermore, on occasion Bourassa was openly critical of some Liberal speeches on Imperialism[146] and in turn was criticized by Liberals as that "extremist" Bourassa.[147] As might be expected, Laurier himself was politically diplomatic and personally friendly, but his confidence in Bourassa was never restored. According to Willison, Laurier had seen in him his "natural and inevitable successor",[148] and certainly he had been groomed for political promotion. In 1904 it was Rodolphe Lemieux and not Bourassa who became Solicitor-General, and in the same year Bourassa's request for the Speakership was refused.[149] Nothing could efface the mutual suspicions of Laurier and Bourassa; on the issue of Imperialism there could only be an uneasy truce. The political separation because of the Boer War explains the political breach over the Naval Bill in 1910.

[139] O. Héroux, *Vérité*, 11 Feb., 1905.
[140] *Le Devoir*, 14 May, 1913.
[141] *Canadian Annual Review*, 1903, 326, quoting program.
[142] *Commons Debates*, 15 Mar., 1904, 120.
[143] *La Vérité*, 11 Feb., 1905.
[144] *Canadian Annual Review* 1904, 436.
[145] Rumilly, *Histoire*, XI, 24.
[146] *Le Nationaliste*, 13 March, 1904.
[147] Montreal *Le Canada*, no date, quoted Rumilly, *Histoire*, XI, 129.
[148] Willison, *Reminiscences*, 307.
[149] *Le Devoir*, 27 June, 1911. Jealousy may explain in part the political bitterness between Lemieux and Bourassa by 1911. This same article is an example of Bourassa's feelings in this respect.

8.
A Liberal Quebec

Satisfactory political compromises, at least from the point of view of the politician, are those which suppress controversial issues and at the same time alienate as few people as possible. The Manitoba school question and the Boer War had been controversial issues, and by this definition, Laurier's solutions had been satisfactory. But Laurier's increasing political dominance of the province of Quebec cannot be entirely explained by these negative achievements. In matters directly affecting the province, in which the problem of compromising with English-Canadian sentiment was less important, the Laurier government made what might be called positive gains, winning the support of groups which might have been neutral or even opposed to the Liberal party. The most important of such groups was the one somewhat vaguely described as the "school of Cartier" or the "school of Chapleau". The key figures in this section of the old Conservative party were Chapleau, Dansereau and Tarte. As much by his personality as by his policy, Laurier retained the confidence of these men until the "school of Cartier" imperceptibly merged with the Liberal party. At the same time, Laurier had to make these tactics acceptable to the old Liberals. Again his personality and his diplomacy were decisive. Both in the provincial and the federal party in Quebec, party unity was preserved. By 1902, a new "Liberal-Conservative" party had been constructed, and Quebec had become "solid Liberal."

Laurier's immediate problem after the election of 1896 was the formation of his Cabinet. Always a difficult problem after years in Opposition, it was complicated in the province of Quebec by the greatly increased support for the party there. The so-called "old Liberals", the heirs of the *Rouge* traditions, who had fought the party struggles in the days when Liberals were outcasts, could now claim political benefits on the basis of effort and loyalty. In the decade before 1896, however, the *Rouge* element had become a minority in the party. The representatives of the "new Liberals" would be dissatisfied with a *Rouge* Cabinet. Laurier's views on the subject were not likely to be made public; there could be no public debate about the selection of his colleagues. But if we can only surmise his views on the subject, we have positive evidence as to his intentions in the representative nature of the colleagues he selected.

The choice of Sydney Fisher as Minister of Agriculture was a logical one. Fisher had long represented the Eastern Townships county of Brome, and in addition to his influence in that region he had connections with the English in Montreal through the Montreal *Herald*. There is nothing to indicate that Fisher was a powerful political figure either in Quebec or in the federal Cabinet. The political importance of the Eastern Townships had been steadily declining. Men of the stature of Galt, Holton and Huntingdon had been succeeded by lesser men such as Pope and Ives. The increasing proportion of French Canadians in this region may account for this, since representatives of the Townships could no longer rely upon the support of a homogeneous body of electors on controversial issues. The political independence of a man like Galt was no longer possible. But Fisher was not a nonentity. He administered the Department of Agriculture for fifteeen years with no accusations of inefficiency or corruption. He was a determined man, as Dundonald was to learn. His political management of the Eastern Townships must have been satisfactory, for only rarely did Laurier receive letters directly from this region. On these occasions, a typical reply was that, "Fisher is the only one who can attend to this matter, and I have no doubt that he will do so."[1]

Among the French-Canadian representatives, Israel Tarte must have been an automatic choice. He represented the recent Liberal adherents and was on very close terms with Chapleau and Dansereau. If the "school of Chapleau" was to be incorporated in the Liberal party, Tarte's influence would be necessary. As a former Castor he was also in contact with many prominent clergymen,[2] although we may assume that his influence had been lessened by his recent campaign. Certainly Tarte was one of the earliest Cabinet selections, since he could write to Willison that "we are having some trouble" about the problems of Cabinet representation.[3] Tarte's connections with the "new Liberals" did not endear him to many of the *Rouges* and his selection was not welcomed. To them, his defeat in Beauharnois in 1896 seemed providential,[4] and even after he had been found another seat there was talk among some Liberals of having him disqualified, presumably for some breach of the Elections Act, and so eliminated from politics.[5] Nevertheless, Tarte was given the important portfolio of Public Works, a department in which he had taken great interest at the time of the Mc-

[1] LP, W. L. to Hon. J. C. McCorkill, 13 March, 1906.
[2] *Ibid.*, Tarte to W.L., no date, 1898, (p. 40500).
[3] Willison Papers, Tarte to Willison, 3 July, 1896.
[4] Dafoe, *Laurier*, 93.
[5] Tarte Papers, Dansereau to Tarte, 16 July, 1897.

Greevy scandals. The *Rouges* may have taken some satisfaction from the fact that C. A. Geoffrion was the other representative of the Montreal district in the Cabinet, since Geoffrion was a member of an old *Rouge* family. As Minister without Portfolio, however his appointment must have been meagre solace to the "old Liberals".

The representation for the district of Quebec was even less popular. In addition to Laurier, Joly became Controller of Inland Revenue, and R. R. Dobell, Minister without Portfolio. Joly was a reassuring appointment from the English-Canadian point of view, for he had opposed the Riel agitation[6] and his honesty was a guarantee that the corruption of the "Mercier wing of the party" would not be condoned.[7] These reasons did not make him popular among the French-Canadians. He was especially criticized for his rigorous stand against wide-spread "dismissals for partisanship in the past."[8] A further fault of Joly's, as Laurier later wrote, was that as a gentleman he was so attentive to his opponents that his friends felt neglected.[9] Nevertheless, Joly had at least been a Liberal for many years. R. R. Dobell was a Conservative who had planned to contest a seat as a Conservative in 1891[10] and had been elected in 1896 with Conservative support.[11] Laurier argued that Dobell had accepted Liberal principles, and that as an influential merchant he was an asset to the Cabinet,[12] especially as he was expected to be able to arrange a "fast line" Atlantic steamship service to the St. Lawrence.[13] No strategic reasons could suppress the Liberal opposition to Dobell's use of patronage for the benefit of the Conservatives.[14] So unsatisfactory was Dobell's appointment that Laurier was considering rewarding him with some office to remove him,[15] when Dobell was removed by death, and was replaced by a British Columbian representative.[16]

Charles Fitzpatrick of Quebec was appointed Solicitor-General, which was not a Cabinet position. Fitzpatrick had run as an Inde-

[6] LP, Joly to W. L., 21 Nov., 1886.
[7] *Ibid.*, Fitzpatrick to W. L., 27 Dec., 1897.
[8] *Ibid.*, Joly to Mulock, 28 Nov., 1896.
[9] *Ibid.*, W. L. to Templeman, 16 Sept., 1905.
[10] P.A.C., Sir John Thompson Papers, Dobell to Thompson, 20 Oct., 1891.
[11] LP, F. Langelier to W. L., 13 March, 1897.
[12] *Ibid.*, Report of interview with Liberal Club of Quebec, 1 Dec., 1896.
[13] *Ibid.*, Dobell to W. L., 27 Nov., 1896.
[14] *Ibid.*, J. B. Laliberté to W. L., 22 Sept., 1896; Dobell to W. L., 4 Oct. 1896.
[15] *Ibid.*, Dobell to W. L., 28 Nov., 1899.
[16] *Ibid.*, W. L. to J. Harper, 8 Feb., 1902.

pendent Liberal rather than a Mercier Liberal in the provincial election of 1892, and had even been offered a post in the Boucherville Cabinet at this time.[17] Tarte was especially hostile to Fitzpatrick, and had once described him as "travelling treachery."[18] Fitzpatrick was expected to represent the Irish Catholics,[19] but there were naturally a few Liberal protests against his appointment.[20]

In the district of Quebec at least two prominent "old Liberals" of Cabinet calibre had been ignored. Senator Pelletier had been a colleague of Laurier's in the Mackenzie administration. Loyal to the party and to Laurier, Pelletier quietly accepted the position of Speaker in the Senate.[21] Francois Langelier had been a provincial minister and had taken for granted that he would be offered a portfolio in 1896. Langelier was temporarily appeased by a written promise that he would succeed Chapleau as Lieutenant-Govenor.[22]

Apart from Laurier himself, the Quebec Cabinet Minsisters included one *Rouge* and two former Conservatives. Mills of Ontario must have expressed the views of many Quebec Liberals when he wrote in his diary: "No man who had heretofore filled the post of first minister has cared so little for those who were his colleagues in opposition."[23] There can be no doubt that Laurier's unusual choice of colleagues was carefully premeditated, since it was certainly not the line of least resistance. One of the reasons probably influencing his choice was the desire to remain free of any connection with the Mercier reputation for corruption. Joly and Fitzpatrick were certainly untainted, and Langelier himself believed that he was suffering for Mercier's sins.[24] Another reason was the desire to conciliate the moderate elements within the Church, and also the Chapleau-Conservatives. The danger of alienating the *Rouge* minority was not great since they had become little more than a radical fringe in the more comprehensive political party of 1896. A few judicious judicial appointments effectively suppressed any *Rouge* intransigence. As Laurier wrote to Tarte, who had complained of Laurier's generosity to "kickers,"[25] "it was quite fair to put Langelier on the bench; it was a good tactic to do the same for Chuoquette...."

[17] Skelton, *Laurier*, II, 9.
[18] LP, Tarte to W. L., 30 Jan., 1894.
[19] *Ibid.*, Fitzpatrick to W. L., 7 Nov., 1898.
[20] *Ibid.*, C. A. Pelletier to W. L., 3 July, 1896.
[21] P. A. Choquette, *Demi-siècle de la vie politique* (Montréal, 1936), 115.
[22] Willison Papers, Tarte to Willison, 16 Dec., 1897.
[23] F. Landon, "A Canadian Cabinet Episode, 1897," *Transactions of the Royal Society of Canada*, XXXII, 2, 49-56.
[24] LP, Langelier to W. L., 15 July, 1896.
[25] *Ibid.*, Tarte to W. L., 21 Nov., 1898.

And for Ernest Pacaud, editor of *Le Soleil* and also a "kicker" at this time, "our best tactic concerning him will be to give him a second paper" – and Tarte was authorized to explain this lesson in politics to Pacaud.[26] With such tactics there was no open revolt by the old Liberals, and Laurier's selection of his Cabinet was the first important step towards consolidating the new "Liberal-Conservative" party in Quebec.

Laurier's greatest asset in gaining the allegiance of the "School of Cartier" was his appeal as a French-Canadian Prime Minister to the *nationalisme* which had been flattered by Cartier's eminence in federal politics. This was the aspect which most influenced Chapleau. With a united Quebec behind him, Chapleau believed that Laurier could accomplish much for his province. After the provincial Liberal victory in 1897, Chapleau pointed out the possibilities as well as the difficulties.

Is the victorious majority going to bury or use the hatchet? Is it going to restore the ruins or level and work in the still smoking wreckage? The problem is in your hands.
I am not abandoning my dream of a united and strong Province. But I can hardly see any more the means to bring it about. The ingredients remain, but the transformation is difficult with the political atmosphere one can observe in Quebec at the moment.[27]

The *nationalisme* latent in Chapleau's political co-operation with Laurier is well illustrated by his remark to Laurier on his departure for the Colonial Conference of 1897. "Our race will profit from the applause for you."[28] To Tarte, also, Chapleau wrote of the destruction of the old party of Cartier's, "which was yours and mine", and of the widespread desire for a "Province of Québec united and strong."[29] Chapeau's desire for a united Quebec which would be influential in determining federal policies could easily be reconciled with Laurier's desire for a Quebec united in its support for Laurier and the Liberal party. Chapleau's defence of the provincial Liberal educational policy is an example of Chapleau's adjustment to the situation; Laurier's attempt to re-appoint Chapleau as Lieutenant-Governor illustrated Laurier's desire to win Chapleau's support. Even such a radical Liberal as P. A. Choquette was temporarily convinced by Laurier that a Tarte-Chapleau combination would be justified by its success.[30]

[26] *Ibid.*, W. L. to Tarte, 23 Nov., 1898.
[27] *Ibid.*, Chapleau to W. L., 15 May, 1897.
[28] *Ibid.*, Chapleau to W. L., 31 May, 1897.
[29] Tarte Papers, Chapleau to W. L., 31 May, 1897.
[30] LP, Choquette to W. L., 6 Dec., 1897.

With the death of Chapleau, the most prominent Chapleau-Conservative apart from the Minister of Public Works, was Arthur Dansereau, postmaster of Montreal. "Boss" Dansereau had not allowed his postal duties to separate him from politics. Even before Chapleau's death, Dansereau's political sympathies had been made clear. Like Chapleau, he wanted a united Quebec – always excepting the Castors. He wrote to Tarte,

The heart of the matter is that we are going to discard this monopolistic and bullying group while we prepare the true Conservatives to rally to you others in Ottawa. Nantel knows that part of it, understands what is going on and accepts the situation....It isn't necessary to say that there is a reconciliation between Le Monde and you; but the campaign which is opening will demand it. Do one thing only: warn La Patrie not to attack Nantel anymore. At a given time if the Niggers of the Liberal Party want to continue their demonstrations against you, you will be able without fear to offer Laurier a Conservative contingent to make up for the losses with which you are threatened. Nothing is urgent; it is a game of patience . . .[31]

As this letter suggests, Tarte was considered a "true Conservative" by the Chapleau group, even when in Laurier's Cabinet, but was suspected of being a false Liberal by many "old Liberals." Indeed, the coalition between the "school of Cartier" and the "old Liberals" caused misgivings on both sides, and could only develop gradually into a united political party. The career of Dansereau himself illustrates how carefully Laurier fostered this growth.

Dansereau's tenure of the Montreal post-office was not secure. Mulock, the Postmaster-General, wrote to Laurier that, "Poor Dansereau, I fear, is not doing everything that he should. I want to be considerate with him, but . . . "[32] Mulock's complaints continued. Later he wrote: "The postmaster (Dansereau) is dissipated, knows nothing of his duties, takes no interest in them whatsoever, comes and goes when he likes and his connection with the office is destructive of all discipline or influence."[33] Mulock was not the man to accept such a situation. As Laurier wrote in another connection, he was so "economical" that Liberal partisans "have some ground of complaint."[34] In the case of Dansereau, Mulock finally decided that, "whilst friendship has its claims, a public trust

[31] Tarte Papers, Dansereau to Tarte, 28 May, 1897.
[32] LP, Mulock to W. L., 7 Dec., 1897.
[33] *Ibid.*, 27 Oct., 1898.
[34] *Ibid.*, W. L. to Fielding, 27 Jan., (1897?).

has its obligations"[35] and informed Dansereau that, "pending final action you are hereby given leave of absence."[36]

Laurier was in Washington at this time. As he knew, Dansereau had been offered the editorship of *La Presse*, the newspaper with the largest circulation in Canada.[37] To have him ignominiously dismissed by the Liberal party might be disastrous. Laurier's action belied the indecision which is traditionally attributed to successful Canadian politicians. He promptly wrote to Mulock, "For reasons which I deem paramount, knowing the situation in Quebec perfectly, I expect that you will at once re-instate Dansereau in his position."[38] Furthermore, he sent Mulock the outline of a letter of apology, which Mulock sent to Dansereau with slight modifications.[39] Dansereau told Laurier that he was well pleased with the "charming letter" of apology which he had received from Mulock,[40] and Mulock received his consolation in a soothing letter from Laurier after the crisis regretting "my perhaps to (sic) hasty action in characterising your own action as hasty."[41] Laurier's "sunny ways" were always in evidence on such occasions.

Possibly fortunately for the welfare of the Montreal post office, Dansereau was more interested in his honour than in his work. Shortly after his re-instatement, he resigned to become editor of *La Presse*. Sir Charles Tupper was hopeful that, in view of the Liberals' treatment of Chapleau and their virtual dismissal of Dansereau, the Conservatives would benefit from Dansereau's influence. "I think that we ought to be able, under all the circumstances, to secure a strong Conservative line on the part of *La Presse* under the editorial management of Mr. Dansereau."[42] Tupper did not understand Dansereau. Dansereau had already informed Laurier that the proprietor of *La Presse*, T. Berthiaume, had promised Dansereau a great deal of latitude in his political editorials and that "I do not despair of your running *La Presse* one day, completely."[43] When arrangements were completed Dansereau wrote that his contract had given him "carte blanche on your account."[44]

One dissident voice was heard from the Liberals in Quebec, the voice of J. Israel Tarte. Tarte had at first agreed with Mulock that

[35] *Ibid.*, Mulock to W. L., 18 Jan., 1899.
[36] *Ibid.*, Mulock to Dansereau, 18 Jan., 1899.
[37] *Ibid.*, G. A. Drolet to W. L., 24 Jan., 1899.
[38] *Ibid.*, W. L. to Mulock, 26 Jan., 1899.
[39] *Ibid.*, Mulock to W. L., 29 Jan., 1899.
[40] *Ibid.*, Dansereau to W. L., 30 Jan., 1899.
[41] *Ibid.*, W. L. to Mulock, 31 Jan., 1899.
[42] Tupper Papers, *Letterbook*, Tupper to H. Dalby, 8 Feb., 1899.
[43] LP, Dansereau to W. L., 30 Jan., 1899.
[44] *Ibid.*, 8 Feb., 1899.

conditions in the Montreal post-office justified Dansereau's dismiss-al,[45] but when Dansereau proposed joining the staff of *La Presse*, the effervescent Tarte modified his views. With his sons now in charge of the Liberal Montreal newspaper, *La Patrie*, his attitude was undoubtedly affected by the fear that Dansereau's *La Presse* would encroach upon its circulation.[46] After Dansereau's resigna-tion, Tarte suddenly decided that the "radical element" of the Lib-eral party in Quebec was betraying the section of the party that he represented, Chapleau having been treated like "a common valet" and now Dansereau had been fired.[47] Tarte's perturbation is illus-trated by a wire to Laurier repeating a fantastic rumor to the effect that there was a plot to replace Marchand as Premier, with *La Presse* as the organ of the schemers.[48] As usual, Laurier was able to restrain his erratic lieutenant. He explained that Dansereau wanted to arrange a peaceful *modus vivendi* with *La Patrie*,[49] and that his motive for leaving the post-office was not because of any injustice but because of the difference between an income of four thousand and of seven thousand dollars.[50] Nevertheless, Laurier agreed with Tarte that it was unfortunate that Dansereau was going to *La Presse*.

He will be led by a word, by an act, gradually and step by step into a course of friendly criticism to begin with, but which will end in open hostility. All this will develop unconsciously, and it will only be when the break has become irreparable that he will notice it. What I regret in all this is that we are going to lose probably – in large part, for sure – the whole of the most sensible and most reasonable element of the school of Cartier, which was about to come in with us once and for all.[51]

Laurier was mistaken. *La Presse* did not unconsciously become an opponent of the Liberal government. In the election campaign of 1900, *La Presse* prided itself on its independence, but the Conserv-ative *Journal* criticized it for open partisanship. The denial of *La Presse* was not convincing. "It (Journal) insists on confusing the performance of the government, on which, during the present cam-paign, we have not said a word, with the person of Sir Wilfrid himself, whom 'La Presse' has always believed worthy of a great place in our politics and our history."[52] The *Journal* can scarcely be

[45] *Ibid.*, Tarte to W. L. 27 Jan., 1899.
[46] *Ibid.*, 7 Feb. 1899.
[47] *Ibid.*, 8 Feb., 1899.
[48] *Ibid.*, 6 Feb., 1899.
[49] *Ibid.*, W. L. to Tarte, 9 Feb., (1899?).
[50] *Ibid.*, 11 Feb., 1899.
[51] *Ibid.*
[52] *La Presse*, 27 October, 1900.

blamed for doubting that such praise for the leader of the Liberal party was proof of political independence. Nor is it irrelevant that *La Presse* repeatedly criticized anti-French Toronto Conservative newspapers.[53] The avowed independence of *La Presse* became even less convincing in the next year, when a series of articles by Dansereau denounced the Conservative betrayal of Chapleau in 1896 and 1897, while at the same time denouncing the Conservative attacks on their compatriot, Sir Wilfrid.

While the other provinces treat one of our own with a respect the sincerity of which is difficult to deny, and which, in spite of the more questioning and sceptical remarks, loses nothing of its original spontaneity, while the prestige of a French-Canadian Prime Minister reflects on our race all that the favourable judgements of England, France and the United States can contain which is particularly flattering and pleasing, Sir Wilfrid's compatriots, without being obliged to, stupidly try to belittle him in every respect, and to refuse him even the average abilities which one usually concedes easily enough to the common run of politicians.[54]

There can be no mistaking the *nationaliste* pride which evoked such sentiments.

Even more important than Dansereau's influence in bringing the "school of Cartier" into the Liberal party, was that of Israel Tarte. Tarte did much to strengthen the identification of the Liberal party in Quebec with French-Canadian *nationalisme*. He took immense pride in Canadian development. Of the proposed exhibit at the Paris Exposition of 1900, *La Patrie* wrote, "We are going to be able to show France and the whole old continent what a vast distance we have travelled, what magnificent progress we have achieved, what an abundant and fortunate land our dear Canada is. . . ."[55] Tarte, whose health was not good, was appointed Canadian Commissioner to the Exposition as a kind of holiday.[56] At Paris, Tarte's pride suffered a severe blow. He found that Canada was forced to share a pavilion in the Imperial section – with the colonies of Western Australia and the Island of Mauritius![57] Tarte himself was subordinate to minor British officials.[58] Tarte's letters to Laurier seethe with indignation.

[53] *Ibid.*, 6 Nov., 1900.
[54] *Ibid.*, 30 Nov., 1901.
[55] *La Patrie*, 23 Sep., 1899.
[56] Laurier, *Commons Debates*, 13 March, 1900, 1788.
[57] LP, Tarte to W. L., 15 May, 1900.
[58] *Ibid.*, 23 April, 1900.

No one recognizes more than I the advantages which we draw from our relations with Great Britain. In addition, no one has realized better, of late, to what inferiority a British colony, however powerful, is condemned in Europe. . . . Our interests have been sacrificed, I say so without apology, in all circumstances where the Royal Commission had to choose between the English of England and us.[59]

The impulsive Tarte could not be expected to accept this affront to his pride. In the many speeches he delivered in Paris that summer he seems to have been carried away. He was reported to have suggested that Canada's future might well be that of an independent country which in the future would become predominantly French-Canadian.[60] In reply to an admonition from Laurier, Tarte replied that "I have great confidence in the future of our race in America, and this confidence I express on all occasions, whether I am speaking before Englishmen or Frenchmen."[61] Laurier defended Tarte in the House of Commons on the grounds that newspaper reports were unreliable,[62] but this was hardly convincing. The reaction in Ontario can be imagined. Suspicion of Tarte's loyalty as a British subject had resulted from his opposition to sending troops to South Africa; these speeches, made while war fervor was still high, confirmed the suspicions. In the election of 1900, Liberal losses in Ontario were widely attributed to Tarte's utterances.[63] In Quebec, Tarte might be considered injudicious[64] but the party would not lose French votes because he was criticized in Ontario for being too French.

It would be misleading to suppose that Tarte's main contribution to the creation of a Liberal Quebec was his appeal to *nationalisme*. As Minister of Public Works and as Laurier's lieutenant for the district of Montreal, Tarte accomplished much. Montreal had been the stronghold of both Cartier and Chapleau, but under Tarte it became more Liberal than Conservative in its political allegiance. One factor in this transformation was Tarte's ambitious policy for the development of the port of Montreal. From a political point of view, Tarte believed that "it is through Montreal, in the future, that you will be able to control more influences, not only in the province

---

[59] *Ibid.*, 31 May, 1900.
[60] Willison, *Laurier*, II, 335.
[61] LP, Tarte to W. L., 25 June, 1900.
[62] *Commons Debates*, 29 June, 1900, 8654.
[63] LP, N. W. Rowell to W. L.; W. E. O'Brien to W. L., 9 Nov., 1900.
[64] *Ibid.*, O'Brien to W. L., 9 Nov., 1900.

of Québec, but in all the other provinces."[65] From the point of view of Quebec, Tarte had analysed the situation in a typical letter.

The Conservative party kept you almost permanently in opposition by means of the big interests and through the influence of the Church. On the latter one cannot rely. We must link as solidly as possible to our chariot the secular influences, the power of capital.[66]

Tarte's enthusiasm often led him beyond the demands of political expediency. So it was in the case of Montreal. He began by continuing the Conservative policy of dredging the St. Lawrence channel as far as Montreal, but such a scheme as the Ottawa and Georgian Bay Canal seemed to him little more than visionary – "for the time being we are engaged in other works."[67] By the next year however, Tarte's unwonted restraint had disappeared.

My opinion is that the government should not hesitate a minute to spend $20,000,000 or even $30,000,000 if necessary, to do for water communications what the Dominion has done for railway communications.

To prepare the Great Lakes harbours, to deepen them to twenty feet, to complete more quickly the digging and improving of canals, to equip Montreal, to complete the excavation and widening of the St. Lawrence channel, to make St. John a first-class winter port, to put the Intercolonial on a paying basis: there is, to my way of thinking, the most national and the most popular program we could offer the country.[68]

A month later, Tarte submitted a memorandum to Laurier, advocating the construction of government grain elevators at Montreal and Port Colborne to secure the western grain trade, and even suggested consideration of some project to secure the construction of a Canadian fleet to carry this trade.[69] By 1902, the memorandum had grown to eighteen pages and also favored "immediate adoption" of the policy of constructing the Georgian Bay canal.[70] Nor were Tarte's efforts restricted to submitting memoranda. During his absence in Paris, the House was informed that in 1898 almost $400,000 had been spent on deepening the St. Lawrence channel[71]

[65] *Ibid.*, Tarte to W. L., 10 July, 1899.
[66] *Ibid.*, 15 Jan., 1897.
[67] *Commons Debates*, 31 May, 1898. 6505.
[68] LP, Tarte to W. L., 3 April, 1899.
[69] *Ibid.*, 19 June, 1899.
[70] *Ibid.*, 22 June, 1902.
[71] Mulock, *Commons Debates*, 19 Mar., 1900, 2191.

and extensive docks were begun in the harbor of Montreal.[72] Even the Georgian Bay canal project seemed likely to become adopted as part of the government program. Laurier admitted in 1903 that it was being considered,[73] and a few years later he still believed that it should be built as soon as the National Transcontinental was completed.[74] What Tarte accomplished fell far short of his plans, but it did achieve the political results he had hoped for. Many business interests in Montreal were attached to the Liberal "chariot."

There was some suspicion that Tarte was more devoted to winning elections than to furthering the national interests. Tarte does not seem to have used his position as Minister of Public Works for his own financial benefit. As the leading Montreal Liberal, he did obtain control of *La Patrie* with the assistance of the Party but this was not necessarily dishonest. The proprietor of the newspaper wished to sell it to a reliable Liberal[75] and Tarte explained that he was authorised by Laurier to arrange for a Liberal organ in Montreal. According to him the Liberal party paid for *La Patrie*, Mr. Greenshields, a Liberal lawyer, delivering the cheque.[76] The newspaper was put in care of Tarte's sons. By coincidence, the government at this time decided to purchase the Drummond County Railway in order to extend the Intercolonial to Montreal. J. N. Greenshields owned this railway. The bill for the purchase was defeated in the Senate in 1897[77] but was passed in 1899.[78] R. L. Borden pointed out the anomaly of a man selling a railroad to the government and at the same time supplying money to the party for a newspaper.[79] This was not conclusive evidence of dishonesty, and Tarte himself denied to Laurier that he had profited by the Drummond affair.[80] Certainly he never became rich while in politics. When he died in 1907, *La Patrie* was suffering a financial crisis.[81]

It was Tarte's work as a political organiser in the province of Quebec that was responsible for his notoriety. He controlled the patronage for the district of Montreal, even the "patronage of a legal nature."[82] He arranged the selection of candidates and organized the election campaign in his district. Laurier did not delegate

---

[72] Tarte, *Commons Debates*, 12 Feb., 1902, 98.

[73] *Commons Debates*, 15 April, 1903, 1303.

[74] LP, W. L. to R. Reford, 16 March, 1907.

[75] LP, Beaugrand to W. L., 2 Feb., 1897.

[76] *Commons Debates*, 26 June, 1897, 5302.

[77] *Ibid.*

[78] Blair, *Commons Debates*, 21 Apr., 1899, 1949.

[79] *Commons Debates*, 18 May, 1899.

[80] LP, Tarte to W. L., 1 July, 1897.

[81] Rumilly, *Histoire*, XIII, 115.

[82] LP, W. L. to Fitzpatrick, 1 Dec., 1900.

this authority unreservedly, and when disagreements arose over the nomination of candidates, Laurier was usually appealed to by all the dissenting factions. Tarte was not always diplomatic. On one occasion he hoped to avoid having the election of a Liberal contested by foregoing the challenging of Bergeron's election as a Conservative for Beauharnois, but found it difficult to restrain the Liberals in Beauharnois. Unable to restrain them, Tarte's solution as he explained to Laurier, might be to help Bergeron financially if an election was forced on him.[83] Nevertheless, at least in the early years, Tarte was usually willing to accept Laurier's decisions and compromises. Of one candidate he wrote: "Note well, however, that if you believe you must make this nomination, I shall take responsibility for it along with you and defend it to the best of my ability. There is this, nevertheless: we will disgust three quarters of our friends in Montreal."[84] Tarte was quite willing to use the Department of Public Works for election purposes if he considered it necessary. When leaving for Paris in 1900, he reminded Laurier that Lemieux had asked to have money voted for work in Gaspé which Tarte considered useless. "All the same, if Lemieux insists and if he must be the candidate in Gaspé, you will do well to vote him a sum of $3,000."[85] On occasion Tarte was also resentful of the regulations which restricted his control of the Department. He wrote to Willison concerning a request made to him, "I will be only too glad to give our friends the dredging work, if my colleagues do not insist on the system of public tenders, which is landing me every day in all sorts of trouble, and in more expenditure in nearly every case."[86] Part of Tarte's difficulty with his colleagues stemmed from his apparent disregard of the principle of economy, which in those days at least, was a Liberal principle. On one occasion in the House, he explained: "We are entering on a new era; it is no use being afraid to spend more money."[87] Mowat, on the other hand, had complained to Laurier that the estimates had "shocked many of our supporters" . . . "I am afraid that our friend of the Public Works has not shaken off Tory ways though on elections as on other matters he has acted so splendidly the part of a Liberal."[88] Nevertheless, Tarte's reputation for unethical political practices seems to have been exaggerated. He had a penchant for the *bon mot*, usually of a cynical nature. He was once quoted as having

[83] *Ibid.*, Tarte to W. L., 16 July, 1897.
[84] *Ibid.*, 13 March, 1897.
[85] *Ibid.*, 20 March, 1900.
[86] Willison Papers, Tarte to Willison, 8 Feb., 1900.
[87] *Commons Debates*, 28 Mar. 1899, 586.
[88] LP, Mowat to W. L., 29 June 1897.

said, "that it is bad to buy votes – when one does not need them."[89] and was credited with similar remarks expressing the cynical view that "politics is a game."[90] But there is no proof that in practice he was as cynical as this would suggest. He was more than willing to exaggerate for effect, without heeding the consequences.

Tarte became a more difficult colleague as the Liberal successes in Quebec continued. The Opposition, criticising the government for being too French, had often called Tarte the "Master of the Administration"; the *Star* commonly spoke of the "Tarte government";[91] and even some French-Canadian newspapers called Tarte "virtually the leader" of the government.[92] Tarte was not immune to flattery. He was soon complaining of encroachments on his Department. "It is the only French department of any importance, and I maintain that it should not be weakened for the benefit of any other department."[93] His special complaint concerned the Department of Railways and Canals, since his transportation projects affected lake harbors and rivers, which were under the jurisdiction of this department.[94] Tarte also challenged Mulock's authority to deal with the Pacific Cable, since he himself was Minister of Telegraphs. He admitted that he had ignored the question while Mulock completed most of the arrangements, but now he intended to do his duty.[95] Tarte, however, did not seem to have any compunction about interfering with other departments. He believed that Blair was endangering the Liberal party by alienating the Canadian Pacific Railway by his determination to develop the Intercolonial as a successful competitor. Laurier characteristically believed that Blair's policy was justified, but that it would be best to arrange a satisfactory compromise with the C.P.R.[96] Tarte, also characteristically, interviewed Shaughnessy,[97] decided that Blair was a fool, and wrote next day that "I refuse, for my part, to concede to any member of the government the right to compromise a whole party by obstinacy."[98] By 1902, a prominent Ontario Liberal was complaining that Tarte was interfering with Ontario candidates. Furthermore, "When not reflecting on the Liberals of Ontario he is lauding his own powers and proclaiming that he has the organization of every

[89] *La Patrie*, 27 Sept. 1899, quoting Montreal *Star*, no date.
[90] Minto Papers, Vol. 20, South Africa Memo.
[91] *Star*, 16 Oct. 1899.
[92] *La Vérité*, 30 Sept. 1899.
[93] LP, Tarte to W. L., 17 April 1899.
[94] *Ibid.*, 1 March 1900.
[95] *Ibid.*, 17 April 1899.
[96] *Ibid.*, W. L. to G. W. Ross, 1 Oct. 1900.
[97] *Ibid.*, Tarte to W. L., 17 Sept. 1900.
[98] *Ibid.*, 18 Sept. 1900.

riding in Quebec in his own hands, and with the locomotive engine and car always at hand, he speeds away to fix any difficulties that may arise."[99] Laurier considered the matter "of such consequence" that he requested an interview on the subject.[100] Nevertheless, while Tarte remained a colleague, Laurier always defended him in public. On one occasion, when Pacaud had criticised Tarte, Laurier reprimanded him. "And, don't forget, Tarte is my colleague, and as much through friendship as tactics, my intention is not only to prevent him being attacked, but even to defend him in all times and in all places, without examining whether he is wrong or right."[101] Laurier practiced the loyalty to the party which he preached. During Laurier's absence from Canada in 1902, Tarte went too far for even his lenient leader. The tariff question had long perplexed the Liberal party. In Quebec, the "school of Cartier" had always considered protection as one of its principles. Arthur Dansereau described the "protection of prosperous and wisely operated businesses" as a major tenet of the group,[102] and the Liberal tariff policy after 1896 had been a factor in gaining the support of this group. Cartwright, the doctrinaire free-trader, had not been appointed Minister of Finance. The Fielding budget which conceded an Imperial Preference without affecting tariff protection against other countries, had been a brilliant political compromise. It had appeased Liberal free-traders without alienating protectionists, while at the same time appealing to the Imperial sentiments of many Canadians. When the British government accepted this tariff preference by denouncing its Belgian and German trade treaties, it was hailed in Quebec as a success for the government but, "above all, it is a great triumph, and a personal triumph, for Sir Wilfrid Laurier."[103] Laurier was well pleased with the tariff settlement. He might argue on occasion that there was still more protection provided for manufacturers than was desirable,[104] but to specific complaints he replied that there should be no "tinkering", that changes could be made only after a careful study of the entire question.[105] Nevertheless, by 1902, Laurier was willing to admit that the tariff question could not long be ignored. Dandurand later reminded Laurier of what he had informed a manufacturer in October 1902.

[99] *Ibid.*, Alex Smith to W. L., 28 Jan. 1902.

[100] *Ibid.*, W. L. to Smith, 29 Jan. 1902.

[101] *Ibid.*, W. L. to Pacaud, 13 Dec. (1900).

[102] *Ibid.*, Dansereau to W. L., 26 Dec. 1901.

[103] *La Presse*, 31 July, 1899.

[104] *Commons Debates*, 18 Mar., 1901, 1619.

[105] LP, W. L. to S. B. Appleby, 9 Aug., 1899; W. L. to R. Millichamp, 22 Oct., 1902.

You declared to him that you were not in favour of a general revision of the tariff but that you were ready to discuss the serious complaints which might exist, and that it would appear reasonable to levy duties on foreign products which are manufactured now in this country and which until now have been admitted free.[106]

To Minto, Laurier admitted that "he himself had practically admitted the possible necessity of a higher tariff against the United States . . ."[107] To another manufacturer, Laurier explained his economic philosophy – "as you know, I am not a doctrinaire, I am always ready to be practical on the tariff as well as on any other question."[108]

The modification in Laurier's attitude may have been influenced by Tarte's refusal to let the issue remain dormant. Tarte had always been a protectionist in principle, as befitted a Chapleau-Conservative. By 1902 he had become convinced that a tariff increase was essential. Laurier as usual restrained his impetuous colleague. As Tarte wrote in April;

I believe that all things considered you were right Sunday evening to tell me that it was as important for me as for the Government that I not give the reply to Sir Richard Cartwright. His harangue of the other day is probably his farewell to political life, for we will be obliged to make a revision of the tariff next year or condemn ourselves to death. And after what he said, I do not see the possibility of his remaining in a cabinet which would make the changes public opinion demands.
I am astonished to see men of the unquestioned worth of Sir Richard Cartwright not understanding more of the reading of public opinion.[109]

With Tarte so firmly convinced that he was right, it is not surprising that he made speeches favoring a higher tariff during Laurier's absence in the summer of 1902. In Ontario and in the Maritimes, he bowed to his conception of public opinion.[110] Many Liberals, even apart from Cartwright, were unwilling to admit that Tarte was politically infallible. The *Globe* in August and Sifton in September denied that a higher tariff was desirable.[111] As might be expected, such contradictions roused the belligerent Tarte to even more dogmatic declarations. In September and October he began an active

[106] *Ibid.*, Dandurand to W. L., 9 Feb., 1903.
[107] Minto Papers, Vol. 2, 18, Memo. of conversation, 20 Oct., 1902.
[108] LP, W. L. to W. Macpherson, 22 Oct., 1902.
[109] LP, Tarte to W. L., 5 April, 1898.
[110] *Canadian Annual Review*, 1902, 21 ff.
[111] *Ibid.*, 22.
[112] *Ibid.*, 25.

tour of Ontario in favour of higher tariffs, even hinting that he would resign from the government if his policy was rejected.[112]

Laurier's biographers have assumed that Tarte's actions can only be explained on the basis that he believed that Laurier's serious illness at this time made it possible for him to aspire to the position as leader of the party. As Tarte he could carry Quebec; as a protectionist, Ontario.[113] A recent historian states that Tarte had learned from private sources that Laurier would be forced to retire because of his health, and so believes 'that this interpretation of Tarte's actions is substantiated.[114] In view of this unanimity among historians, it is surprising that few contemporaries considered the possibility of this explanation. Cartwright was "almost drawn to the conclusion that he has lost his head altogether, or is acting of set purpose to do mischief."[115] Fielding, in London, did not take the problem seriously, since differences between Tarte and his colleagues on the tariff "have not hitherto done us much harm . . .". and all would be well if discussion of the question could be stopped immediately.[116] Blair wrote that Tarte seemed to believe that Laurier agreed with him. "The term 'treachery' has been applied by some to his action. I do not impute any such motive."[117] Certainly Tarte's correspondence in this period does not suggest that he was scheming for the leadership. To one manufacturer he wrote:

The next two or three months will play an important part in the question of the tariff. If the Prime Minister sides with us, as a few months ago I think he was ready to do, there will be a great deal less trouble and work. If he does not, a big fight will be on. We will carry the day triumphantly however. If Sir Wilfrid was in good health, if he could realize the strength of public sentiment, I would not have any anxiety. . . . It is of vital importance that as soon as the Prime Minister is back, he is seen and written to by as many of our friends as possible. A concerted action from all parts of the Dominion will have a good effect.[118]

To Conservative protectionists he expressed the view that the policy of "Canada for Canadians" would sweep the country. "I do not know if I shall remain long in the ministry. If I leave on the question of the tariff, I shall leave with the determination to come

[113] Skelton, *Laurier*, II, 178; Dafoe, *Laurier* 117.
[114] Rumilly, *Histoire*, X, 153.
[115] LP, Cartwright to W. L., 15 Sept., 1902.
[116] *Ibid.*, Fielding to W. L., 18 Sept., 1902
[117] *Ibid.*, Blair to W. L., 8 Oct., 1902.
[118] Tarte Papers, Tarte to G. E. Drummond, 7 Oct., 1902.

back."[119] Tarte's assumption seems to have been that with Laurier's support, the Liberals would adopt a high tariff; otherwise the Liberals would be defeated by a protectionist party. There seems to be no necessity for explaining his actions by a sudden overweening ambition. To historians his actions might seem so unusual as to mean a deep-laid scheme, but to his contemporaries it was merely Tarte being carried away by his convictions again. His career provides many illustrations of a similar nature in which Tarte had committed himself to an extreme position, and when challenged had brazenly confirmed or even exaggerated his statements. His charges of corruption against Langevin had led to a separation from Chapleau; his charges concerning the disallowance of the Manitoba School Act had led to the altercation with Archbishop Taché; only in the case of participation in the Boer War had he retracted or at least modified his statements. In 1899 Laurier had prevented an irrevocable commitment; in 1902 he returned to Canada too late.

When Laurier returned, he acted with a decision which belied his reputation. He had been informed that the Liberal press were united in denouncing Tarte's activities as inopportune.[120] Laurier reached Quebec on the 18th of October; on the next day he told Tarte that he must resign.[121] In view of Laurier's belief that tariff revision might be necessary he was careful to avoid discussing Tarte's statements on that. As he wrote to Willison: "I will not at all discuss the doctrine of protection which he has been preaching. My sole ground will be that his action was unconstitutional, and a violation of the rules of responsible government."[122] The principle of Cabinet unity was easier to defend than the policy of no tariff revision. Tarte promptly resigned, although naturally his official resignation emphasized his views on the tariff as being the reason.[123] There can be no doubt that Laurier had chosen a defensible principle; the question was how the electors would react to the question of the tariff which Tarte had raised.

In the province of Quebec there was also the question as to how much Tarte had contributed to the Liberal success there, and whether he did hold Quebec in the palm of his hand. Most important was the question as to how the "school of Cartier" would react to an anti-Liberal protectionist campaign by their former representative in the Liberal Cabinet. Laurier conceded that "Tarte is most

[119] *Ibid.*, Tarte to A. Gobeil, 22 Sept., 1902 and Tarte to L. P. Pelletier, 30 Sept., 1902.
[120] LP, S. N. Parent to W. L., 29 Sept., 1902
[121] Willison Papers, W. L. to Willison, 20 Oct., 1902.
[122] *Ibid.*
[123] LP., Tarte to W. L., 20 Oct., 1902.

invaluable in many respects, but his actions recently had become a source of great embarrassment."[124] A Quebec Liberal agreed that Tarte's dismissal was unavoidable. "All the same, I suppose that we are also in agreement that it is a tragedy for the party. This *little devil* of a man is certainly invaluable for running a battle."[125] That the Liberals in Quebec were worried is shown by the choice of his successor and by the attention paid to the two by-elections which followed soon after. Raymond Préfontaine replaced Tarte as Liberal representative for the district of Montreal. Préfontaine was a politician of some influence there, having been Mayor since 1898. His influence, however, was not based on a reputation for honesty. In 1898, Laurier had agreed with Tarte that Préfontaine's speculations in the dock area of Montreal were unfortunate.[126] On this occasion, Tarte was pleased to report that if Préfontaine decided to fight him on this issue, "he will destroy himself in a week . . ."[127] Nor was Préfontaine above suggesting to Laurier, albeit unsuccessfully, that the basis of determining the amount of a certain railway bridge subsidy should be altered for his benefit.[128] In spite of this, Préfontaine had one qualification which at this juncture was almost as important as his political popularity in Montreal. He was an avowed protectionist, and so not likely to be harmed by any protectionist campaign by Tarte. He assured Laurier that he had the support of the manufacturers in his by-election.[129] Laurier wrote to the proprietor of the Montreal *Witness*, who was opposed to Préfontaine, to explain that there was no other man available, and that Préfontaine had been a bulwark of the party during the South African crisis. As for his faults, "I make bold to assert that I can reach and bring forth the better man which is in him."[130] It was not often that Laurier had to resort to such a weak defence for his political expediency. Laurier did take the precaution of giving Préfontaine the Department of Marine and Fisheries as being less open to corruption, although at the same time shifting to this department the control of the St. Lawrence channel to reassure Montreal.[131]

[124] *Ibid.*, W.L. to Sen. Powers, 1 Nov., 1902.

[125] *Ibid.*, D. Monet to W.L., 31 Oct., 1902.

[126] *Ibid.*, Tarte to W. L., 30 Nov., 1898; W. L. to Tarte, 4 Dec. 1898.

[127] *Ibid.*, Tarte to W. L., 30 Nov., 1898.

[128] *Ibid.*, Préfontaine to W.L., 29 Sept., 1899, and 27 Jan., 1900.

[129] *Ibid.*, 21 Nov., 1902.

[130] P.A.C., J. R. Dougall Papers, 8 Nov., 1902.

[131] LP, Dansereau to W.L., 6 Nov., 1902. Laurier later praised Préfontaine's "untiring activity" (L.P., W.L. to C. Lugrin, 3 Jan., 1906) but admitted that his department was "in very bad shape" at his death in December, 1905 (LP, W. L. to J. Stratton, 23 May, 1908).

The by-elections went well. Préfontaine in Maisonneuve and another Liberal in Argenteuil were both elected, Préfontaine with a slightly increased majority. Of Argenteuil, Fitzpatrick admitted that it had been an expensive election, but at least it had proved "that elections can be won without the aid of the man who owned the province of Quebec."[132] Similar remarks were made concerning Maisonneuve.[133] Dandurand admitted that he had been nervous, since "I knew the importance of not being beaten in the circumstances."[134] The results must have disillusioned Tarte and those Conservatives who believed that he actually was the "Warwick of Canadian politics."[135]

Tarte still might be dangerous. Laurier was willing to continue to treat him as a Liberal, even to the extent of continuing to give some government advertisements to his newspapers.[136] And Tarte was not willing to accept defeat. In Ontario he apparently hoped to rally the protectionist Liberals against Laurier;[137] in Quebec he attended Conservative assemblies advocating protection.[138] Tarte was soon one of the leading Conservatives in the province, writing their campaign pamphlets,[139] and making suggestions as to the conduct of the election campaign.[140] There was some difficulty, since F. D. Monk, leader of the Quebec Conservatives, was unwilling to co-operate with Tarte, but Monk's resignation was finally withdrawn[141] and an agreement was reached that he would not have to speak on the same platform as Tarte.[142] The Conservatives, however, failed to win a by-election in another Montreal constituency even after a vigorous campaign by Tarte—possibly because Laurier took the situation so seriously that he himself spoke on behalf of the Liberal candidate.[143] Finally, in the general election of 1904 the Conservatives won only eleven seats in the province. This seems to have ended the attempt to revive the Conservative party there under Tarte's leadership. Tarte had failed to bring with him the "school of Cartier", Dansereau explaining that "the whole Conservative group

[132] LP; Fitzpatrick to W.L., 4 Dec., 1902.
[133] LP, C.A.P. Pelletier to W.L., 15 Dec., 1902.
[134] Ibid., Dandurand to W.L., 9 Dec., 1902.
[135] Minto Papers, Vol. 20, South Africa Memo.
[136] LP, R.W. Scott to W.L., 19 Jan., 1903.
[137] Ibid., Charlton to Tarte, 31 Jan., 1903 (copy).
[138] Rumilly, Histoire, XI, 31ff.
[139] P.A.C., Sir R. Borden Papers, Memoir Notes, 5773, Tarte to Borden, 23 Sept., 1903.
[140] Ibid., 5779, Tarte to Borden, 2 Nov., 1903.
[141] Ibid., 5795, Monk to Borden, 17 Jan., 1904.
[142] Ibid., 5737, B. MacNab to A.E. Bount, undated.
[143] Rumilly, Histoire, XI, 96ff.

that I represent . . ." had remained faithful to Laurier.[144] In 1905 Tarte supported Laurier's policy on the Autonomy Bills, and was once again asking for government advertising on the grounds that "if 'La Patrie' isn't a ministerial paper, it isn't a bad paper all the same."[145] Laurier was prompt to accede to his request.[146] After 1904, Fitzpatrick's hope had come true, and Tarte had "ceased to be politically."[147] There could no longer be any doubt that Laurier and not Tarte was Master of the Administration, at least where Quebec was concerned.

Laurier's influence in Quebec is not fully explained until it is realized how closely the provincial Liberal government and the federal government co-operated. From the beginning, Laurier and Marchand assisted each other. Laurier explained the reasons for his interest in Marchand's administration to the editor of the Montreal *Witness*. "Should a Liberal Administration at Quebec turn out to be weak and unequal to the very arduous task which awaits it, the Liberal Administration at Ottawa would to some extent and perhaps a large extent suffer in consequence."[148] Immediately after Marchand's victory in 1897, Laurier offered to make any political appointments which might seem necessary to facilitate Marchand's choice of Cabinet ministers, "in order to satisfy the candidates whom it would not be advisable to select in the present circumstances."[149] Later, Marchand thanked Laurier "for the help you have given me and which helped not a little to keep them happy."[150] Marchand in turn made some provincial appointments at Laurier's request.[151] Provincial legislation too, was sometimes modified after consultation with Ottawa. The most important example of this was Marchand's Education Bill; another example was an amendment agreed to by Marchand to a provincial Act which imposed export duties on pulpwood cut on Crown Lands.[152] There is nothing to suggest that Marchand was a puppet, for he was not willing to accede to any request which he believed endangered his own legislative program.[153] The relationship was rather that of two

[144] LP, Dansereau to W.L., 6 Nov. 1902. Dafoe (*Laurier*, 117) is in error in suggesting that Dansereau aided Tarte in the attempt to "rally the Bleu forces against Laurier."

[145] LP, Tarte to W.L., 2 June, 1905.

[146] *Ibid.*, W.L. to W. Cory, 5 June 1905.

[147] *Ibid.*, Fitzpatrick to W.L. 30 Nov. 1902.

[148] Dougall Papers, W.L. to J.R. Dougall, 5 May 1897.

[149] LP, Marchand to W.L., 14 May 1897.

[150] *Ibid.*, 28 May, 1897.

[151] *Ibid.*, 28 Dec. 1898.

[152] *Ibid.*, 16 Feb. 1900.

[153] *Ibid.*, 1 March 1899.

men of similar moderate temperaments who made no distinction between the interests of the federal and provincial Liberal parties.

Marchand's successful administration, especially his achievement of balancing the provincial budget after years of deficits, helped both wings of the party. Heavy railway expenditures had created a large provincial debt. Under Marchand, as later under S. N. Parent and Lomer Gouin, the provincial governments showed an "unwillingness to embark on enterprises that would create debt." The government restricted itself to the regulation of manufacturing and commercial enterprises which developed, especially in the Montreal district, after the revival of national prosperity about the turn of the century.[154] After 1899 there was a steady diminution of the provincial debt, a contrast to the administrations of Chapleau and Mercier. This conservative budgeting was yet another factor in making Quebec Liberal.

With Marchand's death in 1900, the provincial Liberals found it difficult to select a successor. The two leading candidates were J. E. Robidoux and S. N. Parent.[155] Robidoux was a cultivated gentleman and an accomplished speaker. He had been a member of Mercier's last government, and under Marchand he had been the leading advocate of the first Education Bill. With these qualifications he was most acceptable to the "old Liberals", but less desirable from Laurier's point of view. The link with Mercier held out little hope of continued economy in the provincial administration, and possibly more important, his views on education might alienate the episcopacy. S. N. Parent was a less obvious choice. He had no ability as a speaker or a debater and so lacked a talent very highly rated in the province. On the other hand, he was free of the stigma of anti-clericalism, since his interest and his ability were administrative. As Mayor of the city of Quebec since 1894 he had proved his ability to manage civic elections at least, and had also proved himself capable of economical administration.[156] As Minister of Lands, Forests and Fisheries, Parent was responsible for the sale of waterpower and timber rights in the province,[157] and his careful bargaining had been an important factor in the provincial budget surplus. Aside from this, Laurier had personal reasons for favoring Parent's selection as Prime Minister. Parent was even less likely than Marchand to embarrass the federal Liberal party by radical measures

[154] S. Bates, *Financial History of Canadian Governments*, 150. This survey provides a helpful appraisal of provincial financial developments.

[155] Rumilly, *Histoire*, IX, 234 ff.

[156] *Ibid.*, 15.

[157] *Ibid.*, 16.

because of his temperament alone. In addition to this, he had close personal contact with the federal Liberal leaders, since he and Fitzpatrick were law-partners, and he and Laurier represented the same electors in their respective legislatures. Parent, with his other responsibilities as Mayor of the city, and president of the Quebec Bridge Commission, was able to relieve Laurier of petty patronage problems.[158] With regard to patronage, Laurier wrote that, "our friend Parent has a keen eye and a good judgment to determine all these things."[159] And on an issue which seems almost to have become the touchstone of Liberalism for Laurier, Parent had played a leading part in influencing the province to accept participation in the South African War.[160]

There can be no doubt that Laurier welcomed Parent's selection, but it is less easy to determine the degree of Laurier's influence on the choice. According to one historian, Laurier made the choice independently.[161] This does not conform to Laurier's reply that "on this point M. Marchand's colleagues must have the final decision",[162] when he was asked to support a different candidate – but this is scarcely conclusive. There can be no doubt that Laurier was consulted and that he influenced the decision. Indeed, Robidioux, who became a judge almost immediately after the selection of Parent, thanked Laurier personally for his appointment. "I would only have made a fair Premier; I shall be a good judge."[163] A few years later when a similar problem arose, and Laurier's intervention was sought, the argument was used that the provincial deputies had almost unanimously favored Robidoux and yet Parent had been selected.[164] On this occasion Laurier virtually admitted that he had been responsible for Parent's selection. He agreed that he might be compelled to assume responsibility for the choice of a new provincial leader, and "I count on our friends again this time to rely on my judgement whatever it may be."[165] However inconclusive this may be, there can be little doubt that Laurier's political relations with Parent were more intimate than they had been with his predecessor. There was no problem of getting provincial legislation amended, since Parent was not inaugurating legislative reforms. The bulky correspondence between Parent and Laurier was almost ex-

[158] LP, W. L. to Parent, 10 Jan. 1901.
[159] LP Microfilm, c 371, W. L. to Fitzpatrick, 25 Jan. (1899?).
[160] LP, T. Duffy to W. L., 11 Sept. 1901.
[161] Rumilly, *Histoire*, IX, 243.
[162] LP, W. L. to Charles Langelier, 4 Sept. 1900.
[163] *Ibid.*, Robidoux to W. L., 16 Oct. 1900.
[164] *Ibid.*, G. Langlois to W. L., 30 March 1904.
[165] *Ibid.*, W. L. to Langlois, 1 April 1904.

clusively concerned with patronage and matters administrative.[166] With local patronage being managed by an expert, Laurier was free to devote his time to other problems. Meanwhile Marchand's conservative financial administration was continued by Parent.

A glance at a minor political problem will illustrate Laurier's prestige in the province, and also his tactful use of his influence to maintain party loyalty. After 1896, the problem of selecting Liberal candidates to contest constituencies was no longer that of finding a candidate willing to run, but of restricting the choice to one Liberal only, since an official Liberal candidate in Quebec was almost certain to be elected. The coalition with the Chapleau-Conservatives increased the likelihood of candidates representing only party factions, and also increased the danger that this rivalry would weaken party unity. In 1897, in a Temiscouata by-election, two prospective candidates appealed to Laurier for his support.[167] A Liberal organiser then explained that the nominating convention had made its choice, but that the other candidate was not satisfied. What was needed was a letter from Laurier to the parish *chefs* supporting the choice of the convention.[168] Laurier did not wish to intervene unless it was essential for party harmony,[169] apparently because the unofficial candidate was a personal friend. Finally he wrote to this man and advised him to withdraw in his own interests.[170] That was all that was necessary. The official candidate was elected by acclamation. In this case, as always, Laurier assumed a position of neutrality, stating that it was up to the electors to select the candidate.[171] If other Liberal candidates did not then withdraw, Laurier might intervene by sending a letter to the official candidate which was a public appeal to the electors to be loyal to the Liberal candidate.[172] But on rare occasions, Laurier might intervene before a convention if it was obvious that the selection of any single candidate would be difficult. On one occasion he consented to act as arbitrator between four prospective candidates, all of whom consented to accept his choice.[173] The selected candidate was elected by acclamation, and the others received a personal note of thanks from Laurier and a promise to express his gratitude more effectively if the opportunity

[166] *Ibid.*, Patronage files, Series E.
[167] *Ibid.*, C. A. Gauvreau to W. L., 26 Aug. 1897; J. E. Pouliot to W. L., 1 Sept. 1897.
[168] *Ibid.*, C. A. P. Pelletier to W. L., 13 Sept. 1897.
[169] *Ibid.*, W. L. to E. Pacaud, 18 Sept. 1897.
[170] *Ibid.*, W. L. to Gauvreau, 11 Oct. 1897.
[171] *Ibid.*, W. L. to C. DeGuise, 28 Feb. 1899.
[172] *Ibid.*, W. L. to E. Lapointe, 3 Oct. 1904.
[173] *Ibid.*, W. L. to P. A. Choquette, 11 May 1905.

arose.[174] Laurier's influence was not always effective. On one occasion at least, the unofficial Liberal candidate was elected. In this case, Laurier had to decide whether the defeated candidate should control the patronage for his constituency, as was customary, at the risk of losing the promised support of the new member. Laurier decided to give the patronage to the new member, "but after preliminary consultation with me, in each case."[175] To the defeated candidate he explained his predicament, but then asked him to submit his recommendations to Laurier nevertheless, and Laurier would do his best for him.[176] The importance of Laurier's influence over the choice of candidates should not be exaggerated, since the prominent Quebec Liberals needed no assistance. Nevertheless, it shows the importance of Laurier's support to a candidate anywhere in the province, and how his personal intervention was usually so tactful as to alienate no one and to maintain the unity of the party he had created.

Few incidents better illustrate Laurier's political domination of the province than the sale of *La Presse* during the election campaign of 1904. The devious scheming by which the proprietor, Berthiaume, was persuaded to sell the newspaper to a syndicate of English Conservatives was reported to Laurier by Edward Farrer.[177] The significant fact is that in spite of the change in ownership, *La Presse* did not support the Conservative party during the campaign. As an editor of *La Presse* wrote to Laurier, "It is true that it has been sold to a syndicate of capitalists, but its political attitude will not alter in any way. It will remain what it has been in the past and will continue to give its independent support to Sir Wilfrid Laurier. If it were otherwise, I would not stay here."[178]

The syndicate, whatever their political motives may have been had made a sizable investment in purchasing the newspaper with the largest circulation in Canada. If this investment was to be protected, the circulation had to be maintained. In 1904, no newspaper that was interested in mass circulation in Quebec could afford to oppose Laurier. Immediately after the election, one of the syndicate was negotiating with Laurier, offering "to give you the exclusive political control of 'La Presse'."[179] Shortly afterwards, the syndicate signed an agreement to the effect that *La Presse* was to be politically independent but was "to give Sir Wilfrid Laurier a gener-

[174] *Ibid.*, 98240, 98246, 98245.

[175] LP, W. L. to Tarte, 22 Feb. 1900.

[176] *Ibid.*, W. L. to J. Boisvert, 9 Feb. 1900.

[177] Farrer to W. L., no date, quoted in Skelton, *Laurier*, II, 209ff.

[178] LP, T. Côté to W. L., 18 Oct. 1904.

[179] *Ibid.*, 25 Nov., 1904.

ous support."[180] Later, when Berthiaume was negotiating to re-purchase *La Presse*, he made a similar promise.[181] Conditions which in 1898 had made Laurier and Tarte fear that *La Presse* would gradually become an Opposition newspaper had so altered by 1904 that *La Presse* had to be Liberal in spite of itself, because there were not enough Conservatives in Quebec to keep such a newspaper solvent.

It would be wrong to give such Liberals as Laurier and Tarte, Marchand and Parent, the sole credit for creating a Liberal Quebec. The policy of the federal Conservatives was of great importance. In 1896 the Conservatives had relied on the Remedial Bill and Castor leaders to gain the support of the province. After their failure, the party repudiated the policy of remedial legislation, yet continued to ignore the opportunities of regaining the support of the Chapleau group.[182] The Imperialism of the Conservative party had completed its ruin in Quebec. Dansereau's statement may be taken as representative of the French-Canadian Conservative's attitude. "As you know, since Chapleau's death, it is impossible for me to acknowledge any one as Conservative leader."[183] The national Conservative Pary never recovered the support which it had lost in 1900.

If a year was to be selected when Quebec had become "solid Liberal", it would be 1902. In 1902, Laurier's policy at the Imperial Conference had regained the political support of the dissident Liberals led by Bourassa, who had opposed the imperialistic tendencies attributed to Laurier. In that same year, Tarte's failure to take with him into the opposition the "school of Cartier" had proved that the new "Liberal-Conservative" party in Quebec was a reality. As an editor of *La Presse* wrote to Laurier a few years later, "You have succeeded in winning the complete, sincere and unrestricted co-operation of those who, in our province, belong to the school of Cartier."[184] Under Laurier, the tentative alliance of 1896 and 1897 had become a union.

Tarte had played an important part in this new alignment of political groups in Quebec. After the death of Chapleau, he had become the virtual leader of the "school of Cartier". By his reputed influence in the Laurier government and by his flair for publicity he

---

[180] LP, 93729, signed by Mackenzie and Mann, 18 Jan. 1905.

[181] LP, Berthiaume to T. Côté, 29 Oct. 1906.

[182] Tupper Papers, *Letterbook,* Tupper to Rolland, 18 April 1898; *La Presse,* 14 Dec. 1901. Tupper refused to find financial support for Nantel's *Nouveau Monde* and founded the *Journal* instead.

[183] LP, Dansereau to W. L., 15 June, 1900.

[184] *Ibid.*, T. Côté to W. L., 19 Nov. 1907.

had made the Liberal party acceptable to former Conservatives. His tenure of office represented the transition period for the transfer of political allegiance. Especially in the district of Montreal, Tarte had been effective. But Tarte with his flamboyance and his impetuosity had been a political liability on occasion. According to a recent historian, "Tarte was the most intelligent man of his time . . . Tarte had genius."[185] On the other hand, a contemporary observer could describe him as "a political comedian".[186] Dansereau was more discerning when he wrote that Tarte "hasn't the temperament of a reliable partisan."[187] Only Laurier's restraining influence had made it possible to take advantage of Tarte's abilities. It was no coincidence that Tarte's political aberrations occurred when he and Laurier were separated. Laurier had been in Washington when Tarte decided that Dansereau's resignation from the Montreal post-office meant disaster; Laurier had been in Chicago when Tarte denounced the idea of sending troops to South Africa; Tarte had been in Paris when he made his inflammatory *nationaliste* speeches; and Laurier had been in London when Tarte began his tariff campaign. Tarte's subsequent unsuccessful opposition to Laurier proved that his role had been no more than a supporting one.

In spite of the political influence attributed to Tarte in this period, Laurier had always been "Master of the Administration". His role was less obvious than that of Israel Tarte. Apart from the important decisions as to policy, such as South African participation, Laurier had played the part of diplomatist. Outside of the province, this is best illustrated by his settlement of the Manitoba school question. Within the province, in addition to his restraining influence on Tarte, Laurier's tact is illustrated by the judicial appointments which suppressed the protests of Liberal "kickers". Even more significant in the creation of a Liberal Quebec was Laurier's role as the symbol of *nationaliste* pride. In Ontario, in England and in France, Laurier had been acclaimed as a great statesman. For the French-Canadian minority, inevitably conscious of its weakness in numbers and influence in the Dominion, the honors paid to Laurier were an incalculable asset in attracting political support.

After 1902, Laurier's control of the province was never challenged by the national Conservative party. The only political party

---

[185] Rumilly, *Histoire*, VIII, 181.
[186] Willison, Toronto *News*, 9 Nov. 1903, quoted J. G. Harris, *The News and Canadian Politics, 1903-1914* (unpublished M. A. Thesis, University of Toronto, 1952), 129.
[187] LP, Dansereau to W. L., 6 Nov. 1902.

which could weaken Laurier in Quebec would have to be a third party–a provincial party with a French-Canadian *nationaliste* platform so extreme that Laurier would appear almost English in comparison. As long as no issues arose by which Laurier might be forced to compromise Castor principles or anti-Imperialist principles, no such party was possible. Quebec had become "solid Liberal" and seemed likely to remain so.

9.
The Autonomy Bills

In the next few years there was no apparent change in the relative strength of the two national parties in the province of Quebec. Quebec still voted Liberal at the polls. But, for various reasons, the allegiance of French-Canadian voters to the Liberal party was undermined by the suspicion that French-Canadian rights were being compromised. The most important incident was the Autonomy Bills, but there were lesser incidents such as the Keewatin boundary question and the Lord's Day Observance Bill. In each case Laurier seemed to have yielded to English-Canadian pressure at the expense of the minority. The Conservative party could derive no benefit from this in the province since its policy on these questions was even less acceptable. But in the oppositon to these measures can be discerned a new and still inchoate Opposition party, a party *nationaliste* in sentiment and provincial in scope.

The creation of the provinces of Saskatchewan and Alberta in 1905 involved the federal government in another separate school question. As in Manitoba, the problem was to determine the legal rights of the Roman Catholic minority under the provincial adminstration of education. Once more the proponents of completely separate schools and of completely secular schools appealed to incompatible principles, and once more a compromise was reached whereby modified denominational schools were preserved within a secular educational system. But the similarity of the Manitoba school question of the 1890's to the school question of 1905 is misleading. The situation in the Territories in 1905 more nearly resembled the situation in Manitoba in 1870. At both times the problem was the creation of a province, and the determination of the educational system within the province. By sub-section one of section 93 of the British North America Act, the right or privilege to have denominational schools, which existed "by law in the province at the Union", was to be preserved after the entry of the province into the union.[1] The Manitoba school question had arisen because a judicial decision in 1892 had decided that section 93 did not guarantee the privilege of state-supported denominational schools. From the point of view of the minority, there had been a blunder at the time of the creation of the province of 1870; the Manitoba Act of that year had

---

[1] British North America Act, c-3, s. 93.

failed to provide adequate protection for denominational schools. The agitation of the 1890's was intended to remedy this blunder by what constitutional remedies remained open. In 1905, it was determined to avoid the blunder, and by careful wording of the statute creating the new provinces to assure that certain rights and privileges of denominational schools would be carefully preserved.

The failure to make any distinction between the constitutional position of the minority in Manitoba in the 1890's and in the Territories in 1905 has sometimes led to a charge of inconsistency when referring to Laurier's policy on these two occasions. Willison, formerly editor of the Liberal *Globe*, but by 1905, editor of the independent *News*, provides an important example of this. "You know that my estimate of Sir Wilfrid Laurier is based chiefly on his devotion to the federal principles and his resolute resistance to clerical interference in education . . . With the Western Autonomy Acts he turned squarely in the other direction. . . .[2] Like many other Ontario Liberals, Willison mistakenly interpreted Laurier's Manitoba school policy as opposed to denominational schools and as based on the principle of provincial rights. Laurier was not opposed to denominational schools, and he had denied even in the 1890's that the provincial rights principle was relevant.

In 1905, the appeal to the principle of provincial rights was no more than a pretext. The argument used was that the people in the province were legally entitled to determine for themselves what educational system they should adopt, without interference from the federal government. This may have been a sensible solution to the problem, but it was not a defensible constitutional argument. On the other hand, the argument that by section 93, the constitution guaranteed some form of separate schools was equally unsound from a legal point of view. The fact was that there was no constitutional enactment which provided rules governing the situation in 1905. Section 93 clearly restricted the autonomy of the provincial jurisdiction over education and so imposed a limitation upon provincial rights. But section 93 only defined the condition by which a *province* was to be admitted to the union, and so did not apply to a situation whereby provinces were being created within the union. Those who preferred a uniform secular school system might appeal to the principle of provincial rights, and those who preferred separate denominational schools might appeal to section 93, but in each case the choice was determined not so much by the constitution as by the school system preferred. That the opposing groups sincerely believed in the legal arguments they adopted only aggravated the political crisis.

[2] Willison to G. Beer, 29 Nov., 1912, quoted in Colquhoun, *Press, Politics and People*, 84.

The educational system in effect in the North-West Territories in 1905 was based upon a clause in the North-West Territories Act of 1875, which had permitted the creation of a separate school district at the request of a religious minority in an area. Ordinances passed by the Territorial government had resulted in an educational system which was administered by a single Department of Education [3] but which was supervised by an Advisory Education Council which included both Roman Catholics and Protestants.[4] Under this supervision, separate schools were authorised to assess their own ratepayers for school taxes,[5] but privileges such as Roman Catholic school inspectors and teachers, and acceptable text-books were administrative concessions which were not secured by any legal enactment. As the time approached when the Territories would become provinces, some Roman Catholics began to work to secure more comprehensive constitutional guarantees.

Of these Roman Catholics, the most active was the Papal Delegate, Mgr. Sbarretti. Sbarretti collected information as to the educational system in the Territories,[6] and as early as March, 1904, was writing to Laurier on the subject.[7] In public, however, there was little discussion of the subject because the Roman Catholics feared that Protestant agitation might deprive the minority of its rights, especially in an election year. As Scott, the Secretary of State, wrote to Sbarretti, "Our only chance of success is in keeping the subject out of politics by avoiding all reference to it."[8] Sbarretti promised to suppress discussion of the topic in Roman Catholic newspapers,[9] Laurier trying to do the same in newspapers over which he could exert some influence.[10] During this "conspiracy of silence" there were prolonged negotiations to draft a satisfactory educational clause for the Autonomy Bills.

The chief negotiators were Laurier, Sbarretti and Fitzpatrick, now Minister of Justice. Bourassa later claimed that he had played some part in the negotiations,[11] but there is no evidence to suggest that he helped to draft the clause. Of this group there can be no doubt that Laurier played the major role. He had a clear idea as to

[3] School Ordinance, 1901, c. 29, s. 3, cited, *Statutes of Canada*, 4-5 Edw. VII, c. 42, s. 17.
[4] *Ibid.*, s. 8.
[5] *Ibid.*, s. 41.
[6] P. A. C., R. W. Scott Papers, Mgr. Grandin to Sbarretti, 4 Oct., 1903 (copy).
[7] LP, Sbarretti to W. L., 1 March, 1904.
[8] Scott Papers, Scott to Sbarretti, 11 Oct., 1904.
[9] *Ibid.*, Sbarretti to Scott, 12 Oct., 1904.
[10] Willison Papers, W. L. to Willison, 11 June, 1904.
[11] *Le Devoir*, 19 May, 1913.

what his intentions were, and as he wrote to Sbarretti, the final wording of the draft was left "to my judgement and discretion." The actual drafting, however, was left to Fitzpatrick, in whose legal judgment Laurier had implicit confidence.[12]

Laurier's intention was to introduce legislation whereby the Roman Catholics in the Territories would be assured of some form of separate school education which could never be eliminated by provincial legislation as it had been in Manitoba. This aspect of the problem must be stressed because to Laurier it was the most important problem. He had no intention of creating a dual administrative system such as there was in Quebec, or of creating any other form of completely denominational school system. There was to be no attempt to impose upon the majority in the Territories an educational system which they would resent. From the beginning, Laurier made this clear to the Papal Delegate.

My opinion is very clear that when the Territories are admitted as a province, the minority should not be placed in a worse condition than it is today; that its schools ought to receive the same degree of protection as is granted to the minority in Ontario and Quebec, where separate schools existed at the first establishment of Confederation, and that the act of admission of the territories into Confederation should especially provide that the system of schools now in existence shall be secured and beyond the power of provincial legislature as provided by section 93 of the Constitution, either to abolish or even prejudicially affect such schools.[13]

This is a revealing statement. It is based on the assumption that the minority were entitled to some form of separate school system, that the system as it existed in the Territories was satisfactory, and that the only problem was to secure this system against the encroachments of future provincial enactments.

There is no evidence to suggest that Laurier ever changed his mind. The educational provisions of the Autonomy Bills secured the separate schools then in existence by arbitrarily declaring that the Territories should be assumed to have been provinces immediately prior to the concession of provincial status, so that the constitutional guarantees of section 93 would therefore apply to the new provinces. Clause 16 went on to insure that there would be no discrimination between public or separate schools in the collection of school taxes and the distribution of government grants, this being an obvious attempt to prevent the financial discrimination which had destroyed the separate school system in Manitoba in the early

[12] LP, W. L. to Sbarretti, 19 Jan., 1905.
[13] *Ibid.*, 7 March, 1904.

1890s. Laurier's intentions seem to have been carefully incorporated in the Bills.

In view of this it is difficult to explain the protests raised when the Bills were made public. It was to be expected that there would be some opposition from the advocates of completely secular schools. As Laurier wrote, "Whenever the question of separate schools arises, we will always have trouble. We stand, however, as I believe, on firm ground when we take section 93 of the British North America Act."[14] Laurier, as usual, assumed that moderate people would accept the compromise that had already proved satisfactory in the Territories.[15] What was unexpected was the accusation that he was not merely securing the educational system as it existed, but was making a dual system of denominational schools possible. Sifton was the leading figure in the opposition to the original educational clause. As Sifton explained, he had agreed to the principle of maintaining the educational system as it existed in the Territories in spite of a personal preference for allowing the new provincial governments to decide for themselves,[16] but he believed that the Bills went beyond this. His interpretation of the Bills was that they did preserve for the minority the existing privileges but that they "might preserve everything that is set out" in the Territories Act of 1875.[17] Under this Act, a denominational school system had once existed in the Territories. Since the last two paragraphs of section 16 repeated the wording of this Act, Sifton feared that these paragraphs, like the "for greater certainty" section 91 of the British North America Act, might be interpreted so as to modify the meaning of the first paragraph, and so might make possible a denominational school system in the future. Laurier argued that the differences between Sifton and himself were "more of words than of substance,"[18] but Sifton was so convinced of the danger that he resigned from the Cabinet.

Sifton's resignation created a serious crisis. According to Walter Scott, Sifton showed the North-West members for the first time the danger that the clause "would remove separate schools from public regulation."[19] It was even rumored that Fielding would resign.[20] Laurier gave way. As he blandly wrote to Minto, "He (Sifton) was not satisfied with the drafting, and after negotiations we agreed to a

[14] *Ibid.*, W. L. to G. W. Ross, 24 Feb., 1905.
[15] *Ibid.*, W. L. to P. Potter, 25 Feb., 1905.
[16] *Commons Debates*, 24 Mar., 1905, 3120.
[17] *Ibid.*, 3105.
[18] *Commons Debates*, 1 Mar., 1905, 1851.
[19] Skelton, *Laurier*, II, 235, footnote.
[20] *Ibid.*, 230

new drafting, and he has since loyally supported the new measure."[21] To the House, he explained the new clause as a compromise accepted to avoid legal confusion.[22] But Laurier viewed the amendment more seriously than this would suggest. In Committee, he agreed that there was a significant difference between the original and the amended section. He interpreted the original draft to mean that the minority would have some control over the secular as well as the religious instruction given, whereas by the amended draft they would only control the religious instruction in the schools after half-past-three.[23] So seriously did Laurier view the difference that he is reported to have considered resigning rather than accept the amendment. His reason for not resigning was that an unsatisfactory compromise was better than a religious agitation.

There was only one logical position for me after Sifton's resignation, and that was to resign myself. The consequence would only have been that the minority, instead of having what it has now, would have nothing at all; but I believe, and you yourself have been of the opinion, that it would be better to remain in office and face this new situation.[24]

It is difficult to be dogmatic about the constitutional difference between the original and the amended clause. At the time, the opinions of competent lawyers varied widely. Fitzpatrick maintained that the intention had been to "perpetuate the existing conditions", that in his opinion the original clause expressed this intention and implied that the amended clause was only a minor alteration,[25] and Robert Borden also failed to see any difference, in principle at least, between the two clauses. Laurier and Sifton, however, managed to find a considerable difference. It appears that the difference was not in the immediate effect that the Bills would have upon the educational system as it existed in the Territories, but in the possible effect in the future. Laurier's intention was to transform the educational privileges of the minority as they existed, into educational rights guaranteed by the constitution, and thus to give the minority a legal security which the Manitoba Act had failed to give. Sifton was interested in maintaining the legal as well as the educational conditions as they existed in 1905. It would seem that the original clause transformed administrative concessions to the minority into constitutional rights, whereas the amended clause res-

[21] Minto Papers, W. L. to Minto, 8 May, 1905.
[22] *Commons Debates*, 22 Mar., 1905, 2925
[23] *Ibid.*, 8 June, 1905, 7149.
[24] LP, W. L. to F. Béique, 17 June, 1905.
[25] *Commons Debates*, 3 May, 1905, 5344.

tored some degree of administrative discretion to the new provinces. Sifton seems to have exaggerated the possible misinterpretation of the original, but Laurier seems to have minimized its implications. There can be no positive conclusion as to what the clause actually meant since it was never tested in the courts.

From the point of view of Quebec politics, the legal niceties were less important than the fact that Laurier had amended the educational clause because of pressure from Sifton. Sifton's reputation as a prominent member of Greenway's government in Manitoba was enough to suggest that Laurier had sacrificed the rights of the minority in the Territories. The Conservatives in the province naturally depicted Laurier as a traitor to his race. One Conservative newspaper had criticized the original Bill, denying that the existing system which it preserved was a separate school system,[26] but when Laurier accepted the amendment, his action was described as a "pathetic retreat" to conciliate Protestant fanatics.[27] The federal Conservatives from the province were in a difficult position. The national Conservative party was in no position to capitalize on Laurier's vulnerable position in Quebec because the English Conservatives were criticizing Laurier's policy as too Roman Catholic. In the House, Sproule charged that the educational clause had been instigated by the clergy and the Roman Catholics in Quebec.[28] Quebec Liberals were pleased to reprint a cartoon from the Toronto *News* picturing "Whip Sbarretti calling members to vote."[29] Robert Borden had carefully avoided discussing the question of separate schools, but had moved an amendment permitting the provinces "to exclusively make laws in relation to education."[30] In view of the Protestant majority in the Territories, this was tantamount to advocating secular schools, and as Borden himself admitted, was "displeasing" and even "inexplicable" to his supporters in Quebec.[31] The leaders of the provincial party appealed to him to support the principle of separate schools[32] but all in vain. The alternatives for the Quebec Conservatives were to accept the party policy and sacrifice the opportunity of regaining support in Quebec, or to break with the party and try to weaken Laurier in Quebec. They chose the second alternative.

Of course, efforts were made to minimize the seriousness of the schism. Borden was careful not to make his amendment a party

[26] *L'Evénement*, 2 March, 1905.
[27] *Ibid.*, 29 Mar., 1905.
[28] *Commons Debates*, 23 Mar., 1905, 3034.
[29] *Le Soleil*, 8 May, 1905.
[30] *Commons Debates*, 22 Mar., 1905, 2979.
[31] Borden Papers, Memoir Notes, 6073, Borden to W. Ross, 3 April, 1905.
[32] *Ibid.*, 5626, Landry to Borden, 16 May, 1905.

measure,[33] and some Quebec Conservatives argued that Laurier's policy was worse than Borden's although both were reprehensible.[34] But Laurier could not be challenged in Quebec by silent opposition to this measure, and so Quebec Conservatives found it necessary openly to disagree with their colleagues. Both Monk and Bergeron, the most prominent French-Canadian Conservatives, spoke at length against the amended Bills and in favor of separate schools,[35] and as for Borden's amendment, every Conservative member from Quebec voted against it, with the exception of Walsh of Huntingdon, described by Le Soleil as a "fanatical and Orange Protestant."[36] The same group of Conservatives voted for the Bills on the second reading.[37] The division within the Conservative party became more apparent when Bergeron moved an amendment to guarantee separate schools in the new provinces, a motion which did not receive the support of any English Conservatives.[38] Monk also moved an amendment, this time to establish the use of the French language in the provincial Assemblies and courts, which received the support of only six members.[39] Monk could not have expected to pass such an amendment, so it must have been primarily a political gesture to gain political support in Quebec. Laurier rejected the motion on the grounds that the position of the French language had no constitutional protection comparable to the educational guarantees of section 93,[40] but as he wrote to a friend, "the exaggerations contained in this amendment will only make the position more difficult."[41] As far as the Autonomy Bills were concerned, the French-Canadian Conservatives might be called a third party.

This party schism almost resulted in the official separation of the Quebec Conservatives from the national party organization. As Tarte remarked in La Patrie:

How can one wish French Canadians to give their sympathy to a political party the majority of whose parliamentary caucus, newspapers and public men treat them as an inferior race, and threaten to destroy their institutions wherever they can do so?[42]

A party convention of the provincial Conservatives was called in

[33] Commons Debates, 22 Mar., 1905, 2929.
[34] L'Evénement, 27 March, 1905.
[35] Commons Debates, 23 Mar., 1905, 3064ff; 30 Mar., 1905, 3462ff.
[36] Le Soleil, 5 May, 1905.
[37] Commons Debates, 3 May, 1905, 5423.
[38] Ibid., 5 July, 1905, 8831.
[39] Commons Debates, 30 June, 1905, 8530; vote recorded, 8634.
[40] Ibid., 8571.
[41] LP, W. L. to F. Béique, 17 June, 1905.
[42] Rumilly, Histoire, XII, 98.

November, 1905, to consider the formation of an autonomous provincial party, and only after some debate was it decided to remain within the national party.[43]

This challenge to Laurier in Quebec, based on the *nationaliste* pillars of language and religion, was the more serious because of the defection of some French-Canadian Liberals. Laurier received loyal support from the Liberal newspapers in Quebec. The original Bills were warmly applauded,[44] and even after the amendment appeared there was no opposition. *Le Soleil* had denied that Laurier would yield,[45] but a week later described him as the only man who could reach a satisfactory compromise in view of the opposition to the Bills.[46] Even Tarte, in his Parliamentary Letter to *La Patrie* was confident that the amendment secured the rights of the minority, without any ambiguity.[47] Similarly, *La Presse* described the modifications as not affecting the position of the minority, but introduced merely to reassure those credulous Protestant Liberals who had been disturbed by the Protestant agitation.[48] This is not to suggest that these newspapers were a reflection of public opinion in the province. On such an involved constitutional problem, the newspapers are more likely to form than to follow public opinion. And Laurier himself was very conscious of the importance of newspaper support, and had frequently expressed this opinion. "It is certainly my firm belief that the publication of a newspaper is of very great advantage always for the prosperity and well-doing of a political party. In this modern age, the press seems to be essential to the success of anything which requires exertion."[49] Willison had once disagreed with Laurier as to the role of a political newspaper, and his letter to Laurier on that occasion gives an insight into Laurier's theories on party newspapers. "I still think, although I know you do not agree with me that for the *Globe* to be a mere echo of the government on every question makes the paper of little influence with the people when the government really needs effective support."[50] The crisis of 1905 did not change Laurier's opinion. Indeed, he believed that the opposition in Ontario was the fault of the *Globe*'s opposition to his original Bill. "The trouble could have been entirely avoided if the *Globe* had frankly supported us, but as

[43] *Ibid.*, 97; Borden Papers, Memoir Notes, 6125, J. Macdonald to Borden, 23 Nov., 1905.
[44] *Le Soleil*, 23 Feb., 1905; *La Patrie*, 22 Feb., 1905.
[45] *Le Soleil* 3 Mar., 1905.
[46] *Ibid.*, 8 Mar., 1905.
[47] *La Patrie*, 18 March, 1905.
[48] *La Presse*, 21 Mar., 1905.
[49] LP, W. L. to M. Jerome, 12 Aug., 1901.
[50] LP 29861, Willison to Laurier, 21 Jan., 1899.

usual, the *Globe* took fright and simply added fuel to the flame."[51] In view of this conviction, Laurier must have exerted his influence to secure the support of the newspapers in Quebec. It is probable that his powers of tactful persuasion were exerted directly on the Parliamentary correspondents of these newspapers, but he also took care that his friends in the province used their influence to secure the desired comments in the press.[52] The support of the "independent" *La Presse* and *La Patrie* attests to his success.

But there was at least one Liberal from Quebec who could not be influenced by arguments that political compromise was necessary, even to the extent of compromising some of the "rights" of the minority, and who had already shown that he was too independent to be swayed by the seductive influence of Laurier's personality. Bourassa accepted the original Bills as completely satisfactory, and even claimed some credit in later years for acting as "intermediary between the government and several persons who are particularly concerned with the North-West school question."[53] As might be expected, Bourassa's satisfaction with the original Bills made him suspicious of the amendment. But Bourassa always denied the allegation that his resistance to the amendment was a futile refusal to accept a necessary compromise.

I bolted only after I had convinced myself, beyond a doubt, that the government could have pushed through, if it wanted to, the text of the law it had prepared, and I gave assurances of this, with proof, to M. Laurier and to Mgr. Sbarretti.[54]

This assurance appears to have been that enough French-Canadian Conservatives would support the Bill to give the government a majority even after Liberal defections.[55] This was the criticism of most of the opposition in the province – that Laurier could have obtained a majority for the original Bills if he had rejected the amendment.[56] Since this would have split the Liberal party, and virtually created a Roman Catholic coalition to pass the Bills, it is

---

[51] *Ibid.*, W. L. to W. Preston, 23 March 1905. Laurier later wrote of the *Globe*: "Its loyalty is beyond dispute and its devotion to sound Liberal principles cannot be questioned, but the Globe lives in the atmosphere of Toronto, where there is no devotion to Liberal views and principles, and where, though no better than the rest of the community, they all affect to be aiming at the highest purpose . . . ." (LP, W. L. to E. Macdonald, 23 Dec., 1908).

[52] LP, W. L. to L. David, 20 April, 1905.

[53] *Le Devoir*, 27 June, 1911.

[54] *Ibid.*

[55] *Ibid.*, 19 May, 1913.

[56] *L'Evénement*, 17 March, 1905; *La Vérité*, 8 April, 1905.

not surprising that Laurier did not adopt these tactics. In the House, Bourassa forcefully defended the principle of a constitutional guarantee of the right of the minority to attend separate schools,[57] but voted with the majority on the second reading.[58] In Committee, however, he moved an amendment which was "substantially the same" as the original education clause.[59] Seven voted for this amendment, Bourassa and Armand Lavergne from the Liberal party, together with Monk, Bergeron and three other French-Canadian Conservatives.[60] Since Bourassa in turn had supported the principle of Monk's amendment to make French an official language in the new provinces,[61] and had voted for Bergeron's amendment,[62] in effect there was an informal agreement between Bourassa and the dissident Conservatives. The danger was that this *entente* might develop into a formal coalition, into a *nationaliste* third party.

Laurier took a serious view of the situation.

Bourassa has just begun a campaign against us, because, according to him, the clause as amended does not go far enough. I still do not know what effect this new agitation is going to produce. I do believe, however, we shall manage to end it.[63]

To a director of the Liberal *Le Canada* of Montreal, he explained that it was necessary to contradict the argument of Bourassa, "who doesn't seem to understand that it is imperative that compromises be made in these matters."[64] The Liberal press was less sparing of Bourassa than it had been in 1899. *Le Soleil* no longer described him as one of the most promising of young Liberals; instead, it grudgingly admitted that he was a good orator, but suggested that his common sense was less marked.[65]

Bourassa, however, could not yet be described as a political opponent. Years later Bourassa wrote that he had always believed that it was Laurier's sincere intention to preserve the rights of the minority.[66] In speeches made in the province of Quebec at this time, he was always careful to express his admiration for Laurier and to blame the weakness of the Liberal members from Quebec for the compromise. "It is the same with a leader as with a general. What-

[57] *Commons Debates*, 28 Mar., 1905, 3272.
[58] *Ibid.*, 3 May, 1905, 5423.
[59] *Ibid.*, 28 June, 1905, 8341.
[60] Rumilly, *Histoire*, XII, 51.
[61] *Commons Debates*, 30 June, 1905, 8593.
[62] *Ibid.*, 5 July, 1905, 8832.
[63] LP, W. L. to A. Forget, 21 April, 1905.
[64] LP, W. L. to F. Béique, 17 June, 1905.
[65] *Le Soleil*, 24 April, 1905.
[66] *Devoir*, 19 May, 1913.

ever may be his talents, if his soldiers abandon him at the moment of the battle he cannot win the victory."[67] Only personal affection for Laurier, felt by so many of his political associates, can explain Bourassa's unwillingness to criticize Laurier himself. Even after the Boer War and the Autonomy Bills, Bourassa could deny that Laurier's intentions were at fault, and was not even willing to admit that the errors of the government were Laurier's responsibility. Even to Bourassa, the man of principle, Laurier's personality was not a negligible factor in his political attitude.

The attitude of the Roman Catholic episcopacy was of vital importance to the Liberal party in Quebec. Sbarretti argued that the original clause had been satisfactory both to himself and to the members of the episcopacy whom he had consulted, but that he did not approve of the new clause.[68] His suggestion was that Laurier should force through the original clause.[69] Laurier was not likely to be swayed by the Papal Delegate. His view was that Sbarretti, not having experienced the religious crisis of the 1890's, did not understand the dangers of religious agitation in Canada.[70] More important was the message transmitted by Sbarretti on behalf of a large conference of the Canadian episcopacy in Montreal, to the effect that they were not satisfied with the amended clause, but "in view of the circumstances as they are represented to them, they do not intend to oppose the clause . . ."[71] There was at least one exception to this affirmation, since Archbishop Langevin in Manitoba protested against the amendment,[72] but the danger of open political intervention by the clergy was averted. Nonetheless, the dissatisfaction of the clergy was of some importance. In addition to Sbarretti, some religious publications criticized the final solution.[73] There seems to be little doubt that Bourassa's insistence upon the rights of the minority seemed more logical to the Roman Catholic clergy in Quebec than Laurier's decision that a compromise was necessary. The suspicion of Catholic-liberalism could not be allayed in a decade, and certainly not by such a compromise.

Laurier's views on another similar problem again did not conform exactly to the desires of the episcopacy. While the Autonomy Bills debates were dragging on, a delegation arrived from Manitoba to negotiate for the extension of the Manitoba boundaries. It was

[67] Rumilly, *Histoire*, XII, 80, speech of 17 Sept., 1905. See also Bourassa, "Les écoles du Nord-Ouest," (Montréal, 1905).
[68] LP, Sbarretti, to W. L., 7 March, 1905.
[69] *Ibid.*, 9 March, 1905.
[70] *Ibid.*, W. L. to C. Russell, 16 Jan., 1904.
[71] *Ibid.*, Sbarretti to W. L., 7 May, 1905.
[72] Rumilly, *Histoire*, XII, 24.
[73] *Semaine Religieuse de Québec*, 1 April, 1905; *La Vérité*, 8 April, 1905.

alleged that Sbarretti had informed the delegates that negotiations would be facilitated if educational concessions were made to the minority in the province.[74] Laurier promptly denied that there was any such understanding.[75] In fact, in correspondence with Sbarretti, Laurier refused to consider delaying the extension of the Manitoba boundaries merely to preserve the educational rights of the minority in Keewatin, on the grounds that it would be foolish to risk national religious strife for the benefit of the few Roman Catholics in Keewatin.[76] In the House, Bourassa's disciple, Armand Lavergne, expressed sentiments more acceptable to many of the Quebec clergy when he advocated educational guarantees to the minority in Keewatin before any boundary extension was permitted.[77]

Another incident, which received more publicity, was the Lord's Day Observance Bill of 1906. The Bill was the result of agitation by the Lord's Day Alliance in Ontario, and had become a federal issue because there was some doubt as to the competency of the provincial government to pass the desired legislation.[78] The Bill was intended to preserve Sunday as a day of rest by preventing most commercial enterprises and labor on that day. More important, it prohibited the opening of parks and entertainments when an admission fee was charged.[79] The Bill was supported by Archbishop Bruchési, whom Fitzpatrick had consulted, and whose letter of approval to the Minister of Justice was later published in the Quebec press.[80] The reaction in Quebec soon showed that even Bruchési's support was not enough to make the Bill acceptable there. The root of the difficulty was that the day of meditation, idealized by the Lord's Day Alliance, bore no relation to the normal Sunday in Quebec, where after mass, people usually spent the day out-of-doors, playing sports, going to the park or even to horse-races. Some exceptions had been incorporated in the Bill with reference to Quebec, but these were of a minor nature.[81] The opposition to the Bill became apparent in Committee, when both Liberal and Conservative members from Quebec moved numerous amendments.

Leading the assault was Henri Bourassa. To Bourassa, the Bill had been imposed on the government – presumably by Mr. Shearer

[74] *Globe*, 5 Apr., 1905.
[75] *Ibid.*, 6 Apr., 1905.
[76] LP, W. L. to Sbarretti, 10 Dec., 1906 and 23 Dec., 1907.
[77] *Commons Debates*, 10 Dec., 1907, 481.
[78] Fitzpatrick, *Commons Debates*, 12 Mar., 1906, 19.
[79] *Ibid.*, 3 Apr., 1906, 1010.
[80] *La Presse*, 4 July, 1906; quoting Bruchési to Fitzpatrick, 23 Mar., 1906.
[81] Fitzpatrick, *Commons Debates*, 3 Apr., 1906, 1011.

of the Lord's Day Alliance.[82] To him, the Bill in principle meant forcing on Quebec the puritan ideals of the province of Ontario,[83] and he did not hesitate to point out that the Autonomy Bills had been amended because the educational ideals of Quebec were unacceptable elsewhere.[84] Bourassa was able to argue that he, not Laurier, was defending the Liberal principle of freedom of conscience against this "most narrow illiberal measure ever advocated in a Canadian parliament."[85] Bourassa was not alone, since included among the critics of the Bill were three Liberal representatives of Montreal, Gervais, Piché and Rivet. In June, the *Ligue Nationaliste* organised an Assembly on the Champ de Mars to protest the Bill, and these three, together with Bourassa and Lavergne, were invited to speak. Laurier had been warned that this assembly would rival the assembly on the Champ de Mars after the execution of Riel,[86] and certainly the size of the crowd, estimated at ten thousand,[87] illustrates the popular disapproval of the Bill. The meeting however, threatened to be an anti-climax, since it was announced that Laurier had accepted an amendment by Piché which would permit provincial governments to make exceptions to the federal Act.[88] Bourassa prevented the disaster of a protest meeting with nothing to protest, by making a rousing speech against the principles of the Bill, and denouncing the proposed amendment as a delusion.[89] The assembly adopted a resolution which deplored the intention "to impose on the province of Quebec a law contrary to the customs, the sentiments, the interests and the civil rights of its inhabitants."[90] On the third reading, Bourassa introduced an amendment which would prevent the Act from coming into force in any province until the provincial government decided that it should.[91] Fifteen members voted for the amendment, including Monk and Bergeron.[92] Monk then moved an amendment which would leave all Sunday legislation to the provinces, his amendment again receiving fifteen votes.[93] After the Bill had survived these prolonged attacks it went to the Senate, where the French-Canadi-

[82] *Commons Debates*, 21 June, 1906, 5769.
[83] *Ibid.*, 5795.
[84] *Ibid.*, 5799.
[85] *Ibid.*, 5800.
[86] LP, D. Monet to W. L., 28 June, 1906.
[87] Rumilly, *Histoire*, XII, 149.
[88] *Ibid.*
[89] *La Presse*, 4 July, 1906.
[90] Bourassa, *Commons Debates*, 6 July, 1906, 7330.
[91] *Ibid.*, 7333.
[92] *Ibid.*, 7349.
[93] *Ibid.*, 7352.

an Senators also found fault.[94] The Senate amendment to the effect that prosecutions would only be possible with the permission of the provincial Attorney-General was quietly accepted by the government.[95] As Bourassa pointed out, this meant that the Act would now be acceptable in Quebec because it would not be in force there.[96] The observance of the Lord's Day in the province would not be affected.

If the Act had no legal effect in Quebec, its introduction by the government did have a political effect. No provincial newspapers had given the Bill more than half-hearted support. Tarte, in *La Patrie* had unequivocally denounced it;[97] even the Liberal *Le Canada* had criticized it strongly;[98] *La Presse* was willing to accept Bruchési's opinion of the Bill although it too, had misgivings.[99] In view of this, it is difficult to understand why Laurier was so slow to have the Bill modified. Laurier agreed with Bruchési that commercial entertainments and organised excursions on Sunday were undesirable,[100] and also believed that the Bill was much less comprehensive than its detractors declared.[101] In the House, he defended it as a satisfactory compromise.[102] A compromise it may have been, but there was some justification for the critics' suggesting that it was a compromise between what the Lord's Day Alliance demanded and what the government wished to concede. Certainly it ignored the susceptibilities of Quebec. In 1905, Laurier had been described by Bourassa as unwillingly compromising the rights of the minority in the Territories; now he was described as willingly seconding the attempt to force the customs of Ontario on Quebec.[103] The size of the assembly on the Champ de Mars suggests that the argument was effective. *Nationaliste* criticisms of Laurier were beginning to bear fruit when French Canadians could believe that Laurier was willing to sacrifice their pleasures to conciliate the Lord's Day Alliance.

Yet another indication of the *nationaliste* appeal which was weakening Laurier's position in the province was Armand Lavergne's motion that the French language should be "placed on a footing of equality with the English language in all public mat-

[94] LP, J. P. B. Casgrain to W. L., 13 July, 1906.
[95] Aylesworth, *Commons Debates*, 11 July, 1906, 7686.
[96] *Ibid.*, 7689.
[97] Rumilly, *Histoire*, XII, 147.
[98] *Le Canada*, 28 Mar., 1906.
[99] *La Presse*, 22 June, 1906.
[100] LP, W.L. to Bruchési, 16 June, 1906.
[101] LP, W.L. to G. Langlois, 3 April, 1906.
[102] *Commons Debates*, 21 June, 1906, 5798.
[103] Rumilly, *Histoire*, XII, 153.

ters."[104] Lavergne was the promising son of Laurier's former law-partner in Arthabaska, who had been elected for Montmagny in 1904. There had been two prospective candidates in Montmagny at this time, but Lavergne had promised to accept the decision of the nominating convention "for I am, in spite of everything, a good soldier."[105] Laurier was not convinced that he would be a loyal Liberal, telling Bourassa that "under your auspices, he is going to be, 'another thorn in the flesh'."[106] But nonetheless Laurier made no attempt to influence the convention for or against Lavergne.[107] Lavergne was Bourassa's disciple[108] in spite of his almost filial relationship with Laurier,[109] and had invariably voted with Bourassa on each occasion that the latter had opposed the government. His motion on the French language was in turn supported by Bourassa. Their argument was that government enterprises such as the Intercolonial Railway and the Post-Office issued their regular forms in English only.[110] Laurier graciously conceded that there was some justice in these statements but deplored any pedantic insistence upon the use of French where the use of English caused no inconvenience.[111] Changes were made in the government departments, and the government used its influence upon the privately-owned railway companies so that all railway schedules in the province would be printed in both languages.[112] The *nationalistes*, with some justification, claimed the credit for these changes,[113] but there was less justification for the implication that the government had unwillingly ended this discrimination.

The more probable explanation is that the government had merely been slow to recognise a new situation. Vocal elements in the province of Quebec had made French Canadians more conscious of any implied discrimination, and *nationalisme* in Quebec was becoming more aggressive. The Autonomy Bills and the Lord's Day Observance Bill had provided the opportunity for *nationalistes* to exploit the suspicions of the minority. Logically, the next step was to discover long-standing but as yet unrecognised grievances; hence the French language motion. From the point of view of a national party or a national politician, this aggressive attitude was not only

[104] *Commons Debates*, 25 Feb., 1907. 3642.
[105] LP, Lavergne to W.L., 23 Jan. (1904).
[106] *Ibid.*, W.L. to Bourassa, 5 Feb., 1904.
[107] *Ibid.*, W. L. to E. Roy, 27 Jan., 1904.
[108] A. Lavergne, *Trente ans de vie nationale* (Montreal, 1934), 94.
[109] Rumilly, *Histoire*, x, 67.
[110] Lavergne, *Commons Debates*, 25 Feb., 1907, 3646.
[111] *Commons Debates*, 25 Feb., 1907, 3655.
[112] LP, Dandurand to W.L., 14 April, 1908.
[113] Lavergne, *Commons Debates*, 14 Jan., 1908, 1211.

futile but dangerous to political unity. Since Lavergne and Bourassa often found themselves isolated from the rest of the House, or supported only by the few French-Canadian Conservatives, even they must have felt the futility of the situation. Their political interests were becoming more and more restricted to the province of Quebec, where their *nationaliste* sentiments commanded more support. By 1908, both Bourassa and Lavergne had tacitly admitted this and had returned to provincial politics. Since 1904, Laurier's prestige in the province had certainly declined because of *nationaliste* criticisms, but politically he was still invulnerable there. The province would still have no difficulty choosing between the two national parties or the two national leaders. In the general election of 1908, the Conservatives again elected only eleven candidates. From Laurier's point of view, the danger of the *nationaliste* campaign was that it made the support for the national Liberal party less enthusiastic. Even among Liberals, pride in the party and in its leader tended to be replaced by an apologetic attitude; the argument that they were supporting the lesser of two evils. While the two national parties continued to dominate politics, this transition would scarcely be reflected at the polls; only if a *nationaliste* party challenged the Liberals would the degree of disaffection be discovered.

10.
The Provincial
Opposition

The years following Bourassa's return to provincial politics were significant years in the political history of the province. The provincial government found itself opposed by dissident Liberals as well as provincial Conservatives. The agreement between the federal French-Canadian Conservatives and Bourassa in connection with the Autonomy Bills and the Lord's Day Observance Bill was duplicated in provincial politics, and became an active and open collaboration. Once again the basis of the *entente* was *nationalisme* – this time reflected in the criticism of colonization in the province.

In the province of Quebec, colonization was like the weather; everybody talked about it, but nobody seemed to do anything about it. Colonization was one of the most important aspects of *nationalisme*. If French Canadians were to avoid assimilation it was essential that the ratio of French to non-French Canadians in Canada should be maintained and if possible increased. This directly involved the federal government immigration policy, since it might be possible to increase the proportion of French-speaking European immigrants. Other aspects of the problem were more directly the responsibility of the provincial government. French-speaking immigrants were likely to be assimilated by English Canada if they settled on the prairies, so it was desirable that they should be persuaded to settle in the province in the uncultivated areas north of the St. Lawrence. Since this region was forested it was less attractive than the prairies to immigrants anxious to put their homestead under cultivation as soon as possible. Special incentives would have to be provided by the provincial government. The reverse side of this immigration problem was the French-Canadian emigration to the New England states. Here again it was desirable, in this case doubly so, to make colonization in Quebec more attractive than industrial employment in the United States. From the point of view of *nationalisme*, colonization was even more significant than the maintenance of French-Canadian numerical influence would suggest. Numerical survival was only a means to the end of maintaining a distinct French-Canadian society. This society was believed to be founded upon the French-Canadian *habitant* who was not susceptible to the temptations of the materialistic philosophy of his fellow Canadians. As Bourassa wrote in 1902, "this colonising spirit has preserved, as the basis of the French-Canadian race, a sturdy and a sober population of land-owners...."[1] The social units by which the *habitant* preserved the integrity of the French-Canadian society were the family and the parish. The French language helped to prevent contacts which might lead to the intrusion of ideas destructive of this ideal society, but more important was the pervading influence of the Roman Catholic church at the parish level, which provided and preserved the philosophical basis of French-Canadian society. Thus to the *nationalistes*, intent upon maintaining this society, colonization would not only maintain or even increase the proportion of French Canadians in the Dominion, but would also maintain or increase the proportion of rural French Canadians within the province. In view of the urbanization in the Montreal region, and the consequent tendency towards secularization there, this rural extension had become very important. Thus, since the days of Mercier and Curé Labelle, *nationalistes* had co-operated closely with the authorities of the church in attempts to stimulate colonization.

The success of Sifton's immigration policy was another factor which increased the interest in colonization after the turn of the century. Most of these immigrants came from the United States, Great Britain or central Europe, and so were reducing the proportion of French-Canadians within Canada. Since Sifton's career in Manitoba had given him the reputation of being an assimilationist, some French-Canadians believed that the small number of French-speaking immigrants was intentional. According to Dandurand, "just between us, your colleague appears – perhaps wrongly – not to be very anxious to increase the French language population in the West."[2] It is not difficult to provide more probable explanations for the small proportion of French immigrants. In theory, there was no discrimination, as Laurier reminded an immigration agent. "As you are aware, our policy has always been to ignore the religious line, but to get able-bodied, strong active men. We trust that in the long run, they will come out right true Canadians."[3] In fact, special efforts were made to attract immigrants from France and Belgium to avoid criticism. Priests were unobtrusively authorized to go to these countries to publicize the opportunities for emigrants in Canada,[4] and a permanent agent was maintained in Paris. After pro-

[1] *The French Canadian in the British Empire,* (London, 1902), 4.
[2] LP, Dandurand to W. L., 8 July, 1903.
[3] *Ibid.,* W. L. to Preston, 21 April, 1906.
[4] *Ibid.,* Father George to W. L., 31 July, 1898; Tarte Papers, Father Lacombe to Tarte, 27 July, 1900.

longed negotiations, a direct steamship service was arranged between France and Canada, partly in the hope that it would facilitate the immigration of French-speaking settlers.[5] But more active measures were impossible. As Lemieux explained:

As long as Wiallard could claim that the clergy and other representatives who came to France and spread out into the provinces were unofficial agents, voluntary recruiters, operating on their own behalf, the damage – though great – was not irreparable: Wiallard disavowed them, and that was that.[6]

Whenever the Canadian propaganda became more obvious, the French government interfered to prevent possible depopulation.[7] Under such circumstances, it was unfair to criticize the government immigration policy for the small proportion of French immigrants.

Some French-Canadian critics of the federal policy seem to have decided that since French-speaking immigrants could not be obtained, the best solution was no immigration at all. This attitude may have influenced Bourassa to support the Conservative attacks upon Sifton's North Atlantic Trading Company.[8] Certainly in 1907 he gave expression to this preference. "I claim, as I have always done, that the best settler you can have for the North-West is the Canadian settler."[9] At the same time Bourassa claimed that he did not object to foreign immigrants in general, but this was qualified by Lavergne's claim that the bonus system was attracting undesirable immigrants,[10] and by statements of both Bourassa and Lavergne that the English- and French-Canadian races should not be swamped by foreign immigrants in the North-West.[11] The unseemly haste to settle the prairies seemed to be modifying the racial structure of Canada, which to the *nationalistes* at least, was of more lasting significance than the economic benefits to be derived from a quickly-populated prairie region. Thus an avowed *nationaliste* listed as one of the four principles of his creed: "The settlement of the country with the sole view to the strengthening of Canadian nationhood."[12]

Another criticism of the federal government was that the federal

[5] LP, W. L. to H. Garneau, 10 April, 1908.
[6] *Ibid.*, Lemieux to W. L., 16 Nov., 1909. Wiallard was the Canadian agent in France.
[7] LP, W. L. to H. Garneau, 26 Sept., 1910.
[8] *Commons Debates*, 4 June, 1906, 4530
[9] *Ibid.*, 15 Apr., 1907, 6725
[10] *Ibid.*, 9 Apr., 1907, 6156
[11] Bourassa, *Commons Debates*, 9 Apr., 1907, 6183
[12] O. Asselin, *A Quebec View of Canadian Nationalism*, (Montréal, 1909).

immigration policy discriminated against the province of Quebec as well as against French Canadians. Immigration advertising was concerned mainly with the opportunities of settlement in the west; the province of Quebec paid its share of federal immigration expenses but received almost no direct benefits.[13] This argument of course, applied equally well to the province of Ontario, which suggests that the real objection was to immigration in general. The federal government, in fact, was not averse to assisting colonization in the province of Quebec. In general, Laurier opposed grants to private colonization companies on the grounds that the money was wasted,[14] but on one occasion at least, a colonization railway in Quebec was given an increased mail subsidy because of its colonization efforts.[15]

To some extent the National Transcontinental Railway was a colonization railway. To Laurier, another transcontinental railway seemed to be "a national as well as a commercial necessity",[16] and there can be no doubt that his intention was to have an all-Canadian railway constructed which would deliver prairie wheat to a Canadian port by the shortest possible route. Nevertheless he did not ignore the colonization opportunities which such a railway would provide in the province of Quebec. Years before, Curé Labelle had dreamed of a railway running westward from Northern Quebec through Ontario which would create a new area for French-Canadian settlement.[17] A colonization railway running north from the city of Quebec had even planned an extension westwards to the Pacific under the name of the Trans-Canada railway. This was the route of the National Transcontinental. Of the area served by the Quebec-Winnipeg section of the new railway, Laurier wrote, "If you hope that the settlers from Europe are going to locate in a forest, you are wrong. All the timbered regions in Québec and even in Ontario are the patrimony of the French Canadians. They alone, in our day, still love the forest and are clearers of the land."[18] Laurier defended the Quebec-Moncton section, not only on the grounds that it would be a shorter route than the Intercolonial, but also because it would open up "good timber and farming land."[19] To Willison, he stated that "it would pass through a fertile, already

[13] A. Lavergne, *Commons Debates*, 9 Apr. 1907, 6149.
[14] LP, W. L. to Gouin, 4 Dec., 1908.
[15] *Ibid.*, W. L. to J. G. Scott, 19 Jan., 1897.
[16] *Commons Debates*, 20 July, 1903, 7658.
[17] Rumilly, *Histoire*, VI, 11.
[18] LP, W. L. to H. Garneau, 10 April, 1908.
[19] *Ibid.*, W.L. to C.M. Hays, 23 Nov., 1903.

rapidly settling country" south of the St. Lawrence.[20] According to Lemieux this area would become a "New Quebec."[21] As far as railway construction was concerned, there was no justification for claiming that colonization in Quebec was being ignored by the federal government.

It would be wrong to exaggerate the importance of the colonization problem as far as the federal government was concerned. Colonization was mainly the responsibility of the provincial government. It was against the provincial government that the most serious criticisms were levelled, and it was only indirectly, by the effect of the colonization problem upon the provincial parties, that Laurier's political relations with the province were affected.

Within the province of Quebec, those interested in colonization were more concerned with the emigration of French Canadians to the United States than with the small number of French-speaking immigrants. If colonization in northern Quebec could be made more attractive it was assumed that this depopulation of the province would cease, and French Canadians in the United States might even be persuaded to return. Luring colonists to the north had become the responsibility of the provincial government. Mercier had given much publicity to this aspect of his administration, and succeeding governments had continued this emphasis. Railroads, roads, surveys and colonization agents were items in most provincial budgets.[22] Under the economical Liberal administrations beginning in 1897 the expenditure on colonization railways had declined, and this in itself might have led to severe criticism by those who believed that the extension of French-Canadian settlement was more important than balanced budgets. Under S. N. Parent, however, the critics attacked a different aspect of the provincial administration. Parent had leased large areas of the province to pulp and lumber firms, as well as selling water-power rights to the highest bidder. This was not a new policy in the province, but Parent had been more successful than his predecessors in finding customers.[23] The "limits" were not sold but leased, so that in theory they did not interfere with colonization. A settler might obtain the concession of a lot within the "limit" and within a year the lumber merchant's right to cut trees on this lot was withdrawn.[24] In practice, however, there

[20] Ibid., W.L. to Willison, 29 Jan., 1904.

[21] Commons Debates, 15 April, 1907, 6743

[22] G. Vattier, Esquisse Historique de la colonization de la province de Québec (Paris, 1928), 96 ff.

[23] "Speech of the hon. S.N. Parent on the Pulp Question," (Québec, 1903), 39.

[24] Ibid., 37.

was usually friction between the settler and the limit-holder. This was a serious political problem because *nationaliste* sympathies were always with the settler, and it was easy to depict the government policy as a restriction upon the "rights" of the colonist whenever such friction developed.

The provincial Conservative party naturally took advantage of this situation to criticize the Parent government. Colonization became prominent in the Opposition platform. Thomas Chapais, son-in-law of Hector Langevin and former Castor,[25] was a leading Opposition critic of the Liberal colonization policy. "I accuse M. Parent of having dealt a fatal blow to the work of colonization in the province of Québec. I accuse him of having injured, if not mortally at least gravely, the prosperity of our country."[26] At the same time, the provincial Conservatives were assisted by the young *nationalistes* in the province. The platform of the *Ligue Nationaliste* of 1903, in addition to its emphasis on national autonomy, advocated a provincial policy which implied a criticism of Parent's administration. One clause of the platform read as follows:

Adoption by the provinces of a more active colonization policy and one more in harmony with their respective needs. Exclusive control by the Ministers of Colonization of the sale of lands for agricultural purposes.[27]

Bourassa, in his exposition of the *Ligue* platform, described colonization as the most important duty of the Quebec government, and denounced the sale of timber-limits and waterpower sites to speculators. A provincial Commission, appointed to study the problem of colonization, gave additional publicity to criticism of the treatment of the settlers, Conservatives, *nationalistes* and above all, Bourassa, appearing before the Commission to state their opinions.[28] Thus, as early as 1903, Bourassa and the provincial Conservatives were united in their criticism of Parent and the provincial Liberal government.

This apparent alliance between the *Ligue* and the provincial Conservatives was less obvious because even within the Liberal party there were severe critics of Parent. As one Liberal wrote to Laurier, "Apart from his colonization policy, I acknowledge and admit that Mons. Parent has been a good Premier; but the time has come when he must of necessity busy himself with the beautiful and

[25] Rumilly, *Histoire*, IV, 141.
[26] *Ibid.*, XI, 31; Speech, 30 Aug., 1903.
[27] *Canadian Annual Review, 1903*, 161.
[28] Rumilly, *Histoire*, XI, 114ff.

great cause of colonization."[29] Lemieux pointed out the danger that the dissatisfaction with Parent might harm the federal Liberal party.[30] Only the English Liberals in the province seem to have been well satisfied with Parent.[31] Laurier agreed that it was a serious problem, and admitted that he would have to concern himself with it,[32] but he was not eager to see Parent replaced, especially since there was no obvious successor.[33] So difficult was this problem that by 1904 Laurier had decided that he would have to select a successor in order to prevent factional quarrels.[34] However, 1904 was an election year, and apparently nothing was done. Then Parent himself took steps to strengthen his position. The day after the federal Liberal election victory, Parent announced that the provincial elections would be held at a date only three weeks away.[35] The provincial Conservatives decided to abstain in protest against this high-handed action – possibly influenced by the fact that their position was hopeless. Thirty-seven Liberals were elected by acclamation and in many other constituencies the contest was between Parent and anti-Parent candidates.[36] The result, apparently a sweeping victory for Parent, was less decisive than the Premier must have hoped. When the Assembly met, the dissident Liberals came to an agreement to depose him. His candidate for Speaker was defeated and after prolonged debates on colonization policy, he resigned, to be succeeded by Lomer Gouin.[37] Laurier, while officially neutral, had sympathised with Parent during the crisis[38] and had promptly appointed him chairman of the National Transcontinental Railway Commission after his resignation. Parent retained some of his political influence in the district of Quebec, continuing to deal with patronage problems there for many years,[39] but after 1905, Lomer Gouin shared with Laurier the leadership of the Liberal party in Quebec.

Laurier's relations with Gouin for the next few years were less intimate than with his predecessors. Gouin was too young for the

[28] Rumilly, *Histoire*, XI, 113ff.
[29] LP. C. Major to W. L., 24 Oct., 1903.
[30] *Ibid.*, Lemieux to W. L., 30 Nov., 1903.
[31] *Ibid.*, T. Trenholme to W. L., 15 Nov., 1903.
[32] *Ibid.*, W. L. to Sen. Lagris, 1 Dec., 1903.
[33] *Ibid.*, W. L. to W. Edwards, 31 March, 1904.
[34] *Ibid.*, W. L. to G. Langlois, 1 April, 1904.
[35] Rumilly, *Histoire*, XI, 185.
[36] *Ibid.*, 191.
[37] P. A. Choquette, *Un demi-siècle de la vie politique* (Montréal, 1936), 164 ff. has a detailed account of the conspiracy.
[38] LP, W. L. to G. Langlois, 11 Jan., 1905.
[39] LP, W. L. to Parent, 11 March, 1911.

close friendship developed among Liberals in Quebec who had shared the long years of almost hopeless opposition to the Conservatives; and he was a more independent and a more enterprising politician than Parent. Laurier's intimacy with Parent must also have affected Gouin's relations with Laurier. Certainly the two men observed a careful formality in their correspondence for some years, Gouin for example writing for permission to suggest a candidate for a judgeship before mentioning his candidate's name.[40] Gouin's independence is illustrated by his demands for increased provincial subsidies. Since the days of Gouin's father-in-law, Mercier, Quebec politicians had sought increased subsidies. Parent had even called an Interprovincial Conference in 1902,[41] although the federal government had ignored the resolutions passed. Gouin was less amenable, Laurier describing his insistence as showing "impatience or dictation".[42] However, since the *Ligue Nationaliste* platform had emphasized this question of federal subsidies,[43] and since additional expenditures on colonization would be facilitated by increased subsidies, Gouin may have believed that his agitation was a political necessity. At his instigation,[44] Laurier convened a Conference in 1906, and in 1907 the provincial subsidies were modified, the subsidy for the province of Quebec being increased by one-half.[45] There were subsequent incidents of less importance upon which Laurier and Gouin disagreed,[46] but as with the provincial subsidies, an agreement was always reached, and within a few years the two party leaders were firm political allies. In later years, Gouin became Laurier's principal adviser for the province of Quebec.[47]

The close connection between the provincial and federal Liberal parties was illustrated by a federal by-election in Quebec County in 1906. The Liberal party in the Quebec district had not yet recovered from the schism between the Parent and the anti-Parent factions. A Liberal candidate who was not identified with either faction was selected[48] and his nomination was arranged by the party

[40] LP, Gouin to W. L., 30 Sept., 1907.
[41] Canada, *Dominion-Provincial and Interprovincial Conferences, 1887-1926* (Ottawa, 1951), 31
[42] LP, W. L. to G. Murray, 30 Jan., 1906. 43 *Canadian Annual Review., 1903*, 160.
[44] LP, R. McBride to W. L., 4 Oct., 1905.
[45] W. Eggleston and C. T. Kraft, *Dominion-Provincial Subsidies and Grants* (Ottawa, 1939), 122.
[46] LP, W. L. to Gouin, 22 April, 1909, concerning the appointment of three additional judges for the district of Montreal.
[47] LP, W. L. to Gouin, 17 June, 1916.
[48] *Ibid.*, W. L. to H. Beland, 22 Oct., 1906.

leaders in the face of considerable local opposition.[49] As a rich non-resident,[50] he was not a popular candidate, and a local Liberal candidate refused to withdraw.[51] Bourassa and Lavergne took advantage of this situation to campaign vigorously for the independent Liberal. They avowed that they were sincere Liberals and true friends of Laurier,[52] but when their candidate was elected it was widely interpreted as a personal defeat for Laurier.[53] The division among the provincial Liberals had made possible this defeat in a federal by-election.

When Bourassa in 1907 began to devote himself to the colonization campaign in the province of Quebec, he had not yet admitted that he was opposing Laurier, explaining his Quebec County campaign as a campaign for an independent Liberal who, as a Liberal, could not be repugnant to Laurier.[54] Laurier, too, had avoided any direct repudiation of Bourassa. Armand Lavergne even suggests that Laurier tried to bring Bourassa into his Cabinet after the by-election,[55] but this is scarcely credible. Laurier did not want to alienate Bourassa but party loyalty would have been severely tested if he had been rewarded for his intransigence. Laurier's remarks to the editor of Le Soleil after the by-election suggest that instead of rewarding Bourassa, he recognised the fact that Bourassa was now a dangerous opponent. He did not believe that Bourassa had done himself any political harm by his campaign there.

I know that he is already very poorly regarded in certain quarters where things are carefully thought out. It is not the same, however, with the masses, as you know. He calls on all the passions and his appeals, supported by his fine talents, will do us harm, although in the long run, he will not manage to establish anything permanent and solid.[56]

Laurier's remarks concerning Armand Lavergne at this time might equally well have applied to Bourassa. "I regret as much as you the attitude taken by your M.P., M. Lavergne. He is simply separated from his party and we can no longer consider him one of ours."[57] Control of the patronage of the county was therefore transferred to a

[49] *Ibid.*, Lemieux to W. L., 9 Sept., 1906.
[50] *Ibid.*, G. Amyot to W. L., 21 Sept., 1906.
[51] *Ibid.*, L. Robitaille to W. L., 24 Sept., 1906.
[52] Rumilly, *Histoire*, xii, 175.
[53] *Ibid.*, 179.
[54] *Commons Debates*, 26 Nov., 1906, 107.
[55] Lavergne, *Trente ans*, 137.
[56] LP, W. L. to d'Hellencourt, 27 Oct., 1906.
[57] *Ibid.*, W. L. to L. Martineau, 30 Nov., 1906.

more loyal Liberal.[58] No more overt action was taken at this time. Laurier, with the temperament of a diplomat, could always meet opposition without irritation and without being tempted to issue a political challenge.

This armed truce became an undeclared war in 1907. In that year Bourassa, accompanied by Lavergne and other disciples, began a campaign against the provincial colonization policy. His slogan was "free land for a free settler," a phrase which had seen long service[59] but which was still effective. Bourassa advocated the creation of separate forest reserves and colonization regions in order to end the interference with the settler by the limit-holder. The reply of the government was that this was already being done.[60] But Bourassa's campaign was more denunciatory than constructive. A recent historian, not unsympathetic to Bourassa, describes it as becoming more and more violent.

He accused Gouin, Turgeon and Prévost of dishonouring the province. He left no stone unturned, using when required some newspaper insinuations, the complaints of discharged officials, and some gossip from unlucky settlers – with exaggerations mixed into a basis of truth. After each meeting, the corrections and denials came thick and fast . . . – Bourassa did not pay any attention, and continued, without altering his ways.[61]

So effective was Bourassa's campaign that Turgeon, Minister of Lands and Forests, challenged Bourassa to the political equivalent of a duel. Bourassa resigned from the House of Commons and Turgeon from the Assembly, and the two men fought a provincial by-election in Turgeon's constituency of Bellechasse. The campaign of vilification was intensified, even Bourassa later admitting that he had been unjust.[62] Bourassa was defeated in the by-election[63] but it was only a temporary set-back. In the provincial elections of the next year, he was elected in two constituencies, defeating Lomer Gouin himself in Saint-Jacques.[64] In provincial politics at least, Bourassa was undeniably an opponent of the Liberal party.

Within the provincial Liberal party, Bourassa's campaign had the effect of ending the schism between the Parent and the anti-Parent groups. A. Taschereau, once Parent's law-partner, entered

[58] *Ibid.*, W. L. to J. Lislois, 30 Nov., 1906.
[59] Rumilly, *Histoire*, XI, 118.
[60] L. Gouin, "Provincial Politics," (1907), 18, speech by A. Turgeon.
[61] Rumilly, *Histoire*, XIII, 88.
[62] *Ibid.*, XIII, 108, quoting *Le Devoir*, 4 Feb., 1930.
[63] *Ibid.*, 104.
[64] *Ibid.*, 151.

Gouin's Cabinet in 1907.[65] Nor did the federal Liberal party remain silent. In reply to one Liberal, Laurier expressed his "complete confidence in Gouin."

You mention as a conclusion of your letter that the ideal would be a Bourassa government in Québec and a Laurier government in Ottawa . . . but is that Bourassa's ideal? You know that it is nothing of the sort. . . . It is true that for the moment he does not attack me. How long will that last? I am going to tell you right away. That will last until the first difficulty I shall have to solve. What has happened in the past will happen in the future.[66]

At Gouin's suggestion, Laurier publicly asserted his confidence in Gouin's government and in Turgeon's honesty at the time of the Bellechasse by-election.[67] Bourassa continued to argue that federal and provincial politics should be dissociated and that Gouin should not be allowed to use Laurier's prestige to keep himself in power,[68] but the unity of the party was never in danger. In the province of Quebec a Liberal was a Liberal in both federal and provincial politics. By opposing Gouin, Bourassa had completely severed himself from Laurier.

As Bourassa's separation from the Liberal party increased, his connection with the provincial Conservative party became more apparent. After the provincial campaign of 1908, the defeated Opposition leader, E. Leblanc, was replaced by M. Tellier. Evariste Leblanc, later appointed Lieutenant-Governor of the province by Borden, was a loyal Conservative and a firm believer in party unity. Mathias Tellier was a less forceful character, more willing to cooperate with Bourassa and having more in common with Bourassa and his nationaliste policy.[69] Bourassa himself wrote in 1913 as follows:

With the provincial Conservatives, it was not difficult to agree—especially after the disappearance of M. Leblanc. The Conservatives accepted our program in its entirety; we would not claim in case of victory any share of the spoils: agreement was easy. But I had fairly warned these gentlemen that, while ready to make common cause with them in provincial politics, we would have nothing in common with the Tories of Ottawa.[70]

[65] *Ibid.*, 100.
[66] LP, W. L. to L. Brousseau, 24 Aug., 1907.
[67] *Ibid.*, W.L. to D. Roy, 29 Oct., 1907.
[68] Rumilly, *Histoire*, XIII, 144.
[69] *Ibid.*, XIV, 23.
[70] *Le Devoir*, 20 May, 1913.

Bourassa himself seems to have benefited from this alliance by a promise by Conservatives to give financial assistance for the founding of a newspaper for Bourassa, on condition that he himself run against Gouin in Saint Jacques.[71] Nevertheless, as Bourassa stated, his alliance was with the provincial Conservatives only. If he had become a Conservative it was a peculiar form of Conservatism. The policy was provincial in scope, based upon *nationalisme* and more specifically colonization, a policy which had no connection with the national Conservative program, and which most English Conservatives would have repudiated. Bourassa openly stated his hope that a new provincial party, independent of both Liberal and Conservative parties, would be created.[72] Under Tellier, the provincial Opposition party bore more resemblance to Bourassa's ideal than to a provincial Conservative party. The separation of the provincial from the federal Conservative party, which had been contemplated in 1905, was close to being realised.

Laurier believed that there was a close alliance between the Conservatives and the *Nationalistes*, as Bourassa and the youthful supporters of the Ligue Nationaliste were called,[73] but another aspect of the political developments within the province was suggested by Lemieux, who wrote that the support for Bourassa among the clergy as well as among the Conservatives, "lead me to believe that the Tory-Castor alliance is almost a *fait accompli*."[74] The danger that the Liberal party in Quebec would suffer from the opposition of the Roman Catholic church had declined since 1896. The contrast between the attitude of the episcopacy on the Manitoba school question and the Autonomy Bills is instructive. The Castor belief in the pre-eminence of religious problems in politics had not disappeared, but the Castor group had lost its political influence when the Conservative party forsook the minority in Manitoba. With the emergence of a provincial party dedicated to *nationalisme* it was possible for the Castors once more to unite in support of a political party. A comparison between the program of the *Ligue Nationaliste* of 1903[75] and the *Action Catholique de la Jeunesse Canadienne-française* of 1904[76] shows how easy it was for *nationalisme* to assume a religious emphasis. Both associations stated that loyalty to a political party meant the sacrifice of more important principles. Both associations referred to the importance of colonization. The

[71] Rumilly, *Histoire*, XIII, 138.
[72] *Ibid.*, XIV, 20; speech of 25 Feb., 1909.
[73] LP, W.L. to J. P. B. Casgrain, 26 May, 1908.
[74] *Ibid.*, Lemieux to W.L., 8 May, 1907.
[75] *Canadian Annual Review 1903*, 160, 326.
[76] Rumilly, *Histoire*, XI, 158.

activities of two such associations help to explain the ovations received by Bourassa when campaigning for a better colonization program.

In this connection, it must be remembered that the old suspicion of the Liberal party had never disappeared. In addition to the Liberal compromises on the school questions, provincial issues had helped to keep it alive. Lomer Gouin for instance, was suspected of wanting to create a secular Department of Education,[77] and in spite of his denials, opposition candidates continued to repeat the accusation.[78] Then too, G. Langlois, editor of *Le Canada*, the official Liberal newspaper in Montreal since 1903, was believed to be a republican and an anti-clerical[79] and was finally replaced as editor by a less radical man.[80] Suspicion of the Liberal party was in no way dissipated by the weekly *Le Pays* which Langlois began to publish, and which openly advocated secular education.[81] On the other hand, Bourassa was completely acceptable to those with Castor principles. His anti-Imperialist policy, his denunciation of the Autonomy Bills compromise, and above all, his ardent colonization campaign were as much Castor as *nationaliste* in principle. Bourassa was doubtless correct when he stated that he had not directly sought the support of the clergy, but as he explained, the French-Canadian priests supported the *nationaliste* program because they had nationalist sentiments.[82] *Nationalisme*, founded on race and religion, had found a leader.

The return of Castor attitudes into practical politics is illustrated by the founding of an official daily newspaper for the Archdiocese of Quebec, *L'Action Sociale*. In the Pastoral Letter announcing the new enterprise, Archbishop Bégin explained that the newspaper would place itself above political parties, "discussing political things only with a prudent independence, preoccupied above all with the triumph of the religious idea and of social justice."[83] Laurier however, was certain that the newspaper would be politically partisan.

It is the old movement which begins again after an interval of a decade. This movement will result, as it has always resulted, in a vast exploitation of the clergy who, heedless of past experience, will allow themselves to be fleeced. This new newspaper will be

---

[77] *Ibid.*, 219.

[78] "Provincial Politics" (1907), 12; speech by A. Turgeon.

[79] *L'Action Sociale*, 17 July, 1908.

[80] Rumilly, *Histoire*, XIV, 121.

[81] *Ibid.*, 122.

[82] *Le Devoir*, 28 Jan., 1911.

[83] "L'Action Sociale Catholique," (Québec, 1907), quoting Pastoral Letter, 31 March, 1907.

*like all the other publications of this type; it will end with a
resounding crash. Until then it will do a great deal of harm.*[84]

Certainly it was not long before *L'Action Sociale* was carrying on a
public controversy with the Liberal newspapers in the province.[85] It
might be argued that the fault lay with the Liberals who were
prompt to find partisan opinions where none may have been intended,[86] but the fact that two of the editors were *nationalistes* and
disciples of Bourassa suggests that political impartiality was unlikely. On the colonization question especially, *L'Action Sociale* was in
sympathy with Bourassa. It supported his criticisms of the federal
immigration policy,[87] it criticized the colonization achievements of
the provincial government,[88] and it extolled the idea of "free land
for a free settler."[89] Despite Laurier's prophecy, the newspaper
survived, and was to play an important political role in the future.

Bourassa's intervention in provincial politics is of great importance in the history of the Liberal party in Quebec. Of the two
national parties, the Liberals under Laurier were supreme in the
province. Laurier's personal popularity was well established, and his
policies were at least preferable to those of the Conservatives. Bourassa was a brilliant orator, and when he had opposed Laurier it had
been to advocate a policy more popular in Quebec, but as long as
he remained a Liberal, independent or otherwise, he could accomplish little. Certainly he could never convert either national party to
his policies. In provincial politics he could be more influential. His
importance as an ally had accelerated the separation of the provincial Conservative party from the national party. He had become the
spokesman if not the official leader of a political party. His emphasis on the importance of colonization might weld Castors and *nationalistes* into a party which could utilize the provincial Conservative party organization and could conceivably become the majority
party in the province of Quebec. It is true that Gouin and the
provincial Liberals had won the elections of 1908 by a large majority but a few more years of agitation might have been effective.
Certainly the provincial session of 1909 was a stormy one, in which
the government was on the defensive.[90] Bourassa failed to persevere
—in practical politics, at least, Laurier may well have been correct in
saying that he "certainly will not succeed in establishing anything

[84] LP, W. L. to d'Hellencourt, 27 April, 1907.
[85] *L'Action Sociale*, 24 Oct., 1908.
[86] Rumilly, *Histoire*, III, 119.
[87] *L'Action Sociale*, 6 July, 1908.
[88] *Ibid.*, 12 Nov., 1908.
[89] *Ibid.*, 1 Dec., 1908.
[90] Rumilly, *Histoire*, XIV, 35.

permanent and solid."[91] By 1910, Bourassa was once more concentrating upon a federal issue. But between 1907 and 1910 he had accomplished a good deal. To many he had become almost the personification of *nationalisme*. He had discarded his compromising affiliation with the Liberal party, and had close connections with an organized political group. By 1910, Bourassa had become a much more potent political force than he had ever been before.

[91] LP, W.L. to d'Hellencourt, 27 Oct., 1906.

11.
The Naval Bill

The Conference of 1902 had not solved the problem of defending the Empire, although it had removed it from Canadian politics for some years. With the ambitious German naval construction program, the defence of the Empire became once more an urgent issue. British naval supremacy was considered more important than military efficiency for the preservation of the Empire, and so Imperialists became more concerned about the danger than they had been in 1902. As Lord Grey pointed out, sixty million Germans might well defeat forty million Englishmen in a naval armaments race. "The danger menacing the Empire appears to be sufficiently grave to call for consultation between the governments of its component self-governing parts, as to what steps shall be taken to secure the continuance of our naval supremacy."[1] Laurier was no more anxious than he had been in 1902 to become involved in the vortex of militarism; his "well-known horror of war"[2] and his faith in reasonable compromise as a solution to controversies had not been weakened by the responsibilities of office. On the general question of Imperialism, however, his attitude had gradually changed. In 1890 he had believed that Canadian independence was inevitable and even imminent. By 1909 the goal of independence had been modified to autonomy within the Empire, with independence as no more than a distant eventuality. He is quoted as having written in 1911 that "We are making for a harbour which was not the harbour I foresaw twenty-five years ago, but it is a good harbour. It will not be the end."[3] Laurier had made no attempt to accelerate the ship of state. At the Conferences he had opposed any constitutional changes within the Empire. As he said when defending his Naval Bill, no change was necessary.

Well, if we were in a position of inferiority, if we were not a nation when we have a population of eight millions, I would say that we would have to ask for a revision of the connection which unites us to Great Britain. We are not in that position. The two things are compatible . . .[4]

[1] LP, Grey to W.L., 3 May, 1909.
[2] *Ibid.*, 10 Jan., 1910.
[3] Skelton, *Laurier*, II, 290.
[4] A. D. DeCelles, ed., *Discours de Sir Wilfrid Laurier, 1889-1911* (Montréal, 1920), 166, speech of 30 Oct., 1910.

There had been no sudden transition in Laurier's attitude towards the Empire. In the 1890's he had been impatient to clarify the anomalous relationship, but twenty years later he could accept the anomaly calmly since it caused no inconvenience.

The naval issue forced Laurier again to consider the problem of Imperial relations. With his confidence that British diplomacy was peaceful in intention, he could agree with Canadian Imperialists that British naval supremacy was desirable.

That the superiority of the British navy should be maintained at its present strength over all nations is a proposition to which I am quite prepared to agree, but this policy should not be taken up in a panic. . . . The whole Canadian people will stand behind England in her troubles if it comes to that, but we are very far from that.[5]

He would have liked to evade the question, to have believed that the German danger was being exaggerated in England.

I should like to find out exactly what is going on and know the root cause. Is this movement of military imperialism simply an election ploy, or is it really a serious preparation, on Germany's part, for taking England by the throat, as it did with France?[6]

The decision was made to allocate funds for naval defence, so we may assume that Laurier had decided that the German threat could not be ignored. Nevertheless his naval policy cannot be described as an Imperialist policy. Once more, Laurier sought a compromise.

His policy had been foreshadowed at the Colonial Conference of 1902. On that occasion, Laurier had refused to consider a direct contribution to the British Navy in spite of the argument that this would be the most efficient policy. The Canadian delegates submitted a memorandum which acknowledged that Canada should accept an increasing responsibility for its naval defence,[7] but Laurier explained that the government was "contemplating the establishment of a local naval force in the waters of Canada. . . ."[8] In the same year, Borden expressed a similar view.

I took the stand . . . in 1900, when I was speaking only for myself, in favour of a Canadian Naval Militia. It seems to me that a proposal of this kind is likely to encounter less opposition in the

[5] LP, W.L. to G. Wrong, 25 March, 1909.
[6] *Ibid.*, W.L. to Dansereau, 11 June, 1909.
[7] *Papers relating to a Conference between the Secretary of State for the Colonies and the Prime Ministers of Self-governing Colonies, June to August, 1902* (London, 1902, Cd. 1299), 74.
[8] *Ibid.*, 18.

province of Quebec than any other form of assistance to the naval defence of the Empire.[9]

But to Laurier no naval expenditure seemed the best policy of all, and in 1907 the government had not passed the stage of "contemplating" the establishment of a local navy. Laurier attended the Conference of that year with the intention of resisting "the highly sentimental fads of Imperialism and militarism ..."[10] and in London he defeated a resolution favoring naval commitments by the Dominions.[11] By 1909, however, the German naval threat in Europe, and the Imperialist sentiment roused by it in Canada, ended the procrastination.

The government was committed to some form of naval expenditure in 1909. George Foster introduced a resolution that Canada should accept the financial responsibility for the defence of her seacoast.[12] Laurier substituted a resolution which rejected any regular financial contributions to the Imperial treasury but approved of "the organisation of a Canadian naval service in co-operation with and in close relation to the British navy ... and in full sympathy with the view that the naval supremacy of Great Britain is essential to the security of commerce, the safety of the empire and the peace of the world."[13] Robert Borden suggested minor amendments, and the resolution was then passed unanimously.[14] With this unanimous support for its policy of a separate navy, the government was in a strong position to negotiate the details of its composition with the Admiralty.

Laurier still feared that the British authorities would insist on an integrated Imperial navy. When F. W. Borden and Brodeur left for the Naval Conference of 1909, he expressed his apprehension. "I confess that I am somewhat nervous as to the outcome of the Conference ... A big effort will be made to bring us into the maelstrom. I am confident however, that you and Brodeur will weather the storm successfully."[15] Laurier was right. Brodeur informed him that the Admiralty wanted them to begin by supplying a dreadnought and then three cruisers instead of beginning on a small scale with coastal protection units.[16] It is interesting that Brodeur's objec-

[9] Borden Papers, Memoir Notes, Vol. 7, 5666, Borden to W. Evans, 16 Dec., 1902.
[10] LP, W.L. to J. Young, 22 Feb., 1907.
[11] *Minutes of the Proceedings of the Imperial Conference of 1907* (London, 1907, Cd. 3523), 542.
[12] *Commons Debates*, 29 Mar., 1909, 3484.
[13] *Ibid.*, 3512.
[14] *Ibid.*, 3564.
[15] LP, W.L. to F. W. Borden, 17 July, 1909.
[16] *Ibid.*, Brodeur to W.L., 10 Aug., 1909.

tion to this plan was not that the province of Quebec would oppose it, but that the new Canadians on the prairies, and especially those of American origin, were hostile to such militarism.[17] This analysis of western sentiment was widespread.[18] Laurier agreed with Brodeur that the Amiralty's recommendations were unacceptable, and he would not even consent to a resolution that the Canadian Navy, "designed for local purposes", should be so organised as to be able to render aid in any emergency "which might threaten the integrity of the Empire."[19] It was not that Laurier was opposed to this principle, but that he considered it impolitic to draw attention to the proposition. F. W. Borden and Fielding had been willing to accept the resolution but after Laurier's advice agreed that it was inopportune.[20] The result of the Conference was all that Laurier had hoped. The Admiralty acceded to the proposals of the Canadian delegates to create a partial fleet unit which did not include a dreadnought, and which was therefore more suitable for coastal defence than for Imperial naval strategy. Nor was there any official commitment of the Canadian navy for Imperial defence. Laurier was pleased, believing that the Canadian "jingoist" sentiment had suffered a complete defeat. He expected opposition from urban centres such as Toronto and Halifax, but believed that elsewhere the results would be welcomed.[21] As a diplomatic precaution, he advised against any organised demonstrations in the province of Quebec to welcome Brodeur on his return, since he saw no need for emphasizing the defeat of the Imperialists.[22] Clearly, he believed that his compatriots would rejoice at this latest victory over the forces of Imperialism, and that the most serious opposition would come from the Canadian Imperialists.

The Naval Service Act of 1910 in no way modified the policy that Laurier had already adopted. By this Act, Canadian naval forces could only be placed on active service when the Governor in Council decided that an emergency had arisen, and if such a state of emergency was declared, Parliament was to meet within the next fifteen days to sanction the measures taken if it saw fit to do so.[23] Thus the navy was truly Canadian. The Act also authorized the

[17] Ibid.
[18] J. S. Ewart, "Canadian Independence," The Kingdom Papers (Ottawa, 1911), 18. A. Siegfried, The Race Question in Canada (London, 1907), 260.
[19] LP, Brodeur to W.L., 13 Aug., 1909, W.L. to Brodeur, 16 Aug., 1909.
[20] Ibid., Brodeur to W.L., 26 Aug., 1909.
[21] Ibid., W.L. to Brodeur, 26 Aug., 1909.
[22] Ibid., W.L. to Dandurand, 23 Aug., 1909.
[23] Statutes of Canada, 9-10 Edw. VII, c. 43, s. 22 and 24.

Governor in Council to place the Canadian navy at the disposal of the British Admiralty, although this was not obligatory.[24] In this way, Canada could rally to the defence of the Empire if it appeared necessary or desirable. Laurier had described the question of coastal defence as primarily a Canadian problem, but also affected by the responsibility of Canadians as British subjects,[25] and the Bill translated this principle into specific terms.

"When Great Britain is at war, Canada is at war."[26] In this dictum, Laurier expressed Canada's anomalous position in international diplomacy. A nation at war with Great Britain would make no distinction between Great Britain and the rest of the Empire. Hence the need to authorize the executive to declare a state of emergency. As Laurier said the state of "emergency" was a specific legal term, defined by law, which made it impossible for the Governor in Council to place the navy on active service arbitrarily.[27] Nonetheless, Laurier's dictum so shocked some of his compatriots that on the second reading he made it clear that this was simply a principle of international law, and that Canada would participate actively in any war only if circumstances seemed to make it desirable.[28] At the same time he found it necessary to correct another misapprehension. To charges made in the province of Quebec that recruiting for the navy would involve conscription he gave a blunt denial.[29] Since the Naval Service Bill was clear on this point,[30] Laurier was on firm ground. The Liberals at least found Laurier's arguments convincing, and all in the House voted for the measure.

Nevertheless, the unanimity of the political parties at the time of the Resolutions of 1909 was not maintained. In 1909 Robert Borden had assured his Quebec supporters that the Conservatives did not propose to spend money building dreadnoughts; like Laurier, he believed that "the subject must be approached as one of Canadian rather than Imperial concern."[31] When the details of the Naval Bill became known however, Borden canvassed prominent Conservatives for their reaction to the idea of a dreadnought contribution to the Imperial fleet in addition to the building of a Canadian naval force. Opinion from Quebec was definitely hostile,[32] but Bor-

---

[24] *Ibid.*, s. 23.
[25] *Commons Debates*, 15 Nov., 1909, 49.
[26] *Ibid.*, 12 Jan., 1910, 1734.
[27] *Ibid.*, 1734.
[28] *Ibid.*, 3 Feb., 1910, 2965.
[29] *Ibid.*, 2976.
[30] *Statutes of Canada*, 9-10 Edw. VII, c. 43, s. 12 and 21.
[31] Borden Papers, Memoir Notes, Vol. 12, 6563, Borden to T.C. Casgrain, 26 March, 1909.
[32] *Ibid.*, Vol. 13, 6755, T.C. Casgrain to Borden, 4 Dec. 1909.

den apparently decided to ignore this section of his party. As a conciliatory gesture he recommended that the people should first be consulted as to the desirability of a permanent Canadian service,[33] but he already knew that this was not enough to prevent the French-Canadian Conservatives from voting against his amendment.[34] This was because Borden's policy was clearly more Imperialistic than Laurier's. Borden criticized the clause which permitted the Governor in Council to decide whether the Canadian navy would support the British fleet, for if it was decided not to intervene, "such inaction or declaration will amount virtually to a declaration of independence"[35] – a catastrophe shocking to think of – and while the proposal to submit the issue to the people might be interpreted as anti-militarist, his proposal to donate to the Admiralty the cost of two dreadnoughts[36] could not. Laurier's fear that his policy would be opposed by the "Jingoists" was justified.

Laurier, however, miscalculated when he assumed that the opposition would come only from the Imperialists. Since there was officially only one Opposition party, this was a natural assumption, but the fact was that there were now two such parties. The separation of the French-Canadian Conservatives from the national party was completed in 1910. With the passage of time, there had been a gradual change in the personnel of the Quebec Conservative members, and by 1910 a new group had appeared who knew not Macdonald. The last link with this era of traditional French-English co-operation within the Conservative party had disappeared when Bergeron retired from politics after his defeat in 1908. F. D. Monk was now the unchallenged leader of the French-Canadian section of the party – Monk, whom Laurier in 1902 had believed to be "trying to create a national French party."[37] Laurier may have exaggerated the narrowness of Monk's outlook, but certainly Monk was not willing to compromise his *nationalisme* for the interests of party unity. In January of 1909, Borden tacitly recognized the division within the party. At a conference with his French-Canadian supporters he expressed his readiness "to accept and co-operate with" whatever leader the group selected. He agreed to Monk's proviso that the party would "be obliged to carry out any promise within reason" which Monk might make, and so Monk became leader of

[33] *Commons Debates*, 3 Feb., 1910, 2991.
[34] Borden Papers, Memoir Notes, Vol. 13, 6787, Monk to Borden, 28 Jan., 1910.
[35] *Commons Debates*, 3 Feb., 1910, 29850.
[36] *Ibid.*, 2991.
[37] Minto Papers, Vol. 1, 73, Memo. of conversation, 28 Jan., 1902.

the French-Canadian members.[38] Monk apparently had in mind the possibility of some agreement with Bourassa, for at the same meeting he said that he disagreed with Bourassa's idea of a French-Canadian political party, but believed that Bourassa had modified his views since 1896. The meeting agreed that "without making any alliance with him for the present we could work on parallel lines."[39] In view of the English Conservatives' opinion of Bourassa, this was a remarkable concession. This meeting may be considered the first formal recognition within the party that Monk was no longer a lieutenant but a political ally, and that the French-Canadian Conservatives had a policy distinct from the national Conservative party.

It was not long before this divided leadership was revealed by the difference in political policy. In November of 1909, Monk condemned any naval expenditures as useless, the money being better spent on developing Canada's natural resources.[40] On the first reading of the Naval Service Bill he explained his acquiescence in the resolutions of 1909 as a fear of suggesting that he was willing to desert Great Britain in a time of panic.[41] The panic – "probably artificially created" – had now subsided,[42] and he intended to oppose any policy which would involve Canada in Imperial wars. Monk wrote to Borden that he had conferred with French-Canadian Conservatives.

The convictions we hold upon the naval question differ so greatly from those of our fellow members on our side of the House that it would be difficult to meet on common ground and I think it is perhaps better for each to follow our own course. We feel that we must oppose the principle of the bill uncompromisingly.[43]

On the second reading he moved that the Bill "changes the relations of Canada with the Empire" and so should first be submitted to the people by means of a plebiscite.[44] Monk and six other French Canadians voted for his amendment and then voted with the Liberals against Borden's amendment.[45] The French-Canadian Conservatives did not find it necessary to waste their time denouncing

[38] Borden Papers, Memoir Notes, Vol. 12, 1612, T.C. Casgrain's Memo. of the conversation, 28 Jan., 1909.
[39] *Ibid.*, 6511.
[40] Rumilly, *Histoire*, XIV, 98.
[41] *Commons Debates*, 12 Jan., 1910, 1771.
[42] *Ibid.*, 1772.
[43] Borden Papers, Memoir Notes, Vol. 13, 6787. Monk to Borden, 28 Jan., 1910.
[44] *Commons Debates*, 3 Feb., 1910, 3022.
[45] *Ibid.*, 9 Mar., 1910.

Borden's policy in their own province – condemning the Liberal policy kept them occupied – but they would not consider any face-saving compromise to maintain party unity. Even the proposed national Conservative convention of 1910 had to be cancelled because the French-Canadian attitude would have been too disruptive.[46]

Although Monk was the official leader of the Quebec Conservatives, Bourassa soon became their acknowledged spokesman. A year after the meeting which had decided that Monk and Bourassa would work along "parallel lines", these parallel lines had clearly merged. The money for Bourassa's newspaper was finally subscribed, and Le Devoir began publication before the second reading of the Naval Service Bill. For the first time, Bourassa's political influence extended beyond those who were able to attend his political meetings, and for the first time, Bourassa became openly critical of Laurier. No longer was Laurier a man of good intentions who compromised his principles because he was weak or because his followers lacked principles; now his principles were at fault and his speeches were no more than "golden clouds in which M. Laurier envelops the betrayals, weaknesses and dangers of his policy."[47] And most treasonous and dangerous of all his policies was the Naval Bill.

As with the South African War, Bourassa and Laurier did not differ greatly on the broad principles involved. On the issue of Imperialism, Bourassa too had believed that Canada would eventually become independent but that her status within the Empire was satisfactory for the moment.[48] Bourassa would never have accepted the view expressed in the Resolutions of 1909, that British naval supremacy was essential to the safety of the Empire or the peace of the world. He had no such confidence in the intentions of British governments. Nor did the safety of the Empire or the peace of the world seem important to him as a Canadian. According to Bourassa, the Naval Bill would involve Canada in the wars provoked by the Chamberlains and the Rhodeses, the Canadian Parliament being able only to approve once our forces were committed.[49] As for the German peril it was an illusion, and even if it did exist, it was no affair of Canada's. "Did the Imperial authorities consult us when they prepared this situation?"[50] To the argument that Canada

[46] Borden, Memoirs, I, 263.
[47] Le Devoir, 11 Jan., 1910.
[48] "Great Britain and Canada" (1902), 46.
[49] "Le projet de loi navale," (Montréal, 1910), 9, speech of 20 Jan., 1910.
[50] Ibid., 15.

was being protected by the British fleet and that we should accept a share of the burden, he replied that England would have to maintain her naval supremacy even if Canada was independent, and furthermore that Canada could only be threatened by one power, the United States, and that Great Britain would be unable and unwilling to provide protection in such a crisis. *"England will never fire a shot in our defence against the United States."*[51] As for other potential enemies, "the Monroe Doctrine is our best defence."[52] Thus the naval expenditure was a useless waste of money. But much more serious were the constitutional consequences of the Naval Bill. This participation in Imperial wars would necessarily lead to a compensation to Canada in the form of Imperial preference for Canadian wheat, and then to Imperial Federation.[53]

To some extent Laurier would have agreed with Bourassa's isolationism. He had been suspicious of the gulf of European militarism[54] and he believed that with only one neighbor and with no territorial ambitions, Canada would never precipitate a war.[55] But Laurier differed with Bourassa as to Canada's ability to decide for herself whether it was necessary to become involved in a British war. Bourassa believed that a Governor-General such as Lord Grey, an ardent Imperialist and an able diplomat, could manipulate his advisers.[56] Laurier not unnaturally disagreed, and there was some justification in his claim that he had confidence in Canada's autonomy whereas Bourassa had suspected the motives of British Imperialists; the next decade had not altered his views on this subject, but by 1910 he had also lost faith in the compromising Laurier.

In the province of Quebec the re-alignment of political groups in provincial politics was now duplicated in federal politics. The official opposition party, under Monk, coalesced with the *nationalistes*, and the new party accepted Bourassa as spokesman. As in provincial politics, the new party was supported by many clergymen in the Roman Catholic church. *L'Action Sociale* from the beginning had denounced the Naval Bill in its editorial columns. It was described as a regression by which Canada would lose its rights and become a recruiting ground for soldiers and sailors to fight Imperial wars. "And the only duty of a colony towards its metropolis is to

[51] *Ibid.*, 22, The italics are Bourassa's.
[52] *Ibid.*, 20.
[53] *Ibid.*, 30.
[54] *Commons Debates*, 15 Apr., 1902, 2759.
[55] *Ibid.*, 29 Mar., 1909, 3504.
[56] "Le Projet de Loi Navale", 34.
[57] DeCelles, ed., *Discours, 1889-1911*, 164, speech of 30 Oct., 1910.,

remain loyal, to see to its own individual development, save for repelling an enemy when he comes to attack her."[58] Like Bourassa, it believed that the only hope was that the members of Parliament would assert their independence and fight this Imperialism.[59] Laurier was prompt to appeal to higher authorities. As he reminded the Papal Delegate, this newspaper "was to be absolutely non-political, and exclusively to guide the faithful on religious questions. The policy of the creation of a navy is a matter which in no way concerns the object for which L'Action Sociale was ostensibly founded. Its present attitude is a flagrant abuse. . . . "[60]

Laurier took the situation seriously. He believed that the attitude of the clergy would once again lead to politico-religious strife. "I doubt, whatever one may do, that one can stop the course of events. It will be stopped as it was in '78 and in '97, later, in some years' time, when the position again will have become intolerable."[61] Lemieux was sent to Rome to explain the situation to Cardinal del Val. Dandurand, who could not accompany him, sent Lemieux a letter in which he analysed the situation much as Laurier had done in the 1880's. According to Dandurand, the classical colleges in the province of Quebec were French-Canadian to the exclusion of all else, and the clergy, when they left the colleges for the parish, might never come into contact with the English Canadians. The result was that they were unaware of any differing political philosophy, and could not comprehend the danger of interfering in a political question in such a way as to suggest to the majority that the Roman Catholic clergy were disloyal.[62] This appeal to Rome, and a subsequent petition by provincial Liberals against the political intervention of L'Action Sociale had little effect. Archbishop Bégin's reply was publicly to commend the editors for their adherence to the program of the newspaper.[63]

Some of the Liberal protests were no doubt exaggerated. Murphy and Lemieux became so perturbed that they saw evidence of "an insidious campaign"[64] in incidents which seem to have been completely non-political. One such incident was the Eucharistic Congress held at Montreal in 1910. According to Murphy, Archbishop Bruchési refused to admit that there was an anti-Laurier campaign or that it was being tacitly supported by the clergy. This

[58] L'Action Sociale, 22 Dec., 1909.
[59] Ibid., 12 Nov., 1909.
[60] LP, W. L. to Sbarretti, 28 Dec., 1909.
[61] Ibid., W. L. to Lemieux, 10 Aug., 1910.
[62] Lemieux Papers, Dandurand to Lemieux, 9 Sept., 1910.
[63] Rumilly, Histoire, xvi, 32.
[64] LP 173813, Lemieux, to W. L., 11 Aug., 1910.

in itself seemed suspicious![65] The invitation to Bourassa to speak at the Congress was easily interpreted as an indication that this feigned neutrality was concealing an anti-Liberal attitude, and that even the Eucharistic Congress was being used for political purposes.[66] Lemieux even believed that Bruchési was inspiring the policy of *Le Devoir*![67] Laurier naturally restrained his lieutenants. "It would seem to me more and more manifest that another religious war is now unavoidable. We would have, however, this great advantage which we did not have before, that cooler heads in the clergy will not sympathise with these belligerents."[68] Certainly there was no clerical intervention comparable to that of the 1890's. The Bishop of Joliet wrote to Laurier that as a private citizen, a Canadian navy seemed to him premature in view of the expense, but as a Bishop it appeared to be a political issue and so none of his business,[69] and this attitude of personal misgiving but official neutrality seems to have been general among the episcopacy.

Bourassa and *Le Devoir* did much to strengthen this personal sympathy among the clergy for his opposition to Laurier's policy. Two members of the editorial staff of *Le Devoir*, Omer Heroux and Georges Pelletier, had previously been on the staff of *L'Action Sociale*;[70] two other editorial writers, Olivar Asselin and Jules Fournier, *Nationalistes* with anti-clerical tendencies, were soon dismissed by Bourassa.[71] *Le Devoir* published articles written by priests on religious and educational problems.[72] Bourassa's resounding defence of the French-Canadian Roman Catholic church at the Eucharistic Congress[73] helped to strengthen the impression that Bourassa and *Le Devoir* provided an official expression of the views of the clergy. Almost as much as *L'Action Sociale, Le Devoir* gained the reputation of being the orthodox Roman Catholic newspaper; among the clergy and the colleges of the province it was often the only newspaper read.[74]

During the summer of 1910, Bourassa continued his campaign against Laurier's naval policy in *Le Devoir* and at political meetings. The most important was held in July at St. Eustache – a place

[65] *Ibid.*, Murphy to W. L., 20 Aug., 1910.
[66] P. A. C., C. Murphy Papers, Murphy to Bishop Fallon, 25 Aug., 1910.
[67] LP 173815, Lemieux to W. L., 11 Aug., 1910.
[68] *Ibid.*, W. L. to Murphy, 28 Aug., 1910.
[69] *Ibid.*, Mgr. Archambeault to W. L., 8 Feb., 1910.
[70] Rumilly, *Histoire*, XIV, 115.
[71] *Ibid.*, 153.
[72] LP 173815, Lemieux to W. L., 11 Aug., 1910.
[73] Rumilly, *Histoire*, XV, 114.
[74] LP, F. Béique to W. L., 20 Nov., 1910.

where emotional appeals to *nationalisme* were re-inforced by the
memories of 1837. At this meeting, federal members such as Monk,
Nantel and Blondin appeared on the platform with Bourassa.
Bourassa's speech was a tirade against Laurier, the man whom
Bourassa had loved, but who had destroyed the right of the Roman
Catholics to educate their children in the faith and who now sought
to push French Canadians into Imperialism.

*I say when a man, whatever his personal qualities may be, when a
man scorns at such a time the confidence and love a people have
placed in him, in order to betray with one blow all his own people,
I say that a man like that is more dangerous for his faith, for his
country, and even for the British Crown, than the worst of Orangemen.*[75]

It had been many years since anyone had dared to call Laurier a
traitor to his race and a danger to his faith in the province of
Quebec!

The Resolutions of St. Eustache, drafted by Bourassa and approved by Monk,[76] were passed at this and at succeeding political
meetings. They were more restrained than the speeches. They expressed opposition to this new policy, which would involve Canada
in foreign wars, as long as Canada had no influence over British
diplomacy.[77] This was the hallowed principle of "no taxation without representation". In view of Bourassa's criticism of Laurier's
policy as too Imperialist and even tending towards Imperial Federation, it is surprising to find these Resolutions advocating Imperial
Federation, at least by implication. In the enthusiasm of Bourassa's
political assemblies such a logical criticism would have gone un-
heard.

Meanwhile, Laurier was making a triumphant tour through prairie settlements by a railway for which his government could take
much of the credit – "in his official chariot, as the Caesars of other
days toured the provinces," according to Bourassa.[78] Laurier was
under no illusion that his naval policy was popular but, confident
that it was the right policy, he assumed that moderate men would
accept it,[79] and that the appeal to the opposite prejudices of Eng-
lish- and French-speaking Canada would not succeed.[80] Laurier
had written to the editor of *Le Canada* that the best reply to

[75] Rumilly, *Histoire*, xv, 74, speech of 17 July, 1910.

[76] Bourassa, "Le *Devoir*, son origine, son passé, son avenir," (1915).

[77] Rumilly, *Histoire*, xv, 70.

[78] *Ibid.*, 74.

[79] LP, W.L. to J. Ewart, 15 March, 1910.

[80] *Ibid.*, W.L. to J. Pouliot, 4 March, 1910.

Bourassa was to reprint articles from the Opposition press in Ontario.[81] These tactics had been successful in prior campaigns, but since Bourassa was in no way identified with the English Conservative policy, they were to prove less effective this time. The reports from Quebec during the tour were not reassuring, and many Liberals advised Laurier to make an aggressive reply to Bourassa on his return.[82] Even Lord Grey reported that Laurier's friends in Quebec felt that "the Bourassa Bubble has been allowed to blow too big."[83]

Laurier made the speech in Montreal at the end of October. He defended his naval policy as being a national duty, pointing out that it was consistent with his policy at the Conference of 1902, at which time even Bourassa had been satisfied.[84] He repeated his assertion that enlistment would be voluntary,[85] and that participation would be at the decision of the government of Canada,[86] while at the same time defending his assertion that "*we must aid England with all our strength*" if English naval supremacy was threatened.[87] But the speech was not merely a defence of his policy; it was also an attack on the opposition. According to Laurier, in the next election the Conservatives planned to have "as many programs as there are provinces."[88] In the province of Quebec, the Conservative party was now composed of Castors; "the Pharisees of Canadian Catholicism, those who set themselves up with ostentation as the defenders of religion, which no one attacks; those who handle the holy water sprinkler like a club, those who have arrogated to themselves the monopoly on orthodoxy" the group who had betrayed Chapleau in the past. With them were now some young Liberals, who "having nothing Liberal in their nature, have found, after several efforts at groping in the dark, their true home in the waters of the Castors."[89] As in the years of Opposition, Laurier denounced the so-called nationalist policy of creating an exclusively French-Canadian party; once more he waxed eloquent about the principle of national unity.[90] It was Bourassa, not Monk, who was treated as the leader of the Quebec Opposition, Bourassa's speeches that were quoted and

[81] *Ibid.*, W.L. to Rinfret, 21 Jan., 1910.
[82] *Ibid.*, J. Prévost to W.L., 8 Sept., 1910; Dandurand to W.L., 4 Oct., 1910.
[83] LP, Grey to W.L., 9 Oct., 1910.
[84] DeCelles, ed., *Discours, 1899-1911*, 155, speech of 30 Oct., 1910.
[85] *Ibid.*, 173.
[86] *Ibid.*, 165.
[87] *Ibid.*, 192. The italics were added by DeCelles.
[88] *Ibid.*, 147.
[89] *Ibid.*, 149.
[90] *Ibid.*, 202.

refuted, Bourassa's policy that was criticized, Laurier had accepted the challenge.

The by-election of Drummond-Arthabaska may well have been another attempt to prick the "Bourassa Bubble". Since 1887, it had returned a Liberal member. In the federal election of 1900, it alone in the province had returned a member by acclamation;[91] in 1904 the Liberal majority for Louis Lavergne had been almost 2,500; in 1908 it was 800 over an independent Liberal opponent. In a campaign which would involve Laurier's character as well as his policy, the constituency could be expected to remain loyal, for Laurier had once represented Drummond-Arthabaska and usually spent his summer holiday at Arthabaska. And Laurier knew local conditions quite well, on rare occasions advising Lavergne as to patronage.[92] On the other hand, Louis Lavergne had not been successful in his political management. Lavergne was notorious for soliciting patronage for his constituents, – in Laurier's words, "Lavergne is never done asking …"[93] – but his distribution of favors had been restricted to a faction in the constituency, and much ill-feeling had been aroused.[94] This accounts for the independent Liberal candidate in 1908, of whom Laurier said "He is going to be beaten in this election, but he is going to sow the seeds of a division which is will be difficult to heal later."[95] In the spring of 1910, Laurier was still worried about the factional strife in Drummond-Arthabaska. "The local situation is far enough from being cleared up, and at present I fear greatly that in the election which must take place shortly there will be divisions in our ranks."[96] Lavergne was less pessimistic. He had wanted a Senatorship for many years[97] and apparently this affected his judgment. At any rate, he informed Laurier that everybody would support J. E. Perrault as candidate.[98] Laurier, on the western tour at the time, later blamed himself for taking Lavergne's word rather than investigating personally.[99] Nevertheless, after the decision was made to open the constituency the Liberals undertook the campaign seriously. Perrault was a successful lawyer who later held a portfolio in a provincial government, and so could have won. Laurier attended the party convention which "selected" Perrault,

[91] Rumilly, *Histoire*, IX, 257.
[92] LP, W.L. to L. Lavergne, 27 Sept., 1904.
[93] *Ibid.*, W.L. to Cartwright, 6 Nov., 1908.
[94] *Ibid.*, J. Desmarais to W.L., 6 Nov., 1910.
[95] *Ibid.*, W.L. to C. Lavigne, 20 Oct., 1908.
[96] *Ibid.*, W.L. to Abbé Tétreau, 8 Feb., 1910.
[97] *Ibid.*, W.L. to Lavergne, 2 Jan., 1906.
[98] *Ibid.*, Lavergne to W.L., 28 Sept., 1910.
[99] *Ibid.*, W.L. to H. Béland, 10 Nov., 1910.

an unprecedented event as *Le Devoir* pointed out,[100] and his speech at Montreal may also be considered part of the by-election campaign. Certainly Laurier was risking his personal prestige in an otherwise minor election in order to silence the *nationaliste* opposition to the Naval Bill. As *La Presse* said, even if the Liberal majority was reduced it would be a moral defeat for the Liberal party.[101]

The *Nationalistes* hesitated before accepting the challenge. The *Nationaliste* Armand Lavergne, son of Louis Lavergne and so a potential local candidate, told Laurier that he did not wish to present himself in view of the "certain defeat."[102] A candidate was finally found in A. Gilbert. As Armand later admitted, Gilbert had no ability as a public speaker,[103] but he had other qualifications. He was a farmer and so could appeal to the rural prejudice against professional politicians such as Perrault; he came from the county of Drummond, which had expected to provide the next candidate;[104] and he was a Liberal, and so could be described as defending the Liberal tradition which Laurier had betrayed.[105] Gilbert was given energetic support; Lavergne, Bourassa and Monk being prominent among the *Nationaliste* speakers.[106] Supporting Perrault were Bureau, Béland, and Louis Lavergne.

Pre-eminent as usual was Bourassa – but by now his emphasis had changed. In January he had ridiculed Laurier's statement that there would be no conscription as irrelevant; of course there would be no press-gangs. "But naval conscription does not exist in any country in the world . . . And it is patently absurd to pretend that we will not enter into the vortex of militarism because we do not have naval conscription."[107] In October however, conscription rather than Imperialism had become the paramount danger inherent in Laurier's naval policy! Bourassa's argument was that once involved in Imperial wars, conscription would soon follow. In the heat of the campaign however, this rational approach gave way to more effective emotional appeals. He talked of the poor mother whose son would be killed in Japan some years hence, and he also pointed out that Laurier had no children, and so was willing to impose conscription at the request of the British – who distribute titles.[108] Other

[100] *Le Devoir*, 24 Oct., 1910.
[101] *La Presse*, 3 Nov., 1910.
[102] LP, A. Lavergne to W.L., 14 Oct., 1910.
[103] A. Lavergne, *Trente ans de vie nationale* (Montréal, 1934), 162.
[104] LP, David to W.L., 15 Oct., 1910.
[105] *Le Devoir*, 19 Oct., 1910.
[106] LP, H. Béland to W.L., 31 Oct., 1910.
[107] "Le projet de loi navale," 28.
[108] Rumilly, *Histoire*, xv, 133, quoting *Le Devoir*, 19 Sept. 1910.

Nationalistes were equally positive that Laurier was a war-mon-ger.[109] The charge of Imperialism was not forgotten. Laurier's state-ment that when Great Britain is at war, Canada is at war, was re-peated while his qualification was ignored. Even more frequently quoted was the statement attributed to Fielding that "The navy would be Canadian in time of peace but Imperial in time of war," although again, Fielding had always been careful to qualify similar statements by such phrases as "whenever the British nation shall be involved in a major war."[110] Although Laurier never stooped to per-sonal invective, there was some justification for his description of the *Nationalistes* as demogogues – "there is no other expression which can be applied to them."[111]

The *Nationaliste* candidate received a majority of two hundred votes.

The comments on the by-election are instructive. Prominent English Conservatives had recommended that Conservatives should vote against Laurier, although Borden had temporised by recom-mending a vote "according to your conscience."[112] In the province of Quebec, the *Star* made no editorial comment whatsoever on the by-election, while the *Gazette* admitted that the naval issue had been the dominant issue but concluded that the destruction of the fable of "Laurier's solid Quebec" was a "good thing."[113] This seems to have been representative of English Conservative opinion; the end was to defeat Laurier and any ally was acceptable. The *nationalistes* were less equivocal. *L'Action Sociale* interpreted the result as a clear condemnation of Laurier's naval policy,[114] while *Le Devoir* described it as a condemnation of Laurier himself.[115] Nor did the Liberals minimize the defeat. Laurier still maintained that the naval policy, although not popular, would be accepted when it was understood, but meanwhile it would be an effective weapon for the opposition.[116] The by-election result itself was more serious. "The psychological effect on the public has been disastrous and this inju-ry can only be healed with difficulty, if it still can be."[117] The only

---

[109] *Ibid.*, 157. Skelton's uniformed census-takers, if they existed at all, were not important enough to attract the criticism of the Liberals at the time. Skelton, *Laurier*, II, 339.

[110] Rumilly, *Histoire*, XV, 154;
Commons Debates, 19 Apr., 1910, 7469.

[111] *La Presse*, 17 Nov., 1910., open letter from Laurier.

[112] Brodeur, *Commons Debates*, 22 Nov., 1910, 127.

[113] *Gazette*, 4 Nov., 1910.

[114] *L'Action Sociale*, 4 Nov., 1910.

[115] *Le Devoir*, 4 Nov., 1910.

[116] LP, W. L. to David, 12 Nov., 1910.

[117] *Ibid.*, W. L. to Béland, 10 Nov., 1910.

consolation was that the Drummond-Arthabaska campaign could be used both in English Canada and Quebec as a horrible example of Opposition tactics.[118]

The defeat in Drummond-Arthabaska cannot easily be explained. Gilbert had some personal advantages but not enough to carry the constituency in the election of 1911. The factional rivalries among the Liberals might have been expected to disappear in the face of a *Nationaliste* challenge. There were some charges of clerical interference in the election, but it was never proved that local priests used their official as well as their personal influence.[119] The effectiveness of Bourassa's oratory must be balanced against Laurier's prestige. The naval policy was not popular, but such a passive attitude was not likely to overcome the inertia of party loyalty. The most important factor seems to have been the issue of conscription.

In view of subsequent events, it is worthwhile to analyse the attitude towards conscription in French Canada in 1910. It is possible to trace a resentment against forms of conscription since the French régime. At that time there was widespread opposition to service in the militia and to the *corvée*. This attitude was still apparent during the years preceding the Quebec Act.[120] During the War of 1812, the Executive Council found it necessary to recommend martial law on the grounds that the small fines and short imprisonments imposed by civil law were inadequate to enforce recruiting.[121] In 1862, it was the French Canadians who defeated the Militia Bill, and at the time the French-Canadian press was bitterly described as conducting a "*holy* crusade" against the Bill.[122] In 1888, Mercier made a revealing speech in which he denounced Imperial Federation because it would mean conscription;[123] This contradicts the assumption that conscription was opposed because it was too Imperialist. Bourassa also provides examples of this attitude to conscription. In 1902 he wrote, "The aversion of French Canadians to war, to militarism, to soldierly rule and manners, is general and deeply seated."[124] But, to Bourassa at least, it was more than anti-militarism. The explanation for British Imperialism and the desire to find soldiers and sailors in the colonies was to be found in the necessity

[118] e.g. Laurier, *Commons Debates*, 21 Nov., 1910, 54ff.

[119] *Le Devoir*, 27 Dec. 1910, quoting Mgr. Brunault's Circular 13 Dec., 1910.

[120] A. L. Burt, *The Old Province of Quebec* (Toronto, 1933), 265.

[121] W. Wood, ed., *Select British Documents of the Canadian War of 1812*, (Toronto, 1920), 200.

[122] C. P. Stacey, *Canada and the British Army, 1846-1871* (London, 1936), 133. See also footnote, p. 151.

[123] Rumilly, *Histoire*, v, 296.

[124] "The French Canadian and the British Empire", 13.

to avoid conscription in Great Britain – conscription which might mean the "disruption of the United Kingdon, the overthrow of the Monarchy and the advent of social revolution."[125] Thus to many French Canadians conscription was more than an exaggerated form of Imperialism; it was a moral evil, wrong in itself, something equivalent to "social revolution". It was to this instinct that Bourassa had directed his appeal. Combined with the anti-Imperial sentiment as it was in Drummond-Arthabaska, the emotional attitude towards conscription makes more comprehensible the surprising defeat of the Liberal candidate. Certainly Laurier believed that it was necessary to deny that there was any possibility of naval conscription, taking the unusual step of writing an open letter to *La Presse* to that effect.[126]

Meanwhile the issue of reciprocity with the United States threatened to replace the naval issue as the most prominent political question of the day. Laurier had always considered himself a freetrader in principle[127] but in view of the high tariff policy of the United States he made no quixotic pilgrimages to Washington. Yet, in spite of the economic and political benefits of Imperial preference, he wrote in 1903, "This fact does not alter my views as to the desirability of better trade facilities between our two countries, and I will always be ready to consider any fair proposal."[128] In 1910, he believed that a possible tariff war with the United States would not affect the Canadian economy greatly, but the idea was naturally repugnant to him – "This commercial war has no attraction for me".[129] To Fielding, in Washington at this time, he explained that the resentment against American pressure was very strong. "We would make ourselves very popular by making no concessions at all. However your policy upon this point is best."[130] Rather than gain a temporary popularity by appealing to anti-American prejudices, Laurier preferred to rely upon the more stable popularity based on prosperity. When the Reciprocity Convention was finally negotiated, Laurier was well satisfied. As in the days of the unrestricted reciprocity campaign, he believed that increased trade meant increased prosperity but could not conceive that better commercial relations with the United States could affect political relations with Great Britain. To Hugh Graham, he even suggested that prosperity always strengthens loyalty.[131] As usual, he assumed

[125] "Great Britain and Canada," (1902), 30.
[126] *La Presse*, 17 Nov., 1910.
[127] Minto Papers, Vol. 1, 73, Memo. of conversation, 28 Jan., 1902.
[128] LP, W. L. to G. Copeland, 6 June, 1903.
[129] *Ibid.*, W. L. to A. Macphail, 21 March, 1910.
[130] *Ibid.*, W. L. to Fielding, 25 March, 1910.
[131] *Ibid.*, W. L. to Graham, 6 Feb., 1911.

that moderate men would agree with his policy when they understood it.

In the province of Quebec, the *Nationalistes* were not eager to focus attention on reciprocity. In Dandurand's words, "Reciprocity disturbs them because it diverts attention from the Navy."[132] Bourassa had long maintained that reciprocity with the United States was eminently desirable.[133] Even when the details of the Convention were made public, Bourassa admitted that the agreement would benefit the agricultural groups without injuring Canadian industries,[134] and denied that it could lead to annexation.[135] That it would prevent any Imperial Zollverein was to Bourassa the main reason for its adoption.[136] By midsummer, however, with an election imminent, reciprocity somehow found less favor. He decided that the Convention should not be ratified because better terms might be obtained.[137] More important, he decided that the question of reciprocity had paled into insignificance before the paramount issue of Canadian autonomy.[138] Nor did Monk attack the Convention directly. In 1906, he had favored some form of reciprocity,[139] and now he merely criticized the introduction of a new policy before the naval issue had been satisfactorily settled.[140] To the *Nationalistes* the danger lay in Laurier's Imperialism, and if necessary, commercial prosperity should be sacrificed in order to eliminate the danger.

The Imperial Conference of 1911 provided an opportunity once more to attract attention to this issue of Imperialism. Not that Laurier behaved like an Imperialist. Once more he reiterated in London that Canada was satisfied with the present situation, although he would "approach with an open mind" any suggested improvements in Imperial constitutional relations.[141] In spite of his open mind, he opposed the creation of any Imperial Council.[142] As for his naval policy, "We have taken the position in Canada that

[132] *Ibid.*, Dandurand to W. L., 1 June, 1911.
[133] Rumilly, *Histoire*, XIV, 42.
[134] *Le Devoir*, 31 Jan., 1911.
[135] *Ibid.*, 1 Feb., 1911.
[136] *Ibid.*, 7 Feb., 1911.
[137] *Ibid.*, 6 Mar., 1911.
[138] *Ibid.*, 2 Aug., 1911.
[139] Borden Papers, Memoir Notes, Vol. 12, 6203, Monk to Borden, 10 Feb., 1906.
[140] Rumilly, *Histoire*, XVI, 49.
[141] *Minutes of the Proceedings of the Imperial Conference 1911* (London, 1911), 24.
[142] *Ibid.*, 56.

we do not think that we are bound to take part in every war and that our fleet may not be called upon in all cases."[143]

Nevertheless, Bourassa found something to criticize. Like Laurier, Bourassa claimed to approach the matter with an open mind, but again the result of this objective approach differed little from the result that would have been reached by appealing only to preconceived opinions. "The system of Imperial conferences tends inevitably towards centralization of the Empire's government and, as a result, to the weakening of the autonomy and liberty of each of the countries which make it up – or rather of the colonies."[144] Thus to attend an Imperial Conference was proof of Imperialism. With this assumption it was not difficult to explain the plan of the Imperial Council as a cunning plot; by permitting the impracticable scheme to be rejected, the Imperialists had forestalled an attack on the Imperial influence exerted by the Colonial Office and the Governors-General.[145] The implication, earlier made explicit, was that Laurier was still fostering Imperialism either "knowingly or blindly."[146]

In the general election of 1911, the schism between the French and English Conservatives was so complete that anti-Liberal candidates in the province of Quebec usually labelled themselves as *Autonomistes* rather than Conservatives. The platform of this *nationaliste* party was distinct from those of the other two parties, being concerned with "autonomy, protection of minorities, immigration, colonization, conservation of national resources, the danger of trusts, overcapitalization of large companies, absorption of our natural resources and public services by American finance."[147] In theory, the *Autonomiste* candidates were to be independent of both national parties, men of good principles who would not be swayed by opportunism or partisanship to support the anti-national policy of Imperialism.[148] One of the *Autonomiste* campaign pamphlets put this in terms of practical politics. "If thirty of these candidates (Autonomistes) are elected on September 21, the policy of Mr. Monk will triumph in the House, for neither one party nor the other will be able to stay in power if it doesn't have the support of M. Monk and his followers."[149] With Sifton and the Toronto capitalists supporting Borden, Bourassa naturally suspected the attitude

[143] *Ibid.*, 117.
[144] *Le Devoir*, 7 July, 1911.
[145] *Ibid.*, 8 July, 1911.
[146] *Ibid.*, 12 May, 1911.
[147] *Le Devoir*, 18 April 1911.
[148] *Ibid.*, 11 Aug. 1910.
[149] "Monsieur Monk," (Montréal, 1911).

of his party to the minority. "Does one see here the fine Tory, imperialist, plutocratic, anti-French and anti-Catholic – I should say anti-Canadian – combination? Are true Conservatives ready to lend a hand to this Holy Alliance and make use of it as an instrument or stepping-stone? I do not believe so. As for me, I know nothing at all about it."[150] Bourassa always insisted that he had emphasized that the *Autonomiste* candidates were to pledge to oppose the Naval Bill, but also the "no less nefarious policy of Mr. Borden."[151] The Autonomistes were expected to form a Quebec bloc, an anti-Imperialist party.

The fact remains that nowhere did Conservative and *Autonomiste* candidates oppose one another. The attempt to create a third party in the province of Quebec was compromised during the campaign. The difficulty was that if Bourassa and the *nationalistes* were to fight for their principles they could only fight Laurier. Restricted to the French-Canadian districts of the province and including in their ranks most of the French-Canadian Conservatives that had survived, there was no other enemy. On the analogy of a military campaign, the armies fighting a common enemy became allies for the duration. Bourassa's reminiscences in *Le Devoir* after his disillusionment with the elected *Autonomistes* provides one account of this alliance. According to Bourassa, he was approached by two prominent Conservatives with the suggestion that reciprocity should be treated as the major issue in the election, but this he refused. However, he explained that he did not intend to present a candidate where a Liberal and a Conservative had been nominated.[152] Such Conservative candidates were presented in the Eastern Townships, Argenteuil and Pontiac, and three districts in Montreal. On the other hand, Bourassa explained that it was clearly understood that in the rest of the province, the *Autonomistes* under Monk would present all the anti-Liberal candidates.[153] Bourassa also claimed that in the heat of the campaign the Conservative party supplied the *Autonomiste* party with campaign funds without exacting any pledges.[154] We may discount the accuracy of such reminiscences, although it seems suggestive that Borden's *Memoirs* make no mention of the *nationaliste* campaign in Quebec in 1911. But whatever the arrangements there can be no doubt that the primary objective of the campaign was to defeat Laurier. Even the Conservative *Gazette* stated that a vote for Monk or for the even more extreme

[150] *Le Devoir*, 3 April 1911.
[151] *Le Devoir*, 30 May, 1913.
[152] *Le Devoir*, 29 May, 1913.
[153] *Ibid.*, 30 May, 1913.
[154] *Ibid.*, 2 June, 1913.

nationaliste, Asselin, "is a vote for the broadest and best interests of Canada."[155] The less immediate problems of Imperialism and reciprocity could wait until after September 21st.

In the campaign in the province of Quebec there could be no doubt that Bourassa was the most prominent opponent of the Liberals, despite the fact that he was not a candidate. His political assemblies drew enormous crowds[156] and his continued emphasis on the issue of Imperialism put the Liberals in the province on the defensive. Liberal newspapers devoted a good deal of space to proving that Bourassa was mistaken in calling the navy an Imperial navy.[157] Le Canada printed a series of political articles ridiculing the policy of Le Maitre, a name referring to Bourassa's apparent assumption of virtue and infallibility.[158] La Presse repeated the theme that the battle was between Laurier and Borden, whatever Bourassa might claim.[159] Towards the end of the campaign the Liberal press seems to have tried to shift the emphasis to the issue of reciprocity, with "Laurier and Reciprocity" as the slogan,[160] but Bourassa was not easily ignored. Nor was the policy of quoting Ontario Conservative newspapers embarrassing to an opposition in Quebec which denounced Conservative as well as Liberal policies. If there were two protagonists in the province, they were not Laurier and Borden but Laurier and Bourassa.

Laurier won the election in Quebec. Of sixty-five seats the Liberals won thirty-seven. Laurier had expected even better results; more than a week before the election he told Fielding that the losses in the province would be "three or perhaps five" more than before the election,[161] whereas actually fifteen additional seats were lost. It was a mathematical victory, but in comparison with previous election results it was a defeat. The "solid Quebec" had been split.

Nevertheless, the Liberal losses should not be exaggerated. With reference to the two national parties, Quebec was still predominantly Liberal. Most of the constituencies lost had been won by Autonomiste rather than Conservative candidates. It is not a coincidence that of the constituencies lost, thirteen were in northern and eastern Quebec – areas in which the nationaliste colonization campaign had played an important part in weakening the influence of the Liberal

[155] Gazette, 21 Sept., 1911.
[156] Rumilly, Histoire, XVI, 77.
[157] e.g. Le Soleil, 5 Aug. 1911, prints four editorials, all concerned with contradicting Bourassa.
[158] "L'Oeil ouvert," (Montréal, 1911) is a reprint of these articles.
[159] La Presse, 19 and 21 Sept., 1911.
[160] Le Soleil, 20 Sept., 1911.
[161] LP, W. L. to Fielding, 12 Sept., 1911.

party.[162] Even against a party, provincial in scope and *nationaliste* in policy, after fifteen years of office had dimmed the novelty of having a French-Canadian Prime Minister, the Liberals had won a majority of the seats. From a national point of view it was at least reassuring that so many electors had voted for a national party.

There was an indirect, but probably more significant, result of the election of 1911 for the province of Quebec. The Liberal ranks had been decimated in the province of Ontario, and so the Conservative party could have formed a government even without an alliance with the *Autonomistes*. The scheme for a third party which would hold the balance of power at Ottawa had failed. The elected *Autonomistes* tamely accepted Borden's leadership, leaving themselves vulnerable to Liberal accusations that they were unprincipled office-seekers. Bourassa tried to console himself by a bold declaration after the election: "We have helped to bring down one government, we will not hesitate to undermine another, if it fails in its duty."[163] But this was cold comfort to the *nationalistes* who had just helped to establish in power the more imperialist of the two national parties, and who would wait many years for an opportunity to undermine it. The third party movement had failed in 1911. It never recovered from the failure.

[162] Pontiac, Labelle, Joliette, Berthier, Maskinonge, Quebec County, Montmorency, Chicoutimi-Saguenay, Dorchester, Bellechasse, Montmagny, Rimouski, Gaspé.
[163] *Le Devoir*, 22 Sept., 1911.

12.
Conclusion And
Epilogue

Laurier's political philosophy would be misunderstood if his emphasis on the problem of national unity was underestimated. The desire to foster national unity is not peculiar to him; most politicians, and Canadian politicians in particular, subscribe to this principle, but with Laurier other principles were consciously subordinated to this end. The instrument by which this unity was to be achieved was the political party, and so the unity of the party became of paramount importance. It would be misleading to suggest that his emphasis on party loyalty was no more than a desire for power; in Laurier's case at least, it was not so much the desire for power as a sense of responsibility. No doubt he was tempted to believe that he was the best qualified man to lead the Liberal party and to govern the country; however, his desire was not merely to govern but to use his authority to consolidate the Canadian federation. A letter written to a friend in 1904 makes explicit this philosophy.

Many thanks for your letter. I know full well that you are not and never can be a party man in the strict sense which we attach to the word. I believe you are wrong but it is no use discussing that as your impossibility to adhere to party lines proceeds from too high ideals.

Remember this, that in politics, the question seldom arises to do the ideal right. The best that is generally to be expected, is to attain a certain object, and for the accomplishment of this object, many things have to be done which are questionable, and many things have to be submitted to which, if rigorously investigated, could not be approved of.

The career of Lincoln as President affords numerous examples of this too often forgotten truth. His object was save the union. He kept that continuously before the public and to reach that object, many things were done which highly conscientious men could not approve, and under which they fretted and worried. They followed him however, and no doubt now, all are agreed that this was the right course.

My object is to consolidate Confederation, and to bring our people long estranged from each other, gradually to become a nation. This is the suprême issue. Everything else is subordinate to that idea. There will be many things in the future, as there were in the past, which you will not approve in my administration, but this, I am sure, and this is the main point for me, will not alter the friendship of yours.[1]

As this letter explains, Laurier saw the problem of national unity in terms of racial harmony. He was not blind to other disruptive issues: with the growing political importance of western Canada, he believed that the cleavage between the free-trade West and the protectionist East was becoming "dangerous politically and nationally."[2] The policy of reciprocity was the solution he had adopted to end this division, and even after 1911 he had persuaded Ontario Liberals to maintain the policy by making the concession that the issue would not be given undue prominence for some time.[3] But this was an exception. Laurier was more conscious of racial than of regional divisions in Canada. As a member of the minority group this was natural, but it would be wrong to assume that this alone can explain his emphasis on the problem. It might be possible to find some correlation with a growing racial tension in Canada and similar developments elsewhere. Thus nationalism, based on race, language and culture, was becoming increasingly important in European politics. It played an important part in the unification of Italy and Germany; it was a factor in the Imperialism at the turn of the century; and it may be said to have reached its apogee in the self-determination theories at the Paris Peace Conference, which attempted to determine political boundaries in conformity to the boundaries of this nationalist sentiment. In Canada, however, any emphasis on the unity of race, language and culture was naturally a divisive element in national politics. Certainly there can be no doubt that the three decades from Riel to conscription were years when racial animosity was becoming increasingly apparent. As a French Canadian and as a leader of a national political party, during those years, Laurier could not but be conscious of the seriousness of the problem.

Broadly speaking, there were three obvious solutions to the problem of racial unity in Canada. The one favored by many of the minority group might be defined as social segregation. This attitude is best illustrated by the insistence upon a completely separate edu-

---

[1] LP, W.L. to W. Gregory, 11 Nov., 1904.
[2] *Ibid.*, W.L. to A. McLeod, 16 Oct., 1916.
[3] *Ibid.*, W.L. to A. Smith, 24 Sept., 1918.

cational system for the two racial groups; in its extreme form it meant a politically independent "Laurentia." The solution favored by many of the majority group was assimilation. This meant a unified public school system, and in its extreme form, the extinction of the French language. The third solution was a compromise between these two incompatible attitudes. It assumed that neither minority nor majority "rights" could be ignored and that a *modus vivendi* could be found which could be accepted by both groups. Like all compromises, this solution had none of the appeal of a cause based on a rigid principle; it was a pragmatic solution which could appeal only to the moderation and tolerance of the members of both racial groups. This policy of compromise was accepted by most Canadian politicians. Differences arose over the details, over the concessions to be made or exacted by the two groups.

Laurier was the foremost exponent of this policy of compromise. According to Bourassa, the first thing Laurier would do on arriving at the gates of Paradise "will be to propose an *honourable compromise* between God and Satan."[4] Few remarks could be more revealing. For austere men with no political responsibilities, such as Bourassa, it was possible to believe that a political decision was merely a choice between right and wrong. An "honorable compromise" was thus a contradiction in terms. The corollary was that political policy should be based on moral principles regardless of the consequences. But Laurier had a better, or at least a more sympathetic, understanding of political problems. He realized that two conflicting groups might both have some justification for their contentions. Like Pascal, he believed "that men are neither angels nor demons, but beings endowed with some faults and, much more, many qualities of heart and mind."[5] Since there was no simple right or wrong, a compromise became necessary.

The assumption that such compromises were possible illustrates an essential aspect of Laurier's philosophy. Like all philosophical liberals, he had faith in the rationality of mankind. He believed that most men were both reasonable and generous, and that periods of emotional hysteria were no more than temporary abberations. Thus, his instinctive anti-militarism was based on the assumption that most international disagreements could be settled by means of a compromise. Similarly in labor relations, strikes appeared to be a form of wasteful industrial strife which wrought "untold misery and mischief."[6] The Lemieux Act, which delayed but did not outlaw

[4] *Le Devoir*, 23 July, 1910.
[5] LP, W.L. to H. Gadsby, 24 Aug., 1916.
[6] *Ibid.*, W.L. to J. Cameron, 12 Nov., 1908.

strikes, was to Laurier "a most meritorious piece of legislation."[7] Laurier was willing to modify his acceptance of the principles of classical economy[8] in order to facilitate a peaceful settlement of labor disputes.

This innate moderation helps to explain Laurier's confidence that national unity was possible in a bi-racial state. It may be surmised, however, that this confidence was strengthened by his years of political apprenticeship under Edward Blake. That an English Canadian, and at that time the leader of a party deriving its strength from Ontario, should be willing to make concessions to French-Canadian opinion, as in the case of the incorporation of the Orange Order and of the Riel rebellion, could not but strengthen Laurier's conviction that reasonable compromises were possible in Canadian politics. The personal relations of the two men – Laurier's admiration for Blake's integrity and sense of justice, and Blake's respect for Laurier's ability and personality – must have influenced their attitude to the social relations of the two races. The loyalty of his English colleagues in later years would further strengthen Laurier's faith in the possibility of amicable compromise.

The goal of national unity by means of compromise can scarcely be criticized as an abstract proposition. Compromise is the essence of politics, and no government can be completely arbitrary. Only when it becomes a concrete proposition, when the concessions demanded of the affected groups can be assessed and compared, is it possible to judge the policy of compromise. The question is not whether the principle is the right one but whether the compromise was the most satisfactory possible in the circumstances, and whether one group was unduly favored at the expense of the other. Since any alternative to the actual policy can be no more than a "might have been", no such assessment can be more than tentative. In the case of Laurier, criticisms have not been lacking. English Canadians, such as J. W. Dafoe, have denounced Sir Wilfrid's "preoccupation" with public opinion in Quebec and the consequent sacrifice of national welfare.[9] On the other hand, such French Canadians as Bourassa have concluded that Laurier actually regretted "that his compatriots had kept their language and their traditions", and believed that Laurier was one of the "Anglicized Catholics".[10] Yet oth-

---

[7] *Ibid.*

[8] Laurier's economic philosophy is illustrated by his belief that the omission of a "due process of the law" clause in the Canadian constitution was regrettable. (LP, W. L. to W. Nesbitt, 3 Nov., 1909).

[9] Dafoe, *Laurier*, 124.

[10] *Le Devoir*, 28 July, 1910.

er critics, such as O. D. Skelton, have maintained that Laurier understood the beliefs and aspirations of both racial groups and maintained a balance between the two little short of the ideal. The reasons for this divergence of opinion are multiple. Canadians have not yet agreed as to what form their bi-racial polity should take, and when people disagree on this point there can be no agreement as to the necessity or the equity of Laurier's compromises. There is also some disagreement as to what Laurier's motives and his policies were. To this it is more possible to suggest an answer.

In the early years of the union the question of provincial rights was a prominent political issue. Exaggerated claims for provincial autonomy might destroy Confederation. The provinces had surrendered some of their authority to the federal government, but it would be some years before personal loyalties were transferred. As the Opposition party of Ottawa, the Liberals represented this latent reaction to Confederation; as heirs of the liberal tradition of individual liberties, Liberals made explicit their opposition to centralization. But while an emphasis on provincial rights might be divisive, a complete denial of provincial authority might have been equally dangerous. National loyalty could not be achieved by ignoring genuine provincial loyalties. Thus a respect for provincial rights was necessary if the union was to be consolidated.

Laurier's view of provincial rights might be described as a qualified approval of the principle. His criticism of the federal power to disallow provincial legislation illustrates his attitude. In 1888 he told Blake that "the power of disallowance is antagonistic to the federative principle. It should not exist in a confederation. . . ."[11] Two decades later, his opinion had not changed.

To give to the central government, which is drawn from the majority race and the majority religion, the authority to interfere in the jurisdiction assigned to the provinces, is to destroy the legislative independence of the provinces and make of it a snare and a mockery . . .[12]

It would be difficult to deny that the arbitrary use of the power of disallowance might destroy the authority of the provincial governments. But under some circumstances, Laurier was willing to invoke the power of disallowance. To critics of the Ontario Hydro legislation he explained that disallowance should only be entertained when the legislation affected the "peace, order and good govern-

[11] Blake Papers, W.L. to Blake, 16 Jan., 1888.
[12] DeCelles, ed., *Discours, 1889-1911*, 25, W. L. to L. M. Gouin, 18 July, 1918.

ment of Canada."[13] As a practical politician, he also pointed out
that disallowance could only be effective if the action was approved
by public opinion within the province.[14] To Laurier a conference
with the provinces on controversial matters seemed more politic.[15]
Again we see the implicit assumption that disagreements could and
should be settled amicably.

Laurier's recognition of provincial rights was not restricted to the
refusal to invoke the power of disallowance, as is shown by his
financial concessions at the Dominion-Provincial Conference of
1906. In other less obvious ways, his administration recognised the
principle. Judicial and senatorial appointments were the responsibility of the provincial representatives in the Cabinet, with the collaboration of the provincial government if it happened to be Liberal.[16]
On the only occasion when Laurier committed to paper a recommendation for an Ontario senatorial appointment, he was informed
that it would be "highly impolitic" to nominate his candidate.[17] In
Quebec, Laurier once described himself as "the first and last judge"
of such appointments[18] but even in this province his colleagues from
Montreal seem to have controlled such patronage in that district.[19]
Only in provinces such as New Brunswick and British Columbia,
where the Cabinet representatives were sometimes factional rather
than party leaders of the province, did Laurier intervene.[20] Laurier,
however, did not carry his belief in the principle of provincial right
to an extreme. He was, for instance, firmly convinced that the
Canadian constitution was superior to the United States constitution because the residual powers had been entrusted to the federal
government.[21] To Laurier, provincial rights was not a sacrosanct
principle, and his adherence to it was no more than a recognition
that local politicians would insist and therefore must be allowed to
manage local affairs.

Provincial rights were only indirectly a means of promoting racial harmony. English Canadians as well as French Canadians
could advocate provincial rights because to some extent it was a
defence of regional autonomy. Because the province of Quebec
contained most of the French-Canadian Roman Catholic population in Canada, provincial rights in this case became a defence of

[13] LP, W. L. to B. E. Walker, 5 June, 1909.
[14] Ibid., W. L. to Dr. Macklin, 26 Nov., 1909.
[15] Ibid., W. L. to Aylesworth, 3 Sept., 1909.
[16] e.g. LP, W. L. to F. Oliver, 5 Sept., 1909.
[17] Ibid., Cartwright to W. L., 4 Feb., 1907.
[18] Ibid., W. L. to J. Young, 6 March, 1899.
[19] Ibid., W. L. to N. Trenholme, 6 March, 1907.
[20] Ibid., W. L. to Pugsley, 11 Aug., 1908.
[21] Ibid., W. L. to E. W. Thomson, 28 July, 1908.

minority rights as well. Laurier was aware of this. Nevertheless, an increasing number of French Canadians were taking up residence outside the province of Quebec, in the Maritimes, in northern and eastern Ontario, and in the West. For these members of the racial minority, the principle of provincial rights was a threat to their survival. For that reason, the problem of minority rights became more important than provincial rights in the attempt to secure racial harmony within the federation.

The term "minority rights" is misleading. French Canadians who used the phrase were not demanding justice in the legal sense. Such justice could be obtained in the courts. The justice they demanded was an appeal to democratic tolerance – or to Christian love. French Canadians thought of Confederation as the federation of two societies. Implicit in this union was the right of each society to survive. Any condition, legal or otherwise, which threatened the survival of the minority, was a contradiction of minority rights.

For French Canadians outside the province of Quebec, the problem of minority rights centred on the question of education. A series of "school questions" bedevilled Canadian politics; the minority demanding sectarian "separate schools, the majority trying to impose secular "public schools." (See above, Chapters 5 and 9.) There can be no doubt that Laurier's sympathies were with the minority. He believed in the value of an educational system based on Christian principles,[22] but he bluntly condemned any attempt to force Roman Catholics to attend Protestant schools. Logically, his preference must have been for sectarian schools of some sort. Nor would Laurier attempt to evade the issue by admitting that the principle of provincial rights left to the provincial governments the determination of the educational rights of the minority. In 1896 and again in 1905 he insisted that the federal government had the right to interfere – his interpretation of section 93 was in conformity with his belief that racial harmony was a national problem. But Laurier's sympathy for his compatriots did not blind him to the equally sincere convictions of the English Canadians; nor did his belief in the federal rights to intervene make him ignore the fact that no federal law could compel a provincial government to administer an unacceptable educational system. So in 1896 Laurier opposed remedial legislation and negotiated a compromise whereby Roman Catholic students would have Roman Catholic teachers and inspectors and acceptable text-books, although the curriculum followed would conform to that of the public schools. In 1905 the original solution proposed in the Autonomy Bills was similar in principle; the difference appears to have been in the constitutional guarantee

[22] *Commons Debates*, 21 Feb., 1905, 1458.

that the provincial government would not be able to modify the system. The amended Autonomy Bills were less satisfactory from this point of view, but again they illustrate Laurier's ability to recognise the fact that emotional convictions could not be dispelled by appeals to what he believed to be logic and justice, and his assumption that a less satisfactory solution was preferable to a continued agitation.

It would be misleading to assume that Laurier believed in compromise for its own sake. Compromise was a means to an end, not a principle. Just as diplomacy seemed preferable to war as a means of settling international disagreements, so compromise seemed preferable to conflict along racial lines as a means of settling domestic problems. As he wrote in 1918:

There are among us some narrow-minded men who cry: "No compromise; all or nothing." What an aberration! When a minority affirms that it will concede nothing, that it demands everything or will accept nothing less than everything, he is blind three times over who does not see that the inevitable result will be: nothing.[23]

At least in the case of Manitoba in 1896, Laurier's method was effective. In spite of the racial animosities engendered by five years of agitation, he managed to ameliorate the position of the minority with the consent of the English-Canadian population of the province.

Even after 1911, when the Manitoba boundary was extended to include Keewatin, Laurier consistently maintained his policy of compromise. He refused to vote for an amendment which was intended to preserve the separate school system already in existence in the Territory, on the basis that it would be impossible to impose such a policy upon Manitoba.[24] Popular as the amendment was in Quebec, even in the Opposition Laurier's "preoccupation" with his province was not so complete as to lead him to ignore political realities. Thus Laurier's educational policy was an attempt to reach a workable compromise between the unacceptable extremes of assimilation and segregation. His faith that such a policy need not endanger the survival of French-Canadian society was expressed in a letter to a defender of sectarian schools.

For me, the safety of the French race lies not in isolation, but in competition. Give our children the best possible education, put them on an equal basis with those of the other race, and give them

[23] DeCelles, ed., *Discours, 1889-1911*, 26, W. L. to L. M. Gouin, 18 July, 1918.
[24] *Commons Debates*, 12 Mar., 1912. 4902.

he legitimate pride they will have in such a competition. There is afety. There is autonomy.[25]

Closely related to the problem of sectarian schools was the problem of language. The Manitoba school question, for example, might ave been expected to affect all Roman Catholics to the same egree but in fact it was the French-Canadian Roman Catholics vho led the agitation. In Manitoba, Archbishop Taché demanded emedial measures and his successor, Archbishop Langevin, denounced the Laurier-Greenway compromise as inadequate; and in Winnipeg, where many of the French-Canadians in the province vere concentrated, the school system of 1897 was not accepted. Outside of Manitoba, it was the French-Canadian episcopacy which was hostile to the compromise; the English-Canadian episcopacy considering it acceptable although not completely satisfactory. The explanation appears to be that the French Canadians had a dual interest in preserving a separate school system: as Roman Catholics they wished to protect their religious beliefs, but as French Canadians they also wanted separate schools in which the French language could be used as the medium of instruction. The importance of the language problem is illustrated by the clause in the Laurier-Greenway compromise which conceded the right to instruction in a language other than English if ten or more students requested it.

This dual nature of the separate school question, religious and linguistic, helps to explain the serious proportions of the agitation against the threat to eliminate French as a language of instruction in Ontario schools. The Merchant Report of 1911 had described the teaching of English as inadequate in many of the Ontario separate schools attended by French Canadians.[26] The Ontario government in 1912, by Regulation 17, prohibited teaching in French beyond the first two years of school unless the chief inspector decided that the students could not understand English.[27] One might have expected protests from French-speaking citizens in Canada, and certainly such protests were forthcoming. In the Quebec Assembly a motion regretting Ontario's policy was passed unanimously.[28] But most active in opposition to Regulation 17 were religious organizations and, among political groups the faction commonly labelled *castor.* Cardinal Bégin and Archbishop Bruchési gave their support

[25] LP, W. L. to C. Angers, 9 Dec., 1896.
[26] See "The Bilingual Schools of Ontario", for a critical review of this Report.
[27] Province of Ontario, *Sessional Paper No. 16*, 1913, 211.
[28] Rumilly, *Histoire*, XIX, 139.

to the agitation;[29] the *Action Catholique de la Jeunesse Canadienne*
française collected funds to be used for the benefit of their compa
triots in Ontario.[30] Among the politicians Senator Landry accepte
the presidency of the French-Canadian Educational Association o
Ontario[31] and shortly after resigned as president of the Senate t
devote his entire attention to this problem.[32] To an Irish-Canadia
Archbishop he wrote that the fight for bilingual schools was part o
the fight for separate schools. The Irish in Ontario were not con
vinced, but the paramount interest of the French Canadians wa
their survival as a separate society resting on the twin pillars o
language and religion; thus a challenge to one seemed to involve
challenge to the other.[33]

Laurier had never confused Roman Catholic schools with bilin
gual schools. He did not believe that there was any constitution
guarantee for the teaching of the French language,[34] and he feare
that any agitation to secure such a guarantee would endanger th
separate school system as it existed in most English-Canadian pro
inces. Thus in 1894 and again in 1905, he had refused to suppo
proposals to make French an official language in the Canadia
West. Laurier did sympathise with the desire of the French-Can
dian minorities to preserve their mother-tongue, but he believed
could be preserved without excluding a knowledge of English. H
argued that in the English-Canadian provinces all children shou
receive thorough instruction in English with the right to be taugl
French also if they desired.[35] He admitted that there had been son
separate schools in Ontario where no English had been taught, b
he was convinced that the proper remedy was to enforce the law
it had existed rather than to enforce Regulation 17.[36] To Lauri
the most serious aspect of the agitation in Quebec over Regulatio
17 was that the issue was being used by Bourassa and the *natione*
istes to strengthen the resentment of the French Canadians, whi
at the same time this intransigence was making more difficult
satisfactory settlement of the problem of bilingual schools in Onta
io.[37] His first hope was that the Ontario Liberals would oppose tl
Regulation. N. W. Rowell's refusal to do so was a great disappoin

[29] *Ibid.*, XX, 20; XIX, 140.
[30] *Ibid.*, XX, 20.
[31] *Ibid.*, XX, 142.
[32] *Ibid.*, XXI, 129.
[33] *Ibid.*, XX, 54ff.
[34] LP, W. L. to S. Lyon, 9 March, 1916.
[35] *Commons Debates*, 9 May, 1916, 3703.
[36] LP, W. L. to A. Drummond, 1 March, 1916.
[37] *Ibid.*, W. L. to D'Hellencourt, 15 Feb., 1916.

ment since it seemed to indicate that the Ontario Liberals had violated the principle of "fair treatment of minorities" which had been maintained by Mowat and Blake.[38] He remained convinced that if the Ontario Liberals had been more courageous, "no harm would result from the bilingual question."[39] Failing that, it was necessary to try to reduce the effect of the *nationaliste* agitation in Quebec. Ernest Lapointe introduced a motion "respectfully" suggesting the wisdom of allowing French to be taught to French Canadians in Ontario,[40] and Laurier made a stirring defence of this "appeal to the sense of justice of the people of Ontario."[41] One Ontario Liberal and eleven western Liberals voted against the resolution.[42]

The attitude of the western Liberals is important, for there too, it appeared that the Liberal traditions had been forgotten. A Liberal Premier in Manitoba had recently repealed the language section of the Laurier-Greenway agreement, although Laurier had described the step as "most reactionary," arguing that judicious administrative measures could have corrected the abuses.[43] Laurier, with his emphasis on racial harmony, might well feel that the Liberal party had "retrograded."[44]

It is interesting, in that year of war, 1916, to find Laurier writing to a friend in Paris, and blaming the *nationaliste* agitation, rather than the enlistment problem or even English-Canadian prejudices, for the growing racial disunity in Canada.

You have every reason to be alarmed at the greater and greater rift between the two groups which make up our country.

The first source is found undoubtedly in nationaliste pretensions, from the Ottawa River to the Pacific; and these nationalistes have succeeded in making the English population believe that the French race wants to impose its language everywhere, as an official language, even in British Columbia, where the French population is not even 2%.

These exaggerations are exploited by the extremists of Anglo-Saxonism, and make up the perpetual theme of the Tory press.

To this first cause of the rift has been added another in the

---

[38] *Ibid.*, W. L. to Rowell, 28 April, 1916.
[39] *Ibid.*, W. L. to E. Macdonald, 27 May, 1916.
[40] *Commons Debates*, 9 May, 1916, 3618.
[41] *Ibid.*, 10 May, 1916, 3701.
[42] Skelton, *Laurier*, II, 483.
[43] LP, W. L. to T. Norris, 22 Feb., 1916.
[44] *Ibid.*, W. L. to Rowell, 11 May, 1916.

fact that clericalism has almost completely suceeded now in linking the language cause to its own. . . .[45]

Only after this did he mention the small proportion of French-Canadian enlistments as a factor in this racial division. Whatever the reasons, Laurier took a very serious view of the situation. To Dandurand he wrote that "Two states of mind are being created at present in Canada, and it seems to me that conflict is inevitable."[46]

Thus, to Laurier, the school and language problem were of major significance in determining the relations between the two racial groups in Canada. Extremists on both sides were the culprits. Such extremists were blind to an obvious fact of Canadian politics, for the French Canadians could not become English, yet nor could they separate themselves from the rest of Canada. Their irresponsible demands served only to foster intra-racial suspicion. Since Laurier assumed that a reasonable solution of racial problems was possible, the irrational and emotional demands of the extremists were to blame for making this reasonable solution impossible in 1916. It is possible that Laurier exaggerated the importance of these problems in explaining the divisions in Canada; to English-Canadians at least, the problems evoked by the Great War seemed more important. But that by 1916 the racial division had been accentuated there can be no doubt. Laurier's life-work seemed to have borne little fruit or, at best, only to have postponed the schism.

The two racial groups in Canada were divided upon another major issue – that of Imperialism. Like so many "isms," Imperialism in Canada was a vague predilection rather than a concrete political theory. In an emotional sense, Imperialism was a confidence in British principles and British policies, and an assumption that the British Empire stood apart from and superior to the rest of the world. The more extreme Canadian Imperialists were not satisfied with the mere assertion of this faith; they sought more concrete and more binding demonstrations of Imperial unity. This more doctrinaire form of Imperialism assumed three forms: Imperial Federation, which meant the creation of a central executive or legislative authority; military Imperialism, which meant participation by the colonies in all wars of the Empire; and economic Imperialism, which meant free-trade within the Empire. To these extreme forms of Imperialism there was opposed the extreme anti-Imperialism, which maintained that Canada had no obligation to and no interest in the Empire, and that Canada's relations with Great Britain should be based upon material self-interest. Implicit was the as-

[45] *Ibid.*, W. L. to P. Roy, 15 June, 1916.
[46] *Ibid.*, W. L. to Dandurand, 24 June, 1916.

sumption that Canada would develop into an independent nation, and that her position within the Empire was only tolerable if it imposed no obligations upon Canadians, financial, military, or otherwise.

Laurier refused to admit that he belonged to either group. In 1917 he wrote, "For my part, I have stated again and again that I was neither an Imperialist nor an anti-Imperialist: I am . . . a Canadian first, last and all the time."[47] Such a statement however, does not mean a great deal. Both Imperialists and anti-Imperialists believed that they were furthering the interests of Canada, the difference being that the two groups disagreed as to what Canada's interests were. Laurier's conception of Canadian interests with respect to the Empire, deduced from his statements and his policy, must provide our conclusions as to his attitude on this divisive factor in Canadian politics.

There can be no doubt that Laurier was opposed to the more extreme forms of Canadian Imperialism. Since the 1890's he had consistently rejected any proposal to modify the constitutional structure of the Empire. Any central Imperial authority would be an encroachment upon Canadian self-government, and so undesirable. At the series of Conferences from 1897 to 1911, he resolutely refused to consider any of the suggested forms of Imperial Federation. Much has been made of the fact that Laurier showed sympathy for the vision of a Parliament of Greater Britain during the Jubilee celebrations of 1897, but this attitude is comparable to that of the businessman who agrees that the applications of Christian ethics to business is "all very well – in theory." To the end of his life, Laurier continued to express sympathy for the ideal but scorn for its practicability. "As to Imperial Federation, whilst the idea is a great one and strongly appeals to the imagination, at present it seems to me a dream." Written in 1918, this is an accurate summary of the sentiments expressed in the House of Commons in 1894.[48]

Laurier was equally opposed to any commitment by Canada to participate in the wars of the Empire. The responsibility of Canada in any scheme of Imperial defence was restricted to ensuring "the efficiency of its own forces as the garrison of the Dominion and thereby perform(ing) its duty as factor in the defence of the Canadian portion of the Empire."[49] While admitting the "when Great Britain is at war, Canada is at war," he consistently maintained that Canada must decide whether its participation in such a war would be active or

[47] Ibid., W. L. to F. Carrel, 24 Aug., 1917.

[48] Ibid., W. L. to D. Macmaster, 5 Aug., 1918; Commons Debates, 4 Feb., 1894, 90.

[49] Minto Papers, Vol. 2, 11, Memo of conversation, 3 June, 1902.

passive, and that such a decision must be based upon conditions existing at the time. Any permanent scheme which would involve Canada in Imperial wars was opposed as strongly as any scheme for Imperial federation.

As regards free-trade within the Empire, with the corollary of Imperial tariffs against foreign trade, Laurier was less uncompromising. His government introduced the Imperial preferential tariff, which might be considered a step towards Imperial free-trade. In fact, Laurier did not intend it as such. In 1903, when Chamberlain was campaigning in England in favor of such a scheme, Laurier explained this to a Canadian Imperialist. "We have approached that question on our side, quite apart from British opinion and we have fought it exclusively on Canadian grounds."[50] While personally favoring free-trade, Laurier believed that free-trade within the Empire was unacceptable to Canadian manufacturing interests and "was, of course, impossible under present conditions and would continue to be impossible for fifty years at least."[51] Laurier's willingness to accept unrestricted reciprocity with the United States in 1890 and the reciprocity agreement of 1911, illustrate the fact that Laurier's economic policy was not directed towards strengthening Imperial bonds.

As an opponent of these three methods advocated by the more extreme Canadian Imperialists, Laurier might be classified as an anti-Imperialist. Nevertheless, from the point of view of the extreme anti-Imperialists, Laurier seemed to be an Imperialist. To anti-Imperialists, the welfare of Canada was in no way connected with the welfare of the Empire. Laurier had more in common with this group than with the exteme Imperialists – as a French-Canadian it was natural that he felt no attraction for the racial implications accepted by the latter – and his opposition to the plans for Imperial centralization was popular among anti-Imperialists. His belief that Canada would become an independent nation was a conviction held by all members of this group. But the difference between Laurier and the anti-Imperialists became more obvious as the years passed by. Laurier was able to recognize the fact that the emotional bonds between the English Canadians and Great Britain created a political factor which could not be ignored. As Lord Minto reported, "He admitted that the sentimental connection was very strong."[52] This was a political reality which many French Canadians ignored or denied. Thus Bourassa could state in 1910 that the religious and

[50] LP, W. L. to G. W. Ross, 6 Oct., 1903.
[51] Minto Papers, Vol. 2, 50, Memo of conversation, 31 Aug., 1903.
[52] Ibid., Vol. 1, 73, memo of conversation, 28 Jan., 1902.

the Imperialist concessions made by the French Canadians had not been necessary.

The defeats which we have suffered since 1867, the concessions we have made, it is not Anglo-Protestant fanaticism which has imposed them on us: we owe them to our own weakness, to our own party spirit, to the obliteration of our national conscience.[53]

This was equivalent to stating that had the French Canadians been stubborn, the desires of the English Canadians could have been ignored. Laurier was not so politically naive.

But Laurier's compromise with English-Canadian Imperial sentiment was not solely based upon this political realism. In addition to this there was a respect for British ideals of justice and liberty which affected his policy where Imperial relations were concerned. It is impossible to assess the influence of this attitude upon his policy; certainly it was a rational rather than an emotional conviction, since he remained suspicious of any blind loyalty to Great Britain. In 1913 he could talk of "the strong pro-British sentiment which exists in Canada and which on this occasion, as on many others, can be misguided in any direction."[54] Yet Laurier was prone to assume that British diplomacy would be based upon the abstract principle of justice. The sending of Canadian volunteers to South Africa had been an admission of the strength of Imperialist sentiment among English-Canadians, but Laurier's belief that they were going to a just war had made his decision easier. Had Laurier accepted Bourassa's theory of economic Imperialism, the decision might well have been impossible for him. Laurier's Naval Bill is another illustration of this intangible influence on Laurier's attitude to Imperial relations. Again, the Naval Bill can be explained as a sop to Imperialist sentiment, and the clause which permitted the transfer of the Canadian Navy to the Imperial navy as an illusory concession. Yet even in Quebec, Laurier made no attempt to conceal the naval commitment implicit in the Bill.

If there was a war in which the naval supremacy of the Empire was placed in peril, I would be of the opinion myself – and I do not want others to be blamed for it, because I take the responsibility – I believe that we should help England with all our strength.[55]

This statement – made at Montreal during the Drummond-Arthabaska campaign – was more than a grudging concession to the politi-

[53] *Le Devoir*, 2 July 1910.
[54] LP. W. L, to Fielding, 20 Feb., 1913.
[55] DeCelles, ed., *Discours, 1889-1911*, 192, speech of 30 Oct. 1910. The italics were added by DeCelles.

cal pressure of Canadian Imperial sentiment. Underlying this was the assumption that the British navy was on the side of justice and world peace. Such an assumption was more compatible with Imperialism than with anti-Imperialism.

Even Laurier's opposition to Imperial centralization, constitutional, military or economic, was not necessarily anti-Imperial. He himself believed that the spirit of the Empire was to be found in the autonomy willingly conceded to the self-governing Dominions, and that the so-called Imperialist policies would destroy the unity of the Empire by challenging this principle. This attitude might be interpreted as hypocrisy or, more charitably, as self-delusion, and it is conceivable that Laurier prevented the strengthening of Imperial ties while claiming to be acting in the interests of the Empire, but some Imperialists agreed with Laurier's policy. Lord Grey, who dominated the Imperial movement in Canada according to Bourassa,[56] described "the well-considered path of sane Imperialism, founded on the ungrudging recognition of the autonomous rights of the Dominions . . . ."[57]

Thus Laurier's policy in connection with Imperial relations was a compromise between Imperialism and anti-Imperialism. It was based on the assumption that Canada's interests were the paramount concern of Canadians, and yet was an admission that Canada's interests could not be separated from British interests as long as British diplomacy and British military might defended the principles of justice and liberty. Like all compromises it was a temporizing policy. It meant a Canadian navy which *might* be Imperial in time of war. To Laurier its virtue lay in the fact that most moderate Canadians, English and French alike, could accept it for this very reason. And whatever Imperialist and anti-Imperialists critics may have alleged, it was not a compromise based soley on political opportunism. Rather, it was based on nationalism, modified by a sincere admiration of Great Britain and a recognition of the fact that Canada could not isolate herself from the rest of the world.

Laurier was not able to ignore the problem of Imperialism after 1911 merely because he was no longer Prime Minister. As leader of a national political party the problem became even more difficult in the next few years. It was not difficult to oppose Borden's naval policy of contributing three dreadnoughts to the British Navy. To depart from the policy of a Canadian navy might "discourage and perhaps disintegrate our party, especially in Quebec . . . "[58] To advocate no naval expenditure might be popular among agrarian

[56] *Le Devoir*, 12 July, 1910.
[57] LP, Grey to W. L., 10 Jan., 1910.
[58] LP, W. L. to Fielding, 3 Feb., 1913.

groups but the "sound sense of the country" would agree that some expenditure was necessary.[59] The Conservative argument was that German naval construction had created an emergency which made an immediate contribution necessary, but Fielding reported from London that the "German scare" was being exaggerated for political purposes.[60] In view of Borden's predicament of having to find some reason for not adopting the Liberal policy of a Canadian navy, Laurier probably agreed with Fielding that "the "emergency" is not that of the Empire, nor that of the Imperial government, but only that of Mr. Borden . . ."[61]

The war, however, was a complication which made Imperial relations of paramount importance and which was to disrupt racial harmony in Canada as no other political issue has done before or since. Laurier was unquestionably in favor of participation in the war. In the special session of 1914 he re-affirmed his confidence in the motives of the British authorities by describing the war as being fought for freedom, for democracy and for civilization.[62] As an indication of national unity, he stated that the Opposition would "offer no criticism as long as there is danger at the front."[63] This declaration was subsequently modified to permit what were considered to be constructive criticisms in the interest of winning the war,[64] but there was never any question of neutrality in any form. To one Canadian who feared the stimulus to Canadian Imperialism engendered by the war, Laurier, while admitting that the strengthening of Imperialism would have to be resisted after the war, pointed out that "looking at it from the broader aspect, the triumph of Germany would be the triumph of Imperialism ten times aggravated by German *Kultur*."[65] Even in 1917, when there was talk of a military stalemate and a negotiated peace, and when such a peace might be expected to end the growing racial divisions in Canada, Laurier expressed a personal opinion to a friend that a negotiated peace at this time would be almost equivalent to a defeat. "I am afraid that there is no help but fighting on until at all events some military advantage has been obtained."[66] Such sentiments from an anti-militarist and a man who had devoted his career to improving national unity, attest to Laurier's sincere support for the Allied

[59] *Ibid.*
[60] LP, Fielding to W. L., 5 Feb., 1913.
[61] *Ibid.*, 3 Dec. 1913.
[62] *Commons Debates*, 19 Aug., 1914, 9.
[63] *Ibid.*, 8.
[64] *Ibid.*, 8 Feb., 1916, 633.
[65] LP, W. L. to J. Walsh, 31 Aug., 1916.
[66] *Ibid.*, W. L. to W. Edwards, 11 Jan., 1917.

cause, as well as to his ability to assess political situations without being influenced by personal predilections.

The difficulty arose when the principle of winning the war threatened to clash with Laurier's principle of preserving national unity. As in a Greek tragedy, there was no escape from the dilemma. The crucial fact was that the French Canadians had not enlisted in numbers proportionate to the rest of Canada. It is impossible to determine the exact number of French-Canadian recruits[67] but even Laurier admitted that French-Canadian enlistments were proportionally fewer as compared to English-speaking Canadians. There were many reasons given for this. The English-born citizens had been prompt to enlist, so that the difference in numbers recruited from Canadian-born French and English was less pronounced; and recruiting had been more successful in urban areas, which again gave Ontario an advantage.[68] There were political factors to be considered too. The *Nationaliste* campaign in Quebec, tacitly supported by the Conservatives in 1911, had roused an isolationism which could not quickly be forgotten.[69] The administration of the recruiting campaign in Quebec had been mismanaged – the chief recruiting officer in the province had been an English Canadian and a Protestant clergyman, French Canadians were assigned to English-speaking units, and French-Canadian officers were not given positions of responsibility.[70] The most important factor was the agitation over Regulation 17. *Nationalistes* such as Lavergne stated publicly that French Canadians should not enlist until the rights of the minority in Ontario had been restored,[71] and Bourassa, who had favored participation in 1914, was concentrating upon the problem of bilingual schools in *Le Devoir* by 1916.[72] Indeed, Bourassa finally concluded that the war was an Imperialist war and so no concern of French Canadians.[73] To all this, Laurier had one reply. He admitted the force of these arguments and used them to explain the situation to English Canadians, but he denied that these reasons justified abstaining from enlistment. Laurier did not confuse these internal problems with the problem of fighting the war. For example, on the bilingual school question he said:

Whether my fellow-countrymen have rights or no rights in Ontar-

[67] See E. H. Armstrong, *The Crisis of Quebec, 1914-1918* (New York, 1937), 247, Appendix.
[68] LP, W. L. to D. Brocklebank, 5 April, 1916.
[69] Laurier, *Commons Debates*, 18 Jan., 1917, 2399.
[70] E. H. Armstrong, *The Crisis of Quebec*, 104.
[71] *Ibid.*, 131.
[72] *Ibid.*, 153.
[73] *Ibid.*, 138.

*io, whether these rights are granted or denied, these considerations
are no bar to the duty which French-Canadians owe to themselves
and to the honour of their race to come forward in their fullest
numbers and take part in the great struggle . . .*[74]

Probably of more importance to Laurier than its effect on the
outcome of the war was his belief that French-Canadian enlistments
were necessary to preserve racial harmony in Canada. For this
reason, Laurier and other Liberals took an active part in recruiting
campaigns within the province of Quebec.[75]

One method of recruiting, however, Laurier could not accept.
He could not support conscription. As a French Canadian, and as
a Liberal with an aversion to coercion, he instinctively opposed it.
"I do not believe in the policy; I do not think it is right in any way.
Upon this my mind is fully made up."[76] But Laurier had made up
his mind before, in 1899 and in 1905, and had changed it when a
compromise seemed necessary. In 1917 no compromise could be
found.

In the province of Quebec, the opposition to conscription, which
had been a prominent factor in Drummond-Arthabaska and in the
election of 1911, had been strengthened in subsequent years. Both
Liberals and Conservatives had deemed it necessary to assure
French Canadians that conscription was inconceivable, Archbishop
Bruchési having been persuaded to support National Registration
on the understanding that it did not mean conscription.[77] Nevertheless, *Nationalistes* continued to evoke the spectre, and in a by-
election in 1917 the supporters of the ministerial candidate and
former Nationaliste, Sévigny, did not hesitate to declare that to
support Laurier would be to support conscription.[78] When one
considers the election successes against Laurier over the conscription issue at a time when there were few grounds for suspecting his
intentions, there can be little doubt that if he had accepted conscription in 1917, he would have lost most of his political support in the
province. To join a coalition government which had as its *raison
d'être* the adoption of conscription was no solution.[79]

It would be absurd to suggest that Quebec would have meekly
acquiesced had Laurier given way. "Now if I were to waver, to
hesitate or to flinch, I would simply hand over the province of
Quebec to the extremists. I would lose the respect of the people

[74] *Commons Debates*, 9 May, 1916, 3701.
[75] Skelton, *Laurier*, II, 436ff., 447ff.
[76] LP, W. L. to W. Martin, 21 May, 1917.
[77] *Ibid.*, David to W. L., 27 May, 1917.
[78] Rumilly, *Histoire*, XXII, 22.
[79] LP, W. L. to Béique, 2 June, 1917.

whom I thus addressed and would deserve it."[80] This was the heart of the matter. Quebec would be lost to the extremists and Canadian unity would be shattered. Laurier might argue that conscription would not secure the number of recruits desired[81] but even if it did "it would be at the cost of the unity of the nation. . . ."[82] To try to increase the number of Canadian soldiers at such a sacrifice seemed illogical; that was not the way to "win the war" nor to plan for the future. The suggestion that Laurier was "intent upon the complete capture of Quebec at the impending elections"[83] is a misinterpretation of his motives. It was Canadian unity and not a victory in Quebec with which Laurier was concerned.

Laurier found justification for his opposition to conscription in the attitude of the advocates of conscription. He did not believe that conscription was popular, even among many English-Canadian groups. Support for this contention is to be found in a letter from Sifton to Dafoe – a more objective source than the opinion of any anti-conscriptionist.

As it stands now it appears to be quite impossible for Laurier to go in (i.e. enter a coalition government) on a policy for conscription. The opposition to conscription in the French Canadian population seems to be intensely strong and the opposition in labor circles is also very strong. I do not know what the attitude will be with a population of foreign origin, but it will be hopeless to expect any enthusiastic support in the villages and rural districts of Ontario . . . . I am definitely of the opinion that no Government can be formed which will succeed in carrying out an effective scheme of conscription without either a referendum or an election although there would be a better chance in the case of the latter. The victory however would be at the cost of arraying the English speaking Provinces against Quebec.[84]

Similar views were expressed in the House of Commons, where one western Liberal voted against the proposed referendum on conscription on the grounds that it would be defeated, and suggested that this was widely understood. His conclusion was that "We must win the war even if ignoring the will of the majority to do it."[85] This was the argument of the conscriptionists – it had become a moral

[80] *Ibid.*, W. L. to Rowell, 2 June, 1917.
[81] *Commons Debates*, 24 July 1917, 3724.
[82] LP, W. L. to W. Jaffray, 9 June, 1917.
[83] Dafoe, *Laurier*, 166.
[84] P.A.C., J. W. Dafoe Papers, Sifton to Dafoe, 5 June, 1817.
[85] J. Turriff, *Commons Debates*, 24 July, 1917, 3719.

necessity to "make the maximum contribution to the war."[86] Laurier believed that this moral principle was based upon a determination to compel the French Canadians to do their part.[87] Conscription thus appeared as an overt expression of the growing prejudice against French Canadians. This belief was substantiated by the attitude of Liberals prominent in the Unionist movement; Rowell had supported Regulation 17, Dafoe had supported the amendment of the Laurier-Greenway settlement, and Sifton's reputation dated back to the 1890's. Laurier may have exaggerated this aspect of the conscription sentiment, but there can be no doubt that it was strongly affected by the resentment against the French-Canadian "slackers". Laurier could not be expected to support such a movement.

In spite of this, Laurier proposed a compromise in the form of a referendum upon conscription, pledging that his province would accept the verdict.[88] Since Laurier appears to have believed that the majority would favor conscription,[89] he must have been relying upon his influence in Quebec and on the law-abiding instincts of his compatriots to ensure that conscription would be accepted there. Whether this is true or not, the suggestion of such a compromise does not conform to Dafoe's description of a man intent only upon capturing Quebec. But upon this issue, compromise was impossible. Even prominent English-Canadian Liberals decided against party and personal loyalty and in favor of conscription without a referendum.[90] Conscription was passed, a Union government was formed, and the election of 1917 left the Liberal party with sixty-two seats in Quebec and twenty seats in the rest of Canada. There was to be no compromise, and the nation was divided. All that remained was to try to persuade Quebec to accept the law peacefully and so avoid further complications.[91] The tragedy had reached its climax, and it seemed time for Laurier to leave the stage.

But Laurier had wrought better than he knew. One national party became an English-Canadian party, but the Liberal party was to re-emerge at the next election as a party which included both English- and French-Canadians. This cannot be fully explained by post-war developments. The significant fact is that even in 1917, English Canadians and even English-Canadian conscriptionists, had remained within the Liberal party. The reconstruction of the

[86] Dafoe, *Laurier*, 174.
[87] LP, W. L. to W. Parrish, 27 Sept., 1917.
[88] *Commons Debates*, 18 June, 1917, 2403.
[89] LP, W. L. to W. Kennedy, 9 June, 1917.
[90] Skelton, *Laurier*, II, 517.
[91] LP, W. L. to E. Lapointe, 18 Jan., 1918.

party in the post-war period did not involve the creation of a new one. The English-Canadian politicians who remained loyal to Laurier even though they disagreed with his policy were the nucleus for the English-Canadian section of the post-war Liberal party. To explain this loyalty to Laurier it is necessary to understand the influence of Laurier's personality, because in 1917 this was the only tie which bound many English Canadians to the party.

Laurier's personal appeal cannot be attributed to heartiness or conviviality. His manner was cordial rather than jovial. He had the reserved charm of a *seigneur*, or, as Lady Minto described him, "he was a great gentleman."[92] His intimate friends were few, and during his term of office he was on a *tutoyer* relationship with only a few of the Liberals with whom he had struggled in the days when Liberals in Quebec were in danger of excommunication. Of these, L. O. David was the closest friend. In the years of Opposition after 1911, Laurier seems to have become less reserved. Former colleagues such as Murphy, Macdonald and Lemieux became Charlie, Ned and Rodolphe in his correspondence. He himself was always addressed as "My Dear Sir Wilfrid" in his letters, although his colleagues customarily talked of him as "the Chief" when writing to his secretary.[93] Yet in spite of this formality Laurier evoked among Liberals a depth of feeling which might be considered unusual among politicians. The thirty years as leader of the party, with a political success beyond the expectations of the 1880's helps to account for the respect and even the veneration of his followers, but these alone cannot account for the affection and love he inspired as no other Prime Minister has done since Macdonald.

Possibly the characteristic which helps to explain this feeling was that indicated by Minto's description of Laurier. "Far the biggest man in Canada is Laurier. He is quite charming, and if there is a change I shall miss him more than I can say – and *he is honest*."[94] Minto seems to have meant honest, not in the sense of financial integrity – Laurier had that quality himself but could accept somewhat lower standards from his colleagues on occasion – but rather in the sense that he was frank. Laurier had the faculty of blending frankness with tact in such a way that disagreements did not lead to animosity. Indecision can be a serious fault in a politician because it may breed suspicion; but even more dangerous is an attempt to imply agreement with every correspondent or solicitor before a decision is made, because this can only lead to disillusionment. Laurier temporized on some occasions, especially on the tariff questions of

[92] J. Buchan, *Lord Minto* (London, 1924), 205.
[93] LP, 195131, 196321.
[94] Buchan, *Minto*, 159.

the 1890's and in 1902, but that was because he had not come to any decision. When he had decided upon a policy he was surprisingly frank. To a man interested in a subsidy for the steel industry, Laurier could explain, "I doubt the wisdom of your policy . . . and to tell you the truth I am the worst opponent that you have to meet at Council. Do not be discouraged by this, but come and see me. I will be open to conviction if you have any good reasons to give me."[95] And to an Archbishop who humbly suggested that no freethinker should be appointed judge, Laurier was even more direct. After explaining that no appointment was being considered at the time, he continued;

Allow me, however, to tell you frankly that your caveat alarms me a little. We judge the qualifications of a lawyer for the magistracy by the rank which he occupies in the profession, the esteem of the Bench and of his colleagues, and the worthiness of his character. Your Eminence asks me to penetrate much further, into the most intimate secret of his conscience. Are you surprised to hear me say that this new realization alarms me somewhat?[96]

As a final illustration we may quote Laurier's letter to the Liberal Senator P. A. Choquette, who had been criticizing the results of recruiting in Ontario as a reply to criticisms of French-Canadian recruiting. "Personally, as you know, I have only the highest regard for you. Politically, I am against you, and especially your methods."[97] In a long career such as Laurier's, such frankness would be far more effective than equivocation or half-promises badly kept.

Even more important than this quality of honesty was Laurier's ability to understand and respect the personal convictions of other people, even though he might disagree with them. This quality, although rare, is not peculiar to Laurier, but he possessed it to such an eminent degree that an appreciation of it is essential to an understanding of his leadership. In the political sphere it was reflected in compromises which cannot be explained by mere expediency; in his personal relations it was also important. According to Skelton, Laurier's lip would still curl at the mention of Bishop Bourget fifty years after the Guibord case,[98] but there is no other evidence of personal animosity as the result of personal differences. Even of Bourassa, Laurier continued to speak in measured, although critical, terms. "Bourassa is a man of great ability, but his ability is

[95] LP, W. L. to L. McCarthy, 24 Feb., 1908.
[96] *Ibid.*, W. L. to Bruchési, 30 Nov., 1909.
[97] *Ibid.*, W. L. to Choquette, 1 May, 1916.
[98] Skelton, *Laurier*, I, 103.

negative and destructive."[99] And Laurier retained his respect for the abilities of Tarte and Sifton long after they had resigned from his cabinet. This tolerance was a political asset. Tarte remained a friend after 1902 and lived to defend Laurier's compromise on the Autonomy Bills in *La Patrie*, and Sifton even voted for the amended Autonomy Bills and remained a Liberal for some years after his resignation.

At no time was this quality more severely tried nor more successfully exhibited than during the conscription crisis. To Laurier, conscription meant the destruction of national unity, and so of his political ideal. To an old man it might well have seemed that his English followers had deserted him and even betrayed him at a critical moment. Instead he understood that they too suffered from the separation. To a loyal English Canadian he even defended their action.

Yesterday it was Pardee and today it will be Graham! Graham and Pardee, as dear to me as my own brothers! Do not, however, think hard of them for I do not. They have behaved all through most honourably, and there is not and there will not be any loss of friendship between us. The pain is not less acute on their side than on mine, and I know only too well the difficulties that faced them.[100]

These sentiments were not inspired by the negative quality of tolerance. To tolerate the desertion of his followers, to avoid recriminations, must have been difficult enough. But Laurier had a genuine and a sympathetic understanding, the positive quality of Christian love. His "sunny ways" were not so much the result of political calculation as of innate charity.

It was this personal factor which prevented the complete destruction of the English-Canadian Liberal party in 1917. Aylesworth, for example, who as Minister of Justice had been respected for his integrity rather than for partisanship, and who had now retired from active politics, had such implicit confidence in Laurier's motives that he could say of the conscription question, "whither thou goest, I will go."[101] Sincere advocates of conscription such as E. M. Macdonald, Frank Oliver and George Graham, remained Liberals during the election of 1917, at a time when to be a conscriptionist and a Liberal was the political equivalent of squaring the circle. These men sacrificed their seats and the respect of many of their friends because their personal loyalty to "the Chief" could not be

[99] LP, W. L. to Botha, 1 Dec., 1916.
[100] *Ibid.*, W. L. to Aylesworth, 22 June, 1917.
[101] *Ibid.*, Aylesworth to W. L., 17 May, 1917.

destroyed by political differences. Even among the Liberal-Unionists friendship for Laurier survived the crisis, and some of them continued to attend social gatherings at Laurier House.[102] Because Laurier understood, he had nothing to forgive. And even before Laurier's death this personal factor had played a part in the rehabilitation of the party. Fielding had been welcomed back into the Liberal fold.[103] To facilitate the return of other errant Liberals, Laurier's last speech was an admonition to his followers to avoid recriminations about the past. "Forget the past, and let us still be well united Liberals, acting only under the direction of their conscience."[104]

Laurier died before the party was completely re-united, but the policy of his successor had already been formulated. The effect on the subsequent history of Canada of this restoration of the Liberal party is incalculable. National unity in the political sphere is illustrated by and fostered by the unity of the various regional and racial groups of the nation within a political party. In the post-war years of reconstruction, there was only one Canadian party which could be a truly national party, since only the Liberal party could include both English - and French-Canadians. But for the personality of Sir Wilfrid Laurier, even this might have been impossible.

Laurier had not created a united nation. Indeed, it might be wrong to say that this had been his goal. Unity – unitas – means oneness. Such unity could never be achieved while two societies continued to exist. It could only be achieved by the absorption of one society by the other. What Laurier aspired to was not oneness, but a nation in which the two racial communities would co-operate harmoniously. It was to be a federal union, founded on mutual respect. In Laurier's own words, "My object is to consolidate Confederation, and to bring our people long estranged from each other, gradually to become a nation."[105] Such a nation could never be created by any definitive act. The survival of two societies with different racial, linguistic and cultural characteristics meant that each succeeding generation would have to face political issues upon which the two ¦societies¦were divided. The contribution of a politician to this form of national unity could only be relative – he could avoid disintegration, and each successful compromise would facilitate other compromises in the future.

Laurier's political career coincides with the two most serious

[102] Rumilly, *Histoire*, XXIII, 104, based on an interview with J. A. Calder.

[103] LP W. L. to Sen. Power, 23 Nov., 1918.

[104] A. D. DeCelles, ed., *Discours de Sir Wilfrid Laurier, 1911-1919* (Montreal, 1920), 14 Feb., 1919.

[105] LP, W. L. to W. Gregory, 11 Nov., 1904.

challenges to Confederation in Canadian history. The first was the divisive emphasis on religion in politics in the province of Quebec. In the 1870's a determined effort was made to identify the Liberal party with Catholic-liberalism. If the effort had been successful, the Liberal party in Quebec would have disappeared. The Quebec Conservative party would have been identified with ultramontanism and, it may be assumed, would have become an isolated regional faction in the federal House of Commons. In the 1890's and again in 1905 the religious question became a central issue in Quebec politics with the challenge to separate schools for Roman Catholic minorities in Manitoba and in Saskatchewan and Alberta. Again there was a danger that French Canadians would unite in one political faction and advocate a policy completely unacceptable to English Canadians. The other challenge to Confederation might be described as racialism in politics – the divergent emotional reactions of English and French Canadians to Imperialism. This, too, was a recurrent problem in Laurier's day, evoked by the Boer War, the Naval Bill, and the conscription issue. Again the danger was that the political parties in Canada might be re-formed along racial lines.

On each occasion, Laurier's policy was consistent. His first hope was always to avoid racial schism by avoiding political controversy. He made no important declaration on Catholic-liberalism until 1877; he tried to focus attention on the tariff question in the 1890's; his first official statement concerning participation in the Boer War was to the effect that there was no problem because participation was unconstitutional; his Autonomy Bills and his Naval Bill were expected to allay agitation; and he constantly reiterated his statement that conscription would never be invoked. Later, when it became apparent that these controversies had become divisive political issues in spite of his tactics, Laurier consistently sought solutions which he believed acceptable to reasonable Canadians of either racial community. To review his specific solutions is unnecessary, since it is generally conceded that this was Laurier's intention. Only in the case of conscription in 1917 is there any doubt, and even on this occasion it is difficult to deny that the proposal of a referendum was an attempt to reach such a compromise.

There can be no definitive conclusion as to how successful Laurier was in his efforts to consolidate Confederation. His intention is clear, but any conclusion as to the results must remain a matter of personal judgment. But with reference to the French Canadians at least, Laurier had advantages that no other national politician possessed. As a minority group, French Canadians have a sensitive pride which attributes to any compromise the submission to the arbitrary will of the majority. As a French Canadian and a Roman

Catholic Laurier could retain the confidence of the French Canadians as could no English Canadian. As the leader of a national party, and a statesman honored in London and Paris, his prominence flattered *nationaliste* sentiments. Such a man could propose compromises and yet retain widespread political support in the province of Quebec. This is presumptive evidence at least that Laurier sustained French-Canadian loyalty to Confederation. Certainly he did avoid disintegration of the union. What is more significant, he avoided the disintegration of the Liberal party. Without at least one political party which included representatives of both racial communities, it is difficult to imagine any consistent formulation of a national policy based on mutual respect and co-operation. And events subsequent to Laurier's death suggest that the compromises accepted during his lifetime have so firmly established Confederation that it can never again be seriously challenged.

A Note on Sources and Suggestions for Further Reading

Detailed references to the full list of items in the author's original bibliography are in the footnotes. There are, however, some sources and works which were of special value to the author and which at the time of writing he considered of particular significance in the study of Laurier and of Quebec politics in his era. In addition, there are some other studies and interpretations – several of which have appeared since the thesis was prepared – to which the attention of readers should be drawn.

I SOURCES

The very extensive Laurier Papers at the Public Archives of Canada were by all odds the most important primary source. Information about Quebec politics has been drawn from the Edward Blake Papers (Ontario Archives) and from a great number of Public Archives of Canada collections – among them those concerning J. I. Tarte, R. Lemieux, Sir John A. Macdonald, Sir John Thompson, Sir Mackenzie Bowell, Sir Charles Tupper and Sir Robert Borden. It should be noted that when Dr. Neatby wrote his thesis, according to his original "Note on Bibliography," several manuscript collections in private and Episcopal hands "were not available for the purposes of this study."[1]

The pamphlet collection of the P.A.C. was a virtual treasure trove. To quote the author:

In the nineteenth century especially, pamphlets were widely used for political and ecclesiastical controversy, and sometimes contain previously confidential correspondence.... Other pamphlets express cogently or even virulently the point of view of a political faction.... Other pamphlets are useful because they illustrate the atmosphere of Quebec politics, and especially the extreme partisanship which is usually moderated in less ephemeral publications.[2]

[1] Thesis manuscript, p. 403.
[2] *Ibid.*, pp. 403-404.

As for newspapers, they were consulted mostly concerning specific topics such as the Riel crisis, the Manitoba School question, the Boer War, etc. But Bourassa's *Le Devoir* was read much more closely, from the time of its founding in 1910.

In secondary material, Dr. Neatby found of most value the first twenty-three volumes of Robert Rumilly's *Histoire de la province de Québec* (Citations were made from the third edition, Vols. I-IV, and the first edition of subsequent volumes). Neatby appreciated that Rumilly had gained access to episcopal archives such as those of Montreal and Three Rivers and to private collections such as that of Athanase David.[3] That, plus the heavy grounding of the earlier volumes in newspaper material and of the later ones in personal interviews with survivors make them required reading and an indispensable source for scholars of the period. Neatby considered that Rumilly's talents in character depiction were "outstanding," that although the characters were sometimes "overdrawn" they were "graphic and memorable."[4] But he thought that Rumilly's objectivity was flawed – that he so strongly favoured *nationaliste* movements in Quebec that he gave too little attention to Laurier's efforts at preserving the Liberals as a national party.[5] He questioned as well Rumilly's practice of neglecting very often to cite his sources of information, especially in the volumes about the post-1900 times, where information which he received from Bourassa often was treated quite uncritically.[6]

On three biographies of Laurier – those by Skelton, Dafoe and Willison – Neatby offered assessments. Skelton's two-volume *Life and Letters of Sir Wilfrid Laurier* (Toronto, 1921; Carleton Library Series, 1965) he thought "the best," but he judged that Skelton had been "so concerned with painting Laurier as a political paragon, and possibly so seduced by Laurier's personal charm, that Laurier emerges as a symbol of racial harmony rather than as a human being with a clearly drawn personality, a man with both virtues and weaknesses."[7] In particular, he believed that Skelton, an English-Canadian Protestant, had been guilty of "evasions" in failing to show how much Laurier while in office tried to cultivate the support of the Roman Catholic hierarchy in Quebec.[8] And, he thought, Skelton unwisely had tried to explain Laurier's opposition to conscription on the basis of a pragmatic assessment by him of its

[3] *Ibid.*, pp. 406-407.
[4] *Ibid.*, p. 407.
[5] *Ibid.*
[6] *Ibid.*, p. 408
[7] *Ibid.*, p. 404.
[8] *Ibid.*, p. 405.

worthlessness as a mechanism for providing manpower. For Neatby: "It seems clear that Laurier began with the almost universal French-Canadian attitude that conscription was wrong, and found rational arguments to support his decision later."[9]

Although Neatby judged J. W. Dafoe's *Laurier: A Study in Canadian Politics* (Toronto, 1922; Carleton Library Series, 1964) "the best analytical essay" in the field, he believed Dafoe's view of Laurier had been "distorted" by their divisions over conscription and Union government. For Dafoe, according to Neatby: "Laurier's talk of compromise for the sake of racial harmony seemed no more than a pretext, since conscription was a moral issue and compromise was therefore impossible. . . . His conclusion that Laurier was obsessed with holding Quebec affected his analysis even of Laurier's earlier policies."[10]

J. S. Willison's *Sir Wilfrid Laurier and the Liberal Party* (2 vols., Toronto, 1903) Neatby described as "a well-written contemporary biography," with the section on Catholic-liberalism especially well done. But, he thought, Willison incorrectly had conceived Laurier's Manitoba Schools policy of 1896 to have been based on a hostility to federal "coercion" of the province, instead of on political pragmatism.

Two other works in English, while not really "sources" for Neatby's own study, drew bibliographical comment from him. On Mason Wade's *The French Canadians, 1760-1945* (Toronto, 1955) Neatby's judgment was that it is "the most complete study in English of French-Canadian history for this period, but it contains little that is original."[12] He had less qualified praise for Elizabeth H. Armstrong's *The Crisis of Quebec, 1914-1918* (New York, 1937; Carleton Library Series, 1973) which he viewed as "a scholarly study" of French-Canadian opinion.[13]

II SUGGESTIONS FOR FURTHER READING

Contributions of French Canadians to the historiography on Laurier have been somewhat disappointing. There have been several sketchy "graceful tributes," of which L. O. David's *Laurier: sa vie, ses oeuvres* (Beauceville, 1919) is perhaps the most distinguished. Others include A. D. DeCelles, *Laurier et son temps* (Montreal,

---

[9] *Ibid.*, pp. 405-406.
[10] *Ibid.*, p. 406.
[11] *Ibid.*, p. 409.
[12] *Ibid.*, p. 408.
[13] *Ibid.*, pp. 408-409.

1920) and Raymond Tanghue, *Laurier: artisan de l'unité canadienne, 1841-1919* (Paris, 1960). This last one is available in translation as *Laurier: Architect of Canadian Unity* (Montreal, 1966). There are four excellent compilations in French of Laurier's speeches: the one edited by U. Barthe, *Wilfrid Laurier on the Platform, 1871-1890* (Quebec 1890); and the three by A.D. DeCelles, *Discours de Sir Wilfrid Laurier,* concerning the 1871-1909, 1889-1911 and 1911-1919 years. An important collection of letters is L. Pacaud, ed., *Sir Wilfrid Laurier: Letters to My Father and Mother* (Toronto, 1935). Robert Rumilly has written a good deal about Laurier in his several volumes of history; but only very early in his career, in his brief *Sir Wilfrid Laurier: canadien* (Paris, 1931) did he deal directly with the subject. A good deal more interesting are his references to Laurier in the first twenty-three volumes of his *Histoire* and in his biographies on *Mercier* (Montréal, 1936), *Mgr. Laflèche et son temps* (Montréal, 1945) and *Henri Bourassa* (Montréal, 1953).

Since the Neatby thesis was prepared, a number of new biographical or analytical writings in English about Laurier and Quebec have appeared. Most important is Joseph Schull's *Laurier. The First Canadian* (Toronto, 1965), which is comfortably in the Laurier-and-national-unity tradition of Willison, Skelton and Neatby, and breaks virtually no new ground, which is not surprising because the research emphasis was on a synthesis of existing treatments and exploitation of the already well known main documentary collections. But, as Donald Creighton, the arch-critic of the "Liberal Interpretation" of Canadian history, has remarked of Schull's study: " . . . the story has been revised, freed of its archaisms and crudities, and given a new and compelling appeal."[14] Two articles should be mentioned. Mason Wade's "Sir Wilfrid Laurier" in C. T. Bissell, ed., *Our Living Tradition: First Series* (Toronto, 1957), pp. 89-104, is a short but interesting re-statement of the familiar theme about Laurier the hero of French-English harmony.[15] Paul Stevens in "Wilfrid Laurier: Politician," pp. 69-85 of Marcel Hamelin, ed., *The Political Ideas of the Prime Ministers of Canada* (Ottawa, 1969) commendably tried a new tack of emphasizing the politician's techniques rather than the statesman's ideals. Predictably, his valuable effort at applying fresh insight drew the rebuff of a shocked Laurier traditionalist that it was a "worm's eye view."[16]

A number of worthwhile studies dealing with or touching on politics and society in Quebec have been written in the last fifteen

[14] *Canadian Historical Review*, XLVII (Dec. 1966), 358.
[15] pp. 89-104.
[16] L. C. Clark, *Canadian Historical Review*, LI (March 1970), 89.

years. Among them a few stand out. P. B. Waite's *Canada, 1874-1896: Arduous Destiny* (Toronto, 1971) is an excellent synthesis of existing material on political history, including Quebec's, but not on much more. Ramsay Cook's volumes of essays, *Canada and the French-Canadian Question* (Toronto, 1966) and *The Maple Leaf Forever: Essays on Nationalism and Politics in Canada* (Toronto, 1971) are stimulating; and his *French Canadian Nationalism: An Anthology* (Toronto, 1969) contains fine translations from writings and speeches of Laflèche, Bourassa and others. J. Levitt's *Henri Bourassa and the Golden Calf: The Social Program of the Nationalists of Quebec, 1900-1914* (Ottawa, 1969) is an interesting attempt to view the *nationalists* as less socially conservative on industrial questions and more "progressive," albeit in a Catholic "utopian corporatist" manner. W. F. Ryan's, *The Clergy and Economic Growth in Quebec, 1896-1914* (Ottawa, 1966) corrects somewhat, for these years at least, John Porter's generalization that "Quebec's Catholic hierarchy assumed a reactionary attitude to the industrialization of the province."[17] Pierre Savard in *Jules-Paul Tardivel, La France et les Etats-Unis, 1851-1905* (Québec, 1967), provides a useful study of the ideas of the late-nineteenth century ultramontane journalist of *La Verité*. J. Levitt *has edited, in English*, a number of Henri Bourassa's statements and writings in *Henri Bourassa on Imperialism and Bi-culturalism, 1900-1918* (Toronto, 1970). J. M. Beck, *Pendulum of Power: Canada's Federal Elections* (Toronto, 1968) has a good deal on Quebec politics. A scholarly biography of one of Macdonald's chief Conservative rivals in the province before 1896 is Andrée Desilets, *Hector-Louis Langevin: un Père de la Confederation canadienne, 1826-1906* (Quebec, 1969). A fascinating work is André Siegfried's *The Race Question in Canada*, first published in 1906 and re-issued in the Carleton Library Series in 1966. André Bergevin, Cameron Nish and Anne Bourassa collaborated on the useful *Henri Bourassa: biographie, index des écrits et index de la correspondance publique, 1895-1924* (Montréal, 1966). A modern biography of the *nationaliste* Olivar Asselin is M.-A. Gagnon's *La vie orageuse d'Olivar Asselin* (2 vols., Montreal, 1962). An excellent unpublished work is Paul E. Crunican, *The Manitoba School Question and Canadian Federal Politics, 1890-1896: A Study in Church-State Relations* (Ph.D., University of Toronto, 1968). Among articles published since 1956 on the Laurier period and Quebec four are especially interesting. The late Barbara Fraser's "The Political Career of Sir Hector Louis Langevin," *Canadian Historical Review*, XLII (June 1961),

---

[17] *The Vertical Mosaic: An Analysis of Social Class and Power in Canada* (Toronto, 1965), p. 333.

93-132 is a fine companion piece to the Neatby and Saywell treatment of Quebec Conservatism, as is that of Andrée Desilets, "La succession de Cartier, 1873-1891," Canadian Historical Association, *Historical Papers 1968*, pp. 49-64. A. I. Silver's "French Canada and the Prairie Frontier, 1870-1890," *Canadian Historical Review*, L (March 1969), 11-36 is very informative. And P. E. Crunican's "Bishop Laflèche and the Mandement of 1896," Canadian Historical Association, *Historical Papers 1969*, pp. 52-61 is excellent.

R.T.C.

Note on the Author

H. Blair Neatby was born in Renown, Saskatchewan, in 1924. He attended the University of Saskatchewan (B.A.), Oxford University (M.A.), and the University of Toronto (Ph.D). He has taught history at Prince of Wales College, P.E.I. (1954-1955), the University of British Columbia (1955-1964) and Carleton University (since 1964). He is currently Chairman and Professor of History at Carleton.

Dr. Neatby is the author of numerous scholarly articles and of *William Lyon Mackenzie King, 1924-1932: The Lonely Heights* (1963). From 1964 to 1967 he was supervisor of research on education for the Royal Commission on Bilingualism and Biculturalism.

Note on the Editor

Richard T. Clippingdale was born in Toronto, Ontario in 1941. He received his B.A. (Hons.) from Trinity College, University of Toronto in 1963 and took his graduate training at Princeton University on a Woodrow Wilson Fellowship and then at the University of Toronto (Ph.D., 1970). Since 1967 he has been a member of the faculty of Carleton University and is now Associate Professor of History.

Dr. Clippingdale's unpublished Ph.D. thesis was on *J. S. Willison, Political Journalist: From Liberalism to Independence, 1881-1905*, and he has written the article "J. S. Willison and Canadian Nationalism, 1886-1902," Canadian Historical Association, *Historical Papers, 1969*, pp. 74-93, and a number of scholarly reviews.

Index

THE CARLETON LIBRARY